PENGUIN BOOKS

FAMOUS TRIALS 4

Over fifty years have passed since the first volume of the Penguin *Famous Trials* appeared. This reissue of nine volumes of the famous series covering notorious crimes and trials from the mid nineteenth century onwards remains true to the original text and just as fascinating to modern readers.

The Penguin *Famous Trials* series has its origins in the *The Notable British Trials Series*, which was founded in 1905 by Harry Hodge. As Managing Director of William Hodge & Co. Ltd, Publishers and Shorthand Writers, Hodge had a vast knowledge of both the Scottish Courts and criminology – he was himself an expert shorthand writer and this is reflected in his careful selection of editors and his insistence on accurate reporting of trials for *The Notable British Trials Series*. As the original editor of the Penguin *Famous Trials* (Volumes 1 and 2), Hodge chose the most intriguing crimes, remaining firm to his belief that a crime should be at least twenty years old before it can prove itself 'notable'. After his death in 1947 his son, James Hozier Hodge, went on to become general editor of the Penguin *Famous Trials* series.

FAMOUS TRIALS 4

Harold Greenwood
William Joyce
Ley and Smith
Dr Pritchard
Robert Wood

EDITED BY JAMES H. HODGE

PENGUIN BOOKS

PENGUIN BOOKS

Published by the Penguin Group
Penguin Books Ltd, 27 Wrights Lane, London W8 5TZ, England
Penguin Books USA Inc., 375 Hudson Street, New York, New York 10014, USA
Penguin Books Australia Ltd, Ringwood, Victoria, Australia
Penguin Books Canada Ltd, 10 Alcorn Avenue, Toronto, Ontario, Canada M4V 3B2
Penguin Books (NZ) Ltd, 182–190 Wairau Road, Auckland 10, New Zealand

Penguin Books Ltd, Registered Offices: Harmondsworth, Middlesex, England

First published 1954
3 5 7 9 10 8 6 4

Printed in England by Clays Ltd, St Ives plc

Contents

Preface

THE ratio of murders committed in Great Britain to the total population has, on the whole, varied little in modern times. There is no sudden upward surge which calls for general alarm, as in certain other classes of crime, and the lack of numbers in our police forces has not left any obvious mark. Serious assault on the person may have increased, and the margin between brutal physical violence and possible death may be slight, but it does appear that a fairly steady, albeit low, murder percentage will continue whatever deterrents we impose and however widespread our reforms may be.

Much of this kind of crime can be traced to human nature, to latent wickedness. And so, until a revolution occurs in man's morality, we can expect the private taking of life to continue. It must be stressed that despite what appears in the press, the murder rate is in reality low. It is a crime that occurs but seldom in any one year, and there is no doubt that it gets publicity out of all proportion, in view of its distressing results. It is the volume of lesser crimes that causes us alarm, especially in young persons, and it is to the prevention of these that our main attention must be given. But even so, there ought to be a diminution of murder as we progress, and if statistics show little or no increase in homicidal activities, that is no ground for complacency. As the world grows older, we expect its peoples to get wiser. There have been vast discoveries in every branch of science, and great progress in the emancipation of the individual human being. Surely we are entitled to look for a decrease in the deeds of evil. Unfortunately the appalling mass crimes already committed this century give us little hope of individual improvement. Modern wars and the comprehensive purges carried out by certain States against sections of their subjects, encourage the worst traits in the human character and cheapen the value of life in the eyes of many, making infinitely more difficult the progress we all hope to see in the elimination of violence. In this country mob law and State terrorism are non-existent, and we shrink with horror at some of the actions reported from less fortunate nations. The freedom of the individual, both in act and speech, encourages the sense of responsibility and regard for the law which is enacted by democratic methods. As long as this is preserved we can hope to sustain our moral values, and murder is unlikely to be a frequent occurrence. Individual acts against Society will still occur, but even these should diminish with improved education, medical enlightenment and the elimination of squalid living conditions. But vicious throwbacks will remain with us, even though their number is minute.

This volume deals with five remarkable trials. In two of these, Wood and Greenwood, a verdict favourable to the accused was returned by the jury; the others resulted in convictions. Treason, poisoning, throat-cutting, abduction, and strangling are all met with, and there are few similarities in the cases which range over a wide period of time. Dr Pritchard, one of the most hypocritical and fiendish of poisoners, was the last person to be hanged publicly in Glasgow; he killed both his mother-in-law and wife, and possibly more. Harold Greenwood died in poverty a few years after being tried for poisoning his wife; he became an outcast, ruined professionally as a country solicitor, despite his acquittal. Robert Wood made history by being the first person to succeed on a murder charge when giving evidence on his own behalf; his defence by Sir Edward Marshall Hall was brilliantly conducted. A precedent was set in the case of William Joyce, which went to the House of Lords, in that it is now established that an alien can be guilty of treason outside this realm if at the time of his alleged activities he in fact holds a British passport; Joyce was proved to be an American citizen at the time he broadcast from Germany during the last war. Ley was a former Minister of Justice of New South Wales, who through insane jealousy arranged for the abduction of a young man from Reigate to London where through the agency of

Smith, a foreman joiner, he was strangled. Ley died of paranoia in Broadmoor, Smith was reprieved and received a life sentence. Each case has its place in the *Notable British Trials Series*, where the individual trials are set out in full and can be comprehensively studied.

To stop human beings from committing such crimes we require a change of heart.

J. H. H.

FAMOUS TRIALS 4

Harold Greenwood

· 1920 ·

BY

WINIFRED DUKE

I

MURDER, almost more than any other operating force, takes the obscure, the uninteresting, the hitherto unknown, and thrusts him or her relentlessly under the full blaze of publicity. A certain locality, previously a dot on the map to the great majority, becomes for a brief period the one name on everybody's lips. The searchlight of inquiry is directed mercilessly into the private lives, loves, and hates of a handful of individuals whose patronymics, during the swift course of a *cause célèbre*, are household words. Carmarthen, a small township in South Wales, was one such spot upon which the attention of the entire British Isles was focused throughout one breathless week. Harold Greenwood's trial at Carmarthen Assizes for the alleged poisoning of his first wife, the probing into the supposed taking of a single life just after the conclusion of four years' wholesale murder in war, distracted the public attention from anything else of moment or importance.

The village of Kidwelly lies some twelve or more miles beyond Carmarthen. Kidwelly is one of the oldest boroughs in the country, and dates back over eight hundred years. The neighbourhood is rich in historical and archaeological interests, boasting a famous castle and much legendary and antiquarian lore, but it is safe to say that at no time in its annals did Kidwelly's name and fame create such intense public excitement and heartburning as during the hectic months of its ill-gotten celebrity through the Greenwood case.

The stranger to Kidwelly alights at its picturesque little station and, in order to visit the village, follows a country road for about a quarter of a mile. Kidwelly's crooked main street, a double row of low-browed houses and small, dark shops, climbs at one end towards the open landscape, and at the other runs over a bridge across a sluggish river. Just before the bridge is reached a substantial three-storeyed stone mansion used to stand back from the road in its own grounds. These now lie a neglected wilderness, while the building itself has been entirely reconstructed inside, and converted into a Wesleyan chapel and manse, but in 1919 the place was Rumsey House, the residence of Mr and Mrs Greenwood.

Harold Greenwood was the second son of William Norman Greenwood, of Greenwood Leigh, Ingleton, Yorks. On 2 July 1896 he had married Mabel, the younger daughter of Mr William Vansittart Bowater, of Bury Hall, Edmonton, Middlesex. Mr and Mrs Greenwood lived in London for the first two years of their married life, and in 1898 came to reside at Broomhill, Kidwelly. Greenwood had been admitted a solicitor the same year, and bought a partnership in the firm of Messrs Johnson & Stead, Llanelly, an industrial town a few miles away. Later, he started to practise on his own account, going regularly to his office at Frederick Street, Llanelly, each morning at 10.30, and returning to Kidwelly in the evening about 5.30. It was his habit to lunch at the office of the *Llanelly Mercury*, the local newspaper, an influential weekly organ, with the proprietor, Mr W. B. Jones, and his sons. Greenwood's practice was not an extensive one, being chiefly concerned with dealings in house property, while among his principal clients were money-lenders. Neither legally nor locally was his reputation too good, and it is significant that when whispers of a criminal charge against him crept abroad no single voice was raised in his defence or favour.

The Greenwoods removed from Broomhill to the Priory, Kidwelly, and in November 1916 Greenwood purchased Rumsey House. Mrs Greenwood seems to have been much liked and esteemed, and somewhat of a personality in the place. She took a sympathetic and practical interest in village affairs, was a regular attendant at St Mary's Church, shared any social activities of the neighbourhood, and despite the handicap of her somewhat frail health, supported local tennis and croquet clubs with enthusiasm. Kidwelly's opinion of her husband was not so favourable. A candid (male) acquaintance described him as not having a single man friend, and being fond of stirring up mischief and trouble. On the other hand, he was exceedingly popular with the opposite sex. Genial and lively, fond of a joke, unable to help making himself pleasant and agreeable, when his character came to be investigated he was accused of 'carry-on' – a convenient term conveying anything from affability to adultery – with sundry ladies in the neighbourhood.

Outwardly the Greenwoods seemed an average couple regarded by their circle of acquaintances and, what is still more important, by their servants, as happy and harmonious in their relations. In June 1919 the occupants of Rumsey House comprised Mr and Mrs Greenwood; Irene, the elder daughter, the oldest of their family of four children, who had come of age the previous April; Kenneth, the younger son, a boy of ten, being educated at home; three women servants, and an outside gardener. The other daughter and son, Eileen, aged seventeen, and Ivor, aged fifteen, were away at their respective boarding-schools. The three maids were Margaret Morris, the cook, aged thirty-eight, who had been in the Greenwoods' service for two years; Hannah Maggie Williams, a girl of eighteen, employed as parlourmaid by them for nine months; and Gwyneira Powell, between-maid, who had been nearly as long as Margaret Morris at Rumsey House. Miss Edith Bowater, Mrs Greenwood's sister, had been living there, paying a certain sum per week and possessing the furniture of one bedroom, but she had gone away about six weeks previously. Greenwood declared that this was in consequence of a quarrel with Mrs Greenwood, a statement unsubstantiated by anyone else. That it cannot have been serious is proved by Miss Bowater's intention, as stated by herself, of joining Mrs Greenwood at Portishead on 24 June for a fortnight's holiday, and afterwards returning with her to Rumsey House. She came back immediately the day of Mrs Greenwood's death, and remained there until Greenwood's second marriage in the following October.

For some considerable time Mabel Greenwood's health had been unsatisfactory. The ordinary relations between husband and wife had had to be discontinued on this account. Greenwood declared that Mrs Greenwood was of opinion that she had never felt fully recovered since the birth of her youngest child ten years before. She was a woman of forty-seven, who suffered from a weak heart, causing prolonged fainting attacks and other disabilities. More than once she expressed a fear of cancer, but declined to take steps to ascertain whether the dreaded malady were real or imaginary. For sixteen years she had been a patient of the Kidwelly doctor, Dr Thomas Robert Griffiths, and she appears to have had complete confidence in his treatment. None of his prescriptions for her at any time contained arsenic. For some months prior to her death she was under his care for a condition which he diagnosed as either a temporary inconvenience incidental to her age, or an internal growth. The subsequent post-mortem revealed that the latter surmise was correct, a small tumour, possibly painful and uncomfortable, but in no sense dangerous to life, being discovered.

Mrs Greenwood was able to go about, and to discharge her social and domestic duties up to the last day of her life. No one associated with her, even her medical man, apprehended any sudden or fatal termination. When it became known in Kidwelly that she had passed away after a few hours' illness in the early morning of Monday 16 June, much sympathy was felt for the widower and his motherless children. A wider circle was apprised of Mr Greenwood's bereavement the following day by a somewhat snobbish announcement in the deaths column of *The Times* for 17 June –

GREENWOOD. – On the 16th of June, suddenly, Mabel Greenwood, the dearly-loved wife of Harold Greenwood, Esq., of Rumsey House, Kidwelly, and the younger sister of Col. and Ald. Sir Vansittart Bowater, Bart.

It is important to consider minutely Mrs Greenwood's state of health for some time prior to her death. Her husband, on oath in the witness-box at his trial, said that 'she would not have lived long because she was broken up.' The post-mortem revealed no trace of natural disease other than the aforementioned non-malignant tumour. The heart was much decomposed, but no signs of disease in the valves were detected by the experts who examined them. Her husband was naturally the person most intimately associated with her, and certainly had the best opportunity of judging of her condition. According to his own statement, as far back as January of 1919 Mrs Greenwood was complaining of pains in her heart, and also of pains internally. She was unable to sleep on her left side for a year before her death, and if she attempted this declared that she felt suffocated. In May 1919 she expressed an opinion that she would not live long, and Greenwood persuaded her to let him write to her brother, requesting him to bring down a specialist to examine her. Mrs Greenwood approved of the letter, but in the end refused to have it posted. It was ultimately decided that after her holiday at Portishead, if her health had not improved, she should submit to a thorough medical overhauling. Unfortunately, Greenwood, who was obviously unable to keep his affairs to himself, told these arrangements to his friends at the *Mercury* office. Stories of Mrs Greenwood's serious state crept about in a garbled form, and on 5 June Greenwood wrote a furious and insulting letter to a Miss Gwyneth David.[1] In it he expressed surprise that she should have told a neighbour, Miss Alice Jones, that Mrs Greenwood was *not* ill, and accused her of telling deliberate lies, and trying to break his friendship with the Joneses, the family into which he subsequently married. The prosecution made a good deal of this letter, alleging that it proved

[1] Miss David was a Llanelly lady, who had been friendly with Greenwood's daughter, Irene, until her father, after the affair of the letter, insisted on her discontinuing the intimacy. According to Irene, Miss David on one occasion came to tea at Rumsey House, and afterwards complained of the tea that she was given, and said that Mrs Greenwood was like an icicle!

that Greenwood was wishful to create the impression locally that his wife was seriously ill in order that her sudden death might occasion no surprise, and also to suggest to another woman that he would soon be free to marry her.

On Sunday 8 June Mrs Greenwood was at church by herself. On Monday 9 June she had tea with a neighbour in the Castle grounds during an Eisteddfod. On Wednesday 11 June she and her husband were out in his car. On Thursday 12 June she attended an antiquarian meeting at Kidwelly Town Hall. Greenwood stated afterwards that several people, whose names he quoted, remarked on how ill she looked, and one especially noticed that she seemed to have great difficulty in mounting the stairs. Poor woman! Little did she reck that exactly a year later that same Town Hall would be the scene of a coroner's inquest upon her decaying and mutilated body. Her husband described her as 'very depressed' that night, and an acquaintance who called at Rumsey House the next evening warned Greenwood that if he were not careful he would not have her long. On Friday 13 June Mrs Greenwood was fitted for a new dress, and alluded to her forthcoming holiday to the dressmaker. On Saturday 14 June she was unusually active, and one person, seeing her so recently and apparently well, at once harboured a grave suspicion as to her very sudden death.

Greenwood stated that his wife never complained of her ailments. She was sensitive and reticent about them, but during the last week of her life she seemed depressed, miserable, suffering, and expressed a constant wish to be in heaven. Kidwelly's candid opinion that her husband had assisted her to obtain this desire led to an exhumation, an inquest, a charge of wilful murder, and a seven days' trial to prove or disprove the same.

On the Saturday morning Mrs Greenwood visited an old servant, Martha Morris, still employed by her former mistress for daily work at Rumsey House. This woman, who had originally been nurse to Irene Greenwood, said in her evidence at the trial that for weeks prior to Mrs Greenwood's death she had noticed her increasing feebleness and loss of flesh, had seen her faint, and heard her complain that she suffered from diarrhoea. On this particular date Mrs Greenwood looked very ill and sat down in Mrs Morris's kitchen. She had seemed depressed the whole week. Greenwood stated that his wife had come to him immediately after breakfast and said that her heart was causing her to feel as if she were suffocating, and she intended to call at her doctor's for a different medicine. Greenwood could not say definitely whether she went, but during the morning she was undoubtedly out. Besides the visit to Mrs Morris, Mrs Greenwood called at the Phoenix Stores, a wine merchant's in Bridge Street, a few yards from Rumsey House, and purchased from Sarah Edwards, the proprietor's wife, a bottle of burgundy. This was wine supplied by Messrs Gilbey, called 'Real Pure Wine', and bearing a red label. The Greenwoods had been regular customers for burgundy and whisky since they had come to Rumsey House, their purchases invariably being a bottle at a time.[1] This particular bottle was placed by Hannah Williams, when laying the luncheon table next day, before Mrs Greenwood's seat, and a good deal of contradictory evidence at the trial concerned it. The maid swore that she put it out when laying the cloth for supper, and never saw it subsequently. She looked for it in the sideboard the following day, but could not find it. She went out on the Sunday evening at 5.30, and on her return the supper things had been taken away, by whom she was unable to state. On her evening off duty Irene Greenwood sometimes performed this domestic task, but Hannah Williams did not know whether she had done so this particular night. As Irene was much occupied with her mother's sudden illness, it seems unlikely. The maid Powell was also out, and the movements of the cook, who was suffering from a gathered finger, were not touched upon. Irene Greenwood swore that she drank burgundy at both

[1] When Miss Bowater was an inmate of Rumsey House she shared the wine ordered from Brigstocke's, a wine merchant in Carmarthen. Greenwood occasionally bought whisky. Between 8 January and 17 April the amount of wine and spirits ordered from Brigstocke's was – 20 bottles of Beaune burgundy, 15 bottles of Pauillac claret, 2 bottles of Scotch whisky, and 6 bottles of sparkling Moselle wine.

lunch and supper on Sunday 15 June, and asked Miss
Phillips, a guest at the latter meal, to have wine which she
refused. Miss Phillips swore that she saw no wine of any kind
on the supper-table, 'as if there had been any she would have
had some.' The prosecution sought to prove that Greenwood
mixed arsenic, in the form of diluted weed-killer, with the
missing bottle of burgundy, and by this means poisoned his
wife.

The alleged motive was undoubtedly the weakest link in
the chain of fact and evidence which the Crown strove to
weave until it became the hangman's noose. Servants, friends,
acquaintances, the family doctor, all described the Greenwoods as a happy couple, and apparently attached to each
other. The only contrary evidence came from two women,
the above-mentioned Miss Phillips, an intimate friend of Mrs
Greenwood's for eleven years, and Miss Mary Griffiths, whose
brother attended Mrs Greenwood in the capacity of her medical adviser. Harold Greenwood was undoubtedly what is
known as a 'ladies' man', and his popularity on this score,
according to these wise virgins, aroused his wife's jealousy.
Miss Phillips averred that he was fond of doing so, and that
she had witnessed 'scenes' which had their origin in Greenwood's attentions to some lady, and Mrs Greenwood's resent-
ment thereat. In the course of the police court proceedings
prior to the trial Miss Phillips was pressed by Mr Ludford, the
defending solicitor, to name one specific instance of these
alleged 'tiffs and brawls'. She became very truculent, refused
at first to answer, and declared that it was most unfair that
Greenwood should be putting Mr Ludford up to the questions he was asking her. Greenwood vowed that Miss Phillips
was known as 'the Kidwelly postman', that she spent her
time largely in collecting and repeating gossip, and that if she
saw him speaking to, or walking with, any women, particularly Miss Griffiths, she went at once to tell Mrs Greenwood.
Miss Griffiths denied that Mrs Greenwood was jealous of her
on account of Greenwood. She stated that 'things were not
very comfortable at times' between the Greenwoods because
of his flirtations. Mrs Greenwood had once said to Miss

Griffiths in Greenwood's presence: 'That is Harold's weakness. He is too fond of women.' Miss Griffiths subsequently admitted to having been on very friendly terms herself with Greenwood, though she indignantly denied the story that she had sat on his knee in a railway carriage. The Griffiths, brother and sister, lived opposite to Rumsey House, a fact which became of importance during the last hours of Mrs Greenwood's life.

2

On Saturday 14 June Mr and Mrs Greenwood lunched early, as she was wishful to attend a tennis meeting at Ferryside, five miles away. Greenwood stated that he did his best to persuade his wife not to undertake such a fatiguing expedition, but she declared herself better, and was determined to go. Greenwood walked with her to Kidwelly Station. On the way she complained of a pain in her heart which she ascribed to flatulence. She sat for some time on a wall near the Railway Inn, then walked the remaining distance to the platform. Greenwood again endeavoured to induce her to give up the Ferryside project, but she was adamant. He left her, on seeing the Kidwelly vicar, the Rev. David Ambrose Jones, coming down the lane, Mrs Greenwood having previously mentioned that she expected him to be at the meeting.

Greenwood's own movements on the Saturday were scarcely touched upon. He stated that he was at home all day, but after tea he went to the local telephone exchange and asked for the *Llanelly Mercury* office. The operator stated that a lady's voice answered, and she heard Greenwood say: 'I am happy, I am satisfied now.' This was not admissible as evidence at the trial, but the fact of Greenwood ringing up the same number every Saturday, and being answered by the same feminine voice, was regarded by the prosecution as proof of a very close association with his second wife prior to the death of his first.

Mrs Greenwood and her clergyman travelled to Ferryside in the same compartment. On reaching the station they walked three-quarters of a mile to the tennis grounds, and the same distance when returning. He described her afterwards as looking unwell, but she made no allusion to her health, and was cheerful, as well as taking a keen interest in the business part of the meeting. A game of croquet was suggested, but Mrs Greenwood whispered to her companion that she would rather not play, so the idea was abandoned. The vicar travelled back with her to Kidwelly, and they parted just outside the station. He never saw her again. Irene Greenwood, who had come from Carmarthen by the same train, but in another compartment, overtook her mother at the station gate, and they walked home together. Irene stated subsequently that she seemed perfectly well, and nothing in any way unusual occurred that evening. Mrs Greenwood retired to bed about 10.15, but, according to her husband, was very restless, and went in several times to see Kenneth, who was sleeping soundly. Poor soul! Had she some prevision of the approaching separation?

Mrs Greenwood was seen by two other people besides the vicar on the Saturday. Martha Morris came to Rumsey House in the evening, found her sitting on the verandah with Miss Phillips, and thought her (Mrs Greenwood) 'very low and very ill.' On the other hand, Miss Phillips, who stayed some little time, during which she and Mrs Greenwood were 'laughing and talking', described her as 'quite bright and unusually well.' Miss Phillips was particularly struck by her friend's complexion. 'It was a lovely sort of pink, which was quite unusual with her.' Mrs Greenwood was not a woman who was given to improving her appearance by artificial aids. On the other hand, arsenic, as testified by such experts as Madeleine Smith and Mrs Maybrick, is a noted beautifier, whether taken internally or applied externally. The latter, in Mrs Greenwood's case, was utterly unlikely. The former possibility was not touched upon.

On Sunday 15 June the Greenwood family spent a leisurely and (so far as their duty to their Maker was concerned) unprofitable morning. They breakfasted at 10 o'clock, the meal consisting of eggs, cooked in various ways, coffee, and bread and butter. Afterwards, Irene attended to sundry domestic duties, and later sat in the garden with a book. At the trial she swore that she never saw her father go into the house the whole forenoon. Mrs Greenwood's Sabbatic occupations and activities up to 1 o'clock are not recorded other than by her husband's subsequent statement that she was reading on the lawn. Hannah Williams said that she saw her mistress writing letters, and this was more or less corroborated by Irene Greenwood's testimony that she took two letters to the post in the afternoon. Mr and Mrs Greenwood had previously arranged to go to church, but she declared herself too unwell, and Greenwood, preferring cleanliness to godliness, was busy overhauling his car, with the assistance of Tom Foy, the manager of the local cinema. Foy both saw and spoke to Mrs Greenwood several times before lunch, and thought her in her usual health. At the trial Hannah Williams swore that at 12.30 Greenwood went into the china pantry, and remained there for half an hour. She was hindered in laying the table for lunch, as the silver basket was kept in the china pantry, and she did not like to go in and fetch it while he was there. She declared that she had never known him to do this before. Greenwood stated, and witnesses were called to prove, that he constantly and frequently used the sink in the china pantry to wash his hands after working at his car or in the garden. A towel was kept behind the door for his special use. On this occasion he went in just as the gong sounded for lunch, and did not remain there for more than a few minutes. The Crown called Foy at the trial, but the defence endeavoured to twist his statements in Greenwood's favour as establishing that the accused man had been in Foy's company the whole morning, thus disposing of the parlourmaid's story of a lengthy sojourn in the china pantry. Margaret Morris, the cook, stated that she was in the kitchen all the forenoon and did not see Greenwood go into the china pantry, the door of which was opposite the kitchen, but admitted that he might have done so without her knowledge. Mrs Greenwood came into the kitchen once between breakfast and lunch, looking very ill. This was the last time the cook saw her alive.

Lunch consisted of a hot joint,[1] vegetables, gooseberry tart, and custard. The meal was served at 1 o'clock, and was partaken of by all the four Greenwoods, and afterwards by the servants. Nobody, excepting Mrs Greenwood, suffered any ill effects. Hannah Williams swore at the trial that Greenwood drank whisky, Mrs Greenwood burgundy, and Irene and Kenneth water. Miss Phillips called at Rumsey House about 1 o'clock. The family were at lunch, but Mrs Greenwood came out from the dining-room. Miss Phillips subsequently described her friend as looking pale and pinched, and speaking in a very low voice. That nothing serious or untoward was apprehended is shown by Mrs Greenwood's invitation to Miss Phillips to return to supper at Rumsey House the same evening.

After lunch, according to Irene Greenwood, Mrs Greenwood first walked round the garden with her, and then retired to lie down. Greenwood stated that his wife went straight to her bedroom from the luncheon-table. Later, she sat on the lawn with a book. Tom Foy, who was giving Irene a lesson in driving the car, took her out in it about 3 o'clock. He saw Mrs Greenwood seated in a deck-chair, reading. 'She seemed to be quite well, and pleased at our going out,' Foy stated. Mrs Greenwood spoke to him, but the noise of the engine prevented Foy's hearing what she said. When he returned at 4.30 he did not see either her or Greenwood, and only heard of her being ill later in the evening. Foy was always emphatic in his declaration that this Sunday, 15 June, was the only occasion when he took Miss Greenwood out in the car, and that he had never confused the date with the previous Sunday, 8 June.

At 3.30 (the statement rests on Greenwood's word alone) Mrs Greenwood came to him and complained that she was suffering from diarrhoea. This is one of the most prominent

---

[1] The cook, Margaret Morris, said in her evidence at the trial that this was a leg of lamb. The between-maid, Gwyneira Powell, described it as roast beef. The parlour-maid, Hannah Maggie Williams, although asked as a special test of her memory whether it were beef or mutton, was unable to say which.

symptoms of arsenical poisoning, and usually manifests itself very early after the poison has been swallowed. The Crown sought to establish the first indications of Mrs Greenwood's fatal illness as soon as possible after lunch, to substantiate their contention that the arsenic was administered in the burgundy drunk at this meal. Against the theory is the undisputed fact, vouched for by several independent and unbiased witnesses, that Mrs Greenwood was apparently quite well so late as 6 o'clock on the Sunday evening. When the parlourmaid brought tea into the drawing-room at 4.30 she noticed nothing amiss. The other maid, before she went out at 6 p.m., saw Mrs Greenwood and her daughter talking together in the garden. At tea, in company with her husband and family, she had some tea and bread and butter, and afterwards lay down for a while. Between 5 and 6 o'clock she was sufficiently well to be in the garden again. Between 6.30 and 7 o'clock, whilst strolling with her husband, she complained of sickness and suffocating pains in the region of the heart. Greenwood administered brandy, which caused vomiting. It was afterwards a disputed point whether he gave her the brandy on the lawn or in the house. He and Irene, with considerable difficulty, took Mrs Greenwood upstairs to her bedroom. Shortly before 7 o'clock Greenwood went across for Dr Griffiths. He came at once, and found the patient sitting on a couch, and vomiting. She told him that the gooseberry tart eaten at lunch had disagreed with her, 'as it always did'. The Crown contended that the suggestion of the gooseberry tart being the cause of her indisposition came from Greenwood, and was said by him in reference to the alleged attack of diarrhoea at 3.30. No mention of this feature of Mrs Greenwood's illness was then made to the doctor. He directed that she should be put to bed and given sips of brandy and soda-water. Whilst her daughter was helping her to undress she had an attack of diarrhoea and vomited again. Greenwood and the doctor, in the meantime, went down to the garden and played several games of clock-golf. Greenwood stated that he was anxious about his wife and wished to detain the doctor on her account. Dr Griffiths saw Mrs Greenwood in bed before returning to his own house, and sent her over a bottle of medicine containing a bismuth mixture, dispensed by himself. On his second visit he considered her better, and the sickness had ceased for the time.

Miss Phillips arrived at Rumsey House about 7.30. She was greeted by Greenwood with the remark, 'The wife is very ill; run upstairs.' The guest did so, and met Irene coming out of Mrs Greenwood's bedroom. Irene announced that her mother was very ill and she was putting her to bed. Miss Phillips, without inquiring the nature of the indisposition, took for granted that Mrs Greenwood was suffering from her heart. She went immediately to fetch the district nurse, Nurse Jones, who lived a short distance from Rumsey House. In her evidence at the trial Irene Greenwood stated that 'Daddy and I' suggested to Mrs Greenwood that Nurse Jones, who had previously attended members of the family and was on friendly terms at Rumsey House, should be sent for, and that Miss Phillips volunteered to bring her. Miss Phillips afterwards claimed the credit for having proposed the nurse. She called at her house with the information that 'Mrs Greenwood was very bad with her heart', and requested her to come at once. On her arrival at Rumsey House, which she subsequently stated was about 8 o'clock, Nurse Jones found Mrs Greenwood very cold and collapsed, with a low temperature. The nurse considered her so ill that she at once desired that the doctor should be summoned. Miss Phillips, who had hurried back without waiting for the nurse, replied that Dr Griffiths had already seen Mrs Greenwood and sent her some medicine. The nurse, believing this to be medicine for a heart case, decided to wait and see what effect it had on the patient. One dose had been taken out of the bottle, and the nurse administered a second. Greenwood told the nurse that 'Mrs Greenwood complained that the medicine caught her at the back of the throat.' Nurse Jones tasted it herself and suffered no ill effects. What ultimately became of this bottle of medicine is not known. Presumably it was thrown away after Mrs Greenwood's death, together with a large quantity of bottles containing patent remedies and Dr Griffiths's other prescriptions, which Martha Morris stated that she got rid of at Miss Bowater's orders.

Nurse Jones remained for an hour with her patient, and then returned home to put her child to bed. At the trial the defending counsel pressed her very hard upon the point, demanding why she left Mrs Greenwood if she considered her so ill. The nurse declared that 'she had to go', and that she left Miss Phillips and Irene Greenwood in charge. Miss Phillips stated afterwards that during the nurse's absence Mrs Greenwood was 'sort of dozing' and very weak. Nurse Jones came back at 10 o'clock, and always averred that at no time from this onwards was Mrs Greenwood any better. Dr Griffiths paid his patient several visits, the hour of one of these subsequently becoming a matter of importance and dispute. On this point his evidence, and that of Greenwood, Miss Phillips, and Nurse Jones, are strikingly at variance. The doctor could only recall four visits – at 6 p.m., at 7 p.m. (before leaving the house), about 9 p.m., and at 3 a.m. He afterwards varied these hours to 6.30, 7.30, 10 or 10.30 p.m., and 3 or 3.30 a.m. Throughout Mrs Greenwood's illness he saw nothing inconsistent with gastric trouble, due to the gooseberry tart. He denied that the nurse ever spoke to him of its being a serious case, or hinted that there was anything wrong. He had no recollection of paying any visit at 1 o'clock a.m. At his last visit the nurse told him that the diarrhoea was 'uncontrollable', but Dr Griffiths did not ask to see the excreta.

Greenwood's conduct on the last night of his wife's life was greatly called in question. It was afterwards alleged against him that when Mrs Greenwood's condition had become materially worse, her husband, sent by the nurse to fetch Dr Griffiths, was so long in returning with or without him that Irene had to go to the doctor's house to discover the reason of his delay. Greenwood swore that he was not absent for more than ten minutes, an opinion endorsed by Miss Griffiths, in whose company he had been. Miss Phillips and Nurse Jones both agreed that he was away for nearly an hour. Still later, when Mrs Greenwood was practically at the point of death, Greenwood, urged to bring Dr Griffiths, came back alone, saying that he could not rouse him. The nurse went over and wakened the doctor at once. The prosecution made much of those two incidents as emphasising that Greenwood's conduct was highly inconsistent with his supposed anxiety about his wife.

It may perhaps be permitted to inquire here: where were the servants? Mrs Greenwood's fatal illness commenced between 6.30 and 7 p.m., and terminated in death about 3.30 a.m. During this time Miss Phillips states that she procured hot water from the kitchen, and herself fetched the nurse. In addition, she and Irene, at Nurse Jones's directions, filled hot-water bottles. It was Greenwood who went repeatedly in person for Dr Griffiths. The two younger maids, Williams and Powell, were both out up to a late hour; but surely when they returned they did not callously go to bed without troubling to ascertain whether they could do anything for their mistress, who, they learned at 9.30, was very ill? All three servants slept together in the same room, immediately over Mrs Greenwood's. Hannah Williams complained that she was kept awake by Mrs Greenwood's groaning, a statement contradicted by her fellow-servants. At about 3 a.m. Irene Greenwood roused the younger maids and sent them to fetch Miss Phillips, who had gone home at 11 o'clock, but Mrs Greenwood was dead before they returned. At the trial all three maids were called as witnesses, but only examined with regard to the laying of the luncheon-table much earlier in the day, and the general relations between their employers.

Much of what occurred in Mrs Greenwood's bedroom that night rests on the testimony of Nurse Jones. According to her sworn and separate statements, Mrs Greenwood grew steadily worse after the nurse's return at 10 o'clock. She was given brandy, milk, soda and brandy at intervals of a quarter of an hour, but could retain nothing. Diarrhoea, of a kind that the nurse stated she had never seen before in her professional experience of over twenty years, continued incessantly up to midnight. Yet at none of his visits did Dr Griffiths express any alarm or call to see the patient without being summoned, and Greenwood, as well as Irene, appears to have felt no undue concern. According to his account, Mrs Greenwood was rational and collected, explaining where anything required for her was to be found, and talking quite composedly.[1] According to the nurse, Greenwood seemed perfectly indifferent to his wife's sufferings, did not suggest at any time sending for the doctor, but had to be told to fetch him, and beyond repeatedly asking Mrs Greenwood how she felt, to which the poor woman, when able to speak, replied 'Very bad', displayed neither interest nor sympathy. The nurse also stated that Mrs Greenwood asked her 'to tell Mr Greenwood not to sit on the bed.' Another version of this request was given by Irene, who stated that she sat on her mother's bed when in the room about 1 a.m., and Mrs Greenwood objected to the weight and desired her to move.

Despite her sufferings and discomfort, Mrs Greenwood seems to have been thoughtful and unselfish to a degree. She repeatedly apologized to the nurse for giving her trouble, and both Nurse Jones and Miss Phillips testified that Mrs Greenwood was 'very considerate about other people' and 'not one to complain'. At 11 o'clock she expressed a wish that her daughter should go to bed, in order to be fit for her work at the bank next morning, and that Miss Phillips should return home. The latter did so, according to her own statement, 'very reluctantly'. Before she went, Nurse Jones mentioned to her about the sickness and diarrhoea. 'She said it was of a very peculiar nature, and she was very worried, as she had never seen anything like it before. She would have to speak to the doctor about it.' Nurse Jones afterwards denied that she had said this. Miss Phillips was seen off the premises by Greenwood, who told her not to worry. He added that he had often

[1] Greenwood stated in his proof: 'During the time nurse was away I kept going into the room and chatted with them all, and my wife seemed quite easy. I asked her several times if she had any pain about her heart, but she replied each time she had none, but that she felt very weak. She showed me how blue her fingers were, and I rubbed them for her several times. ... About 10.30 my wife suggested that nurse should have a cup of tea, and I said I would have one too. About 11 o'clock my wife suggested that Irene should go to bed, and she went. It was a beautiful night. I said I would take a walk round the garden, but my wife said, "Oh, don't leave me", so I did not go."

known his wife much worse, and she would be all right by the morning. This conversation took place outside the gate of Rumsey House. Dr Griffiths, who was taking his customary evening stroll, came up and asked how Mrs Greenwood was. Greenwood replied that she was 'easier', a statement which the nurse subsequently declared she could not understand his making. On hearing this Dr Griffiths did not go in to see the patient, and averred that he had no recollection afterwards of paying her any visit until the last one about 3 a.m., a short time before she died.[1]

By 1 a.m. Mrs Greenwood seems to have realized the seriousness of her condition, if no one else did. She asked the nurse if she were dying, and said that she did wish she could have lived to bring up her children. 'Irene still needed mothering.' The nurse heard her praying, and she afterwards said to her that if she (Mrs Greenwood) did not recover, Miss Bowater was to be told it was her sister's wish that she should look after the children, 'and bring them up in the way I should like to have them brought up.' This conversation took place when Greenwood was out of the room, having been dispatched by Nurse Jones for Dr Griffiths. The nurse subsequently stated that by 1 a.m. 'she had become suspicious that things were not as they should be.' If this were the case, and Miss Phillips, two hours before, had felt similarly uneasy and dissatisfied, why was no suggestion made of calling in another doctor?

During the trial the question was hotly debated of what certain pills, prescribed by Dr Griffiths for Mrs Greenwood, had contained. Greenwood fetched the parcel with them from the doctor's, and at the time of the death no question arose as to their being other than a harmless and necessary remedy. There is considerable confusion as to when they were ordered and administered. Dr Griffiths said that he gave them at his 10 o'clock visit. The nurse and Greenwood both stated that it was at 1 o'clock. Immediately after taking these pills Mrs

---

[1] Miss Phillips stated that between Mrs Greenwood's death and her funeral she heard Greenwood telling Miss Bowater that 'the doctor was so good; he came over every half-hour.'

Greenwood relapsed into coma or sleep, and never woke again. When suspicion had grown rife that her death was caused by unnatural means, Greenwood averred that the pills were 'too strong', and had killed his wife. 'If she had not had the pills she would be all right to-day.' Irene Greenwood stated that, both before and after the exhumation of her mother's body, her father told her that 'morphia pills' had been the cause of her death. Greenwood alleged that he first became suspicious about the pills by Nurse Jones saying 'Damn those pills!' that they had killed Mrs Greenwood, and requesting him not to mention this to Dr Griffiths! Nurse Jones denied on oath that on the morning of Mrs Greenwood's death there had been any talk about the pills, or that she had at any time asked Greenwood not to mention them. Dr Griffiths likewise denied that at the time of the exhumation Greenwood had discussed or alluded to the pills in conversation with him. At the inquest and the police court proceedings the doctor swore that he gave Mrs Greenwood two morphia pills. At the trial he declared on oath that during the previous hearings he had confused morphia with opium, and that the pills were opium pills. From the defence point of view this was both inconvenient and exasperating, as, relying on the statement made at the previous examinations that the pills were morphia pills, the defence was prepared to call two medical experts to swear that Mrs Greenwood died of morphia poisoning.

Mrs Greenwood died at 3.30 a.m. on Monday 16 June. Her illness certainly exhibited two known symptoms of arsenical poisoning – vomiting and diarrhoea – but not its other usual features of cramp and thirst. Nurse Jones declared that the widower did not seem to be put out in any way, though on another occasion she stated that he was 'upset' by the death, and unconcerned throughout the preceding illness. On the other hand, Miss Phillips, when she returned to Rumsey House in the early morning, saw Greenwood walking about the room shedding tears, and Nurse Jones weeping and unable to speak. Dr Griffiths certified the death as due to valvular disease of the heart.

3

About 8 o'clock on the morning of 16 June Nurse Jones called at the vicarage with the news of Mrs Greenwood's death. Whether Greenwood sent her, or she went on her own initiative, does not appear. The vicar stated afterwards that 'he was very much vexed' – whether at the loss of a personal friend or of a wealthy parishioner does not appear either. The earliest hint of a dreadful suspicion which was ultimately to lead to a criminal charge seems to have dated from this conversation between the local clergyman and the district nurse. Mr Jones, having been so recently in Mrs Greenwood's company, when she appeared in her usual health, was perplexed and uneasy at hearing of her very sudden passing. Nurse Jones, agitated and upset, probably let slip more than she intended. Afterwards there was a considerable mystery over 'one thing which she would never tell.' It finally transpired, being wrung from her by the coroner at the inquest, that this was the vicar's inquiry whether she thought there had been foul play in connexion with Mrs Greenwood's death. Mr Ludford, who represented Greenwood at the inquest, asked if the suggestion of foul play had come from the vicar, and sarcastically included him amongst the 'band of gossips' who had been discussing the case in Kidwelly.[1] The nurse admitted telling the vicar that she thought there ought to have been a consultation, and after the funeral regretted that there had not been a post-mortem.

Greenwood's own conduct on the morning of his wife's death was so flagrantly foolish and uncircumspect that it seems more consistent with innocence than guilt. At 10 o'clock he motored to Llanelly, and drove straight to the *Mercury* office. Here he told his friend Mr Llewellyn Jones of Mrs Greenwood's death, and accepted his offer to call at the undertaker's. Greenwood had forgotten the keys of the safe in his

[1] If he were not one of the 'band of gossips', the vicar was undoubtedly among the local prophets. He made the cryptic remark to Sergeant Hodge Lewis: 'When that body is got up people will stiffen their backs, and you will get to know a good deal more.'

Llanelly office. He borrowed twenty pounds from Mr Jones's sister, Gladys, the lady whom he afterwards married as his second wife, and accompanied her to various shops, purchasing his mourning. During his absence the vicar called at Rumsey House, and, finding Greenwood out, paid another visit later in the day. They went together to the churchyard, where Greenwood chose a site for his wife's grave. He told the vicar that heart failure had been the cause of her death, but there was no mention of any feature of the illness. At this time no suggestion was uttered of suicide, but on the day that Mrs Greenwood's body was exhumed Greenwood sent for the vicar, and during their interview some discussion arose as to this possibility. According to the vicar's statement, he was with Greenwood for a quarter of an hour, during which 'Mr Greenwood did the talking and I listened.' At the inquest the vicar indignantly repudiated the suicide theory. Mrs Greenwood had been a cheerful, genial woman, keenly interested in everything, and the last person likely to do such a thing as take her own life. He regarded the suggestion as 'an infamous slander on the character and memory of a deceased lady who was not there to defend herself.' The vicar was probably right. Mrs Greenwood was a religious woman, and, apart from the unlikelihood of her attempting such a terrible act through ill-health and depression, where could she have obtained the arsenic to accomplish her purpose? She was of a reticent nature, and never discussed her husband with her clergyman, who had no reason to suppose that she was other than happy in her married life. Greenwood was a member of the congregation, and, with his first wife and family, had been a regular worshipper at St Mary's Church, but after the exhumation he never attended services there again.

On Thursday 19 June Mrs Greenwood was buried in the somewhat congested churchyard round St Mary's Church. The vicar, assisted by his curate, performed the ceremony. The Rev. Ambrose Jones's smouldering suspicions as to the death were fanned to a steady flame by Greenwood's failure to send him the death certificate. Irene Greenwood had duly registered her mother's death, and the certificate was perfectly in order, so that there was absolutely no reason for Greenwood's neglect in the matter. Unfortunately, it added another to the current rumours that all had not been well, and formed an excellent opening for the interview which the police had with Greenwood on 24 October. Mrs Greenwood was laid in the grave selected for her reception by Greenwood, where her body remained undisturbed until the following April.[1]

The vicar was not the only person to whom Nurse Jones confided her doubts and uneasiness touching Mrs Greenwood's death. To Mrs Smart, president of the District Nursing Association, who had remarked that it was very sad for Mrs Greenwood to die so suddenly, the nurse replied: 'Yes, this case has worried me a lot. I did not quite understand it. I have never seen a case like it before.' On another occasion Nurse Jones said to the same lady: 'I wish I had my time over again. I should insist on a post-mortem, although I don't like them.' Mrs Smart not unnaturally asked if the nurse thought there had been anything wrong, to which her answer was: 'Oh, no, I don't think that. Do what I would I couldn't get Mrs Greenwood warm.' At the inquest Nurse Jones, with the utmost reluctance, admitted that she had said these things in conversation with Mrs Smart, excepting the remark referring to the post-mortem. She also agreed that the conversations between herself and the vicar had taken place, but the admission had almost to be dragged from her by the coroner. She fainted at the inquest proceedings on hearing that arsenic had been found in Mrs Greenwood's remains.

These remarks, no doubt exaggerated, were quoted and

[1] The coffin was placed in a brick cavity about 2 ft 6 ins. deep, which was covered with stone slabs. The bottom of the grave was about 7 ft from the surface. No earth was in contact with the coffin, which bore a brass plate engraved with the name and date of death of deceased. The body was in two coffins, the inner of elm and the outer of oak. When exhumed, there was water in the brick chamber, but none in the coffin, which had not rotted. Nothing was injected into the body before burial for preservation. At the exhumation the undertaker noticed that it was exceptionally well preserved.

repeated about Kidwelly, and came eventually to the ears of the police authorities. Nurse Jones was interviewed by Sergeant Hodge Lewis, and from the police point of view proved unsatisfactory and evasive. At the inquest she denied having said to him: 'You can look through me, sergeant; I am telling the whole truth. I have had many cases like this. There was nothing unusual about the death.' She further denied that at another interview with the officer she told him that she would not say anything more unless compelled. Since Mrs Greenwood's death Nurse Jones had been going to Rumsey House, alleging that Greenwood was looking after some business for her in connexion with the affairs of a recently deceased uncle. On one occasion, between the death and the exhumation of Mrs Greenwood's body, Greenwood asked Nurse Jones: 'What is this rumour that's about?' She told him that people were saying that Mrs Greenwood died an unnatural death. Greenwood replied: 'Anyone that will slander my name will have to pay for it.' Nurse Jones continued to visit Rumsey House, and the night before Greenwood's second marriage she was alone with him up to a late hour. She admitted to telling his fortune, but denied that she had ever said to him that if he knew what people were saying about him his hair would stand on end.

Possibly in time the gossip and rumours touching Mrs Greenwood's end might, unlike the unfortunate subject of them, have died a natural death had it not been for her husband's insane folly in marrying again within four months. At the trial Sir Edward Marshall Hall, Greenwood's counsel, who defended and excused practically every single action on the part of his client except this one, spoke in condemnation of Greenwood's foolish haste, which naturally afforded the prosecution a strong motive for the alleged poisoning of the first wife. On the other hand, the defending counsel stressed Greenwood's 'loneliness', and his difficulties with regard to other women, as accounting for his desire to re-marry so speedily, and, as it proved, so rashly.

Greenwood's position when a widower was a delicate and peculiar one. His earnings as a solicitor would never have sufficed to keep up an establishment such as Rumsey House. His first wife had a comfortable annual income[1] which, if it had passed to Greenwood after her death, would, as his counsel pointed out at the trial, have offered overwhelming motive for compassing her destruction. On the contrary, her husband lost in a financial sense, if in no other, by her demise. Her life was not insured, either by herself or by him. She made no will, and under the terms of her father's the income was hers for life, and afterwards had to go to her children in equal shares. She had no power to dispose of it otherwise. Her mother had left her a few hundreds, her personal estate, when Greenwood took out letters of administration, being sworn at between three and four hundred pounds. Her jewellery was legally his, and the day after her death he divided it between his two daughters. The diamond ring which had been his wife's engagement ring Greenwood gave to his daughter Irene, but subsequently revoked the gift. He decided to have the ring made into something for his own wear, and offered Irene a new ring instead. Ultimately she received the ring originally intended for her, and the newly purchased one, costing £55, became the property of Miss Gladys Jones, later the second Mrs Greenwood.[2]

Life at Rumsey House that summer was scarcely enjoyable. The atmosphere outside seethed with rumours of which Greenwood must have been perfectly aware. The domestic atmosphere inside was strained and uncomfortable. Miss Bowater, as joint mistress of the establishment together with her elder niece, evidently proved uncongenial to her brother-in-law. 'I felt so hopelessly out of it – it was not like a home,' he declared at his trial, when asked whether he showed his

[1] The exact amount of Mrs Greenwood's income was a matter of some dispute at the trial. Greenwood stated in his evidence that he did not know the precise figure, but put it at about £900 a year. I am informed from a private source that it was between £600 and £700.

[2] At the trial Irene was not asked any questions by the defence to corroborate Greenwood's story that the ring had been originally bought for her. Although the marriage did not take place until 1 October, Greenwood proposed to Miss Jones within a month of his wife's death, and the ring was obviously ordered by him as an engagement ring.

alleged affection for his first wife by marrying a second so speedily. There may also have been a grain of truth in his statement in the letter to Miss Griffiths that 'he was fed-up with Miss Bowater, and was going to get rid of her.' The only way in which the wretched widower could assume the mastery of his own house was by a second marriage. Between three and four months after Mrs Greenwood's death Kidwelly tongues were set wagging afresh at the news that he was about to replace her.

Apart from the strong motive of domestic strife and discomfort urging Greenwood to marry again with such unseemly haste, it should be remembered that these events took place less than a year after the conclusion of the Great War. Death had lost its dignity and importance. Mourning was regarded as obsolete, and the outward observances of bereavement were curtailed or disregarded. Speedy marrying and giving in marriage, war weddings, followed by a similar ceremony in a few months' time, had become commonplaces. In Greenwood's case it cannot be stressed too strongly that the usual sordid reason for a hurried wedding was entirely lacking. The element of the *crime passionel* could not be traced. Miss Gladys Jones was a woman of over thirty,[1] whom Greenwood had known intimately since her childhood. The friendship between himself and her family dated back to the year 1898, when he first came to Llanelly. He was completely unknown, but through his aunt, Mrs Treherne, he secured an introduction to Mr W. B. Jones, whose wife was a sister of Mrs Treherne's husband, Dr Treherne. Mr Jones was a well-known and influential figure in Llanelly, being, amongst his many other activities, part-proprietor of the *Llanelly Mercury*. In return for financial help with his paper, at a time when it was in difficulties, Mr Jones assisted Greenwood to build up his solicitor's practice. Mr Jones had a large family of sons and daughters. These were Greenwood's friends over a period of twenty years, and hardly a day passed without his visiting the

[1] The marriage certificate, dated 1 October 1919, describes her as thirty-one. Greenwood, giving evidence at his trial, thirteen months later, described her as 'about thirty-four'.

Joneses' house or the *Mercury* office, or one or other of the sons
going to Greenwood's business premises. There was little or
no social intercourse between Rumsey House and the Joneses.
The first Mrs Greenwood probably looked upon them as her
husband's business acquaintances.

Another motive that may have impelled the bridegroom's
haste was possibly anxiety to wed before he was wedded. A
widower is considered the lawful prey of female tongues and
attentions. Greenwood, always popular with petticoats, in
vulgar parlance, was doubtless 'chased' by every single lady
of his acquaintance, until he sought refuge through marrying
one of them. Kidwelly, like all small villages, was a hotbed of
gossip. Miss Griffiths told Greenwood that she had heard his
name coupled with those of Miss Phillips, Nurse Jones, and
two women unknown to him.

4

In the words of Sir Edward Marshall Hall at Greenwood's
trial: 'No human being could say what the relationship was
between Greenwood and Miss Griffiths.' The night before
Mrs Greenwood's death there had been an extraordinary
conversation between them, vouched for by Miss Griffiths
and emphatically denied by Greenwood. Greenwood went
over to the house to fetch Dr Griffiths at Nurse Jones's request.
The hour was a disputed point, as well as the length of time
which elapsed before his return with the doctor. Miss Griffiths admitted him, and, on hearing that Mrs Greenwood was
ill, inquired if she were suffering from one of her usual heart
attacks. Greenwood, who seemed in excellent spirits, replied
that his wife was worse than usual, and it was possible that she
might not recover. Miss Griffiths denied that she detained
him, or that he was with her for longer than ten minutes.
Ultimately Irene fetched him, and as he was leaving the room
Miss Griffiths made some reference to taking a holiday. Greenwood rejoined that he had been told by a fortune-teller that
his next trip would be a honeymoon. For a man married
twenty-three years the remark was somewhat startling. At his
trial Greenwood averred that Miss Griffiths had been 'got at'

by the police, that the entire conversation as alleged by her to have taken place was a fabrication, and that the observation about the honeymoon was made to her a few days before his second marriage. The prosecution stressed all this heavily as instancing callousness and indifference. In Greenwood's defence it should perhaps be remembered that he was more or less accustomed to his wife's severe attacks of illness, and, if innocent of any hand in this one, probably did not feel anxious about her, while his usual manner was cheerful and jocular.

Two days after Greenwood had intimated to the registrar of marriages at Llanelly his intention of wedding Miss Jones at the Bryn Chapel on 1 October 1919, he wrote the following letter to Miss Griffiths on 26 September:

> *Rumsey House, Kidwelly*
> *Carmarthenshire*
> *(Friday)*

MY DEAREST MAY, – I have been trying hard to get to you this last fortnight, but no luck; always someone going in or you were out. Now, I want you to read this letter very carefully and to think very carefully, and to send me over a reply to-night. There are very many rumours about, but between you and I [*sic*] this letter reveals the true position. Well, it is only right that you should know that Miss Bowater and Miss Phillips between them have turned my children against you very bitterly – why, I don't know. It is only right that you should know this, as you are the one I love most in this world, and I would be the last one to make you unhappy. Under these circumstances, are you prepared to face the music? I am going to do something quickly, as I must get rid of Miss Bowater at once, as I am simply fed up.

Let me have something from you to-night. – Yours as ever,

HAROLD.

At the trial both Greenwood and Miss Griffiths gave his and her separate explanation of this extraordinary production.

Miss Griffiths, for reasons best known to herself, kept the letter. In her evidence at Greenwood's trial she admitted telling Superintendent Jones (of the local police) about it. She was asked for it at the inquest by Mr Seward Pearce, Assistant Director of Prosecutions. Miss Griffiths throughout maintained the attitude that the letter was written in jest, that 'there was nothing in it', and that she was unable to explain it otherwise, or to account for its existence becoming known. Greenwood's versions of the matter most unchivalrously 'give away' the lady. At first he stated that on the Friday prior to his second wedding-day he was over at the Griffiths's house, and in the course of conversation with Miss Griffiths some allusion was made to his motor, which he had recently shown her. Greenwood remarked that he thought of going in the car for his honeymoon. Miss Griffiths, acquainted with the prevailing rumours, asked if it were true that he was to be married the following Wednesday. Greenwood told her not to listen to gossip, inquired from whom she had heard the story, and, finally, very foolishly, observed that he was free enough to propose to her. Miss Griffiths 'dared him to do it', whereupon he promised to write her an offer of marriage. For a solicitor it was surely the height of folly, even though he safeguarded himself by wording the alleged proposal so ambiguously that it might easily have been construed to mean several other things besides matrimony. Greenwood stated that he called in person for his answer on Sunday, and was 'very frightened that she might accept.' Miss Griffiths said 'No', and then asked if he meant to take her refusal seriously. Greenwood replied, 'Oh, no', and made a speedy escape. On the Tuesday, the night before his wedding, Nurse Jones came to Rumsey House with a note from Miss Griffiths,[1] asking if it were true that the marriage was to be next day, and 'was it too late?' Greenwood, by way of proving that it *was* too late, showed Nurse Jones the marriage licence. Nurse Jones went back to Miss Griffiths, returning in a short time with a message from her to the effect that the licence was only a piece of paper and could be torn up. Greenwood refused to agree to this, Nurse Jones carried his decision to Miss Griffiths, and brought over a final message that Miss Griffiths said that there

[1] Had Greenwood been able to produce this note it would have materially corroborated his story.

was nothing to be done, and had retired to bed in tears.[1] The bride's opinion of this imbroglio is not recorded.

Giving evidence at his trial, Greenwood explained the letter by saying that it was written by him at Miss Griffiths's request. When he went to tell her of his forthcoming marriage to Gladys Jones, Miss Griffiths burst into tears, declared that he had 'let her down' by paying her considerable attention, and she had always anticipated becoming the second Mrs Greenwood herself. She was subjected to chaff on the part of acquaintances, and asked Greenwood to propose to her in order to be able to tell people that she had refused him. Greenwood agreed to say that he had done so, but Miss Griffiths demanded a letter, written evidence being unassailable, whereas no one would believe her mere assertion. He acquiesced, and sent the letter, after composing several other attempts, none of which he had kept. Next day she said 'No', 'in a laughing way'. The remark about the honeymoon, alleged to have been made by Greenwood on the night prior to Mrs Greenwood's death, had been confused by Miss Griffiths with his reference to the motor-car trip a few days before he was married for the second time. He acquitted her of any malice in the matter, as he knew that she had not been questioned by the police until some months after his first wife's death, and dates were mixed up in her memory.[2] Miss Griffiths, in the witness-box, asseverated firmly that Greenwood had spoken of a honeymoon and a fortune-teller on the night of Mrs Greenwood's fatal illness, and denied practically everything that he had said regarding the ambiguous letter.

The marriage with Gladys Jones took place on 1 October 1919. Irene Greenwood, only apprised of it by her father two days before the ceremony, was greatly shocked and surprised. Before Greenwood and his second wife had returned from

[1] The conclusion of the whole matter, in Greenwood's elegant phrasing, was: 'May had said "There's nothing to be done", and had gone to bed howling. I was married the next morning.

[2] If the remark about the honeymoon were made to Miss Griffiths on 26 September, and she was questioned by the police so soon after as October or November, it is curious that she should have confused the date when the conversation took place with the night prior to Mrs Greenwood's death.

their honeymoon Irene left Rumsey House, and went to her mother's relatives in London. She and the similarly ousted Miss Bowater did not set up housekeeping together elsewhere. One of the strangest facts in this tangled and obscure story is the undisputed one that when inquiries began to be set on foot regarding the death of the first Mrs. Greenwood, her daughter, a woman of twenty-one, who had been in the house and with her for the greater part of her brief illness, who was present at her death-bed, and might reasonably be supposed to know as much of the circumstances as Miss Phillips, Nurse Jones, Maggie Williams, Tom Foy, or Dr Griffiths, all of whom were interrogated by the police at a very early date, was never interviewed by them, or asked to make any statement.

Despite Greenwood's long friendship and almost daily association with his second wife's family, Irene Greenwood's acquaintance with her stepmother, prior to Miss Jones assuming this relationship, appears to have been very slight. Irene and her sister Eileen once joined Miss Jones for some shopping expedition, and on another occasion the three visited a cinema together. She admitted having, at her father's suggestion, invited Gladys Jones for a week-end to Rumsey House in 1918. This was during Mrs Greenwood's absence, and without her knowledge, though she was told of it afterwards. Miss Jones was accompanied by her sister Gertrude, and as both were engaged to be married Irene saw nothing suspicious or undesirable in her father's wish that Miss Jones should be asked on a visit. Mrs Greenwood had given her daughter permission to invite a friend while she herself was away at the seaside. Irene proposed having Miss Gwyneth David, and Greenwood wanted to include Miss Jones in the invitation. When Miss David proved unable to come, Miss Gertrude Jones was substituted for her. This entirely harmless and natural episode was magnified to appalling proportions afterwards. Irene acknowledged that her mother was 'displeased' when she returned and heard about it, but there was no unpleasantness. On the other hand, local gossip told of 'a dreadful row' as soon as Mrs Greenwood discovered the presence of these unauthorized visitors by 'chocolate boxes all over the house'. The happy party broke up on the Monday morning, Irene and Miss Gertrude Jones departing by an early train to Carmarthen, whilst Greenwood and Miss Gladys Jones went off by a later one to Llanelly. Miss Griffiths related the story of the 'dreadful row' to Sergeant Hodge Lewis, but afterwards admitted that she was speaking from hearsay, based on Kidwelly gossip, and not from any personal knowledge.

The week-end visit was only one of several incidents, harmless in themselves, but capable of a sinister explanation, which the prosecution fastened upon. Greenwood's unlucky purchases of a lady's dressing-bag, weed-killer, and a diamond ring were all gossiped about, magnified, and misinterpreted. Miss Griffiths alleged that before Mrs Greenwood's death Miss Jones was constantly in the habit of ringing Greenwood up on the telephone at Dr Griffiths's, Rumsey House possessing none. There was a tale of a drive in Greenwood's car, with Miss Jones as passenger, on an occasion when Greenwood had been telegraphed for to return home from Pontardulais as his wife was dangerously ill. In the grate at his office Greenwood's caretaker discovered the remains of a partially burned letter containing the phrase, 'It will be nice when I am your wife.' The handwriting was Gladys Jones's. The date on which she saw this letter, which she declared was the morning of Mrs Greenwood's death, and the date of a receipt for the diamond ring bought by Greenwood, also found by Mrs Groves as waste paper, were certainly confused in her mind.

Rumour, especially in a small place, has seven-leagued boots. Greenwood's second marriage gave a fresh lease of life to the sinister whisper abroad in Llanelly, Kidwelly, and the neighbourhood all the summer. The hints and suspicions regarding his first wife's death became so definite that, shortly after the bridegroom's return from his honeymoon, Police Superintendent Jones and Inspector Nicholas, of Llanelly, visited his office on 24 October 1919 and took a lengthy statement from him. There was a further interview on 31 October, when Greenwood produced the death certificate, asked for at the first interview, which he said was in his office safe, but had been unable to find. The first visit by the superintendent lasted from two and a half to three hours. At the conclusion the superintendent informed Greenwood that having regard to the current rumours, and people gossiping so freely, he was afraid that the police would have to apply for an order to exhume the body. Greenwood replied: 'Just the very thing. I am quite agreeable.' Subsequently Greenwood, who had refused to sign the statement which Superintendent Jones took down in a note-book, objected to much of the contents. Certain material points and details, he averred, had been omitted, and things which he had never said appeared in it. At the trial the aforesaid note-book was the cause of a wordy battle between Superintendent Jones and the defending counsel, Sir Edward Marshall Hall. Allegations were made as to leaves having been torn out and other pages substituted. The whole episode, during which the taking of evidence was entirely suspended for a spirited exchange of what is technically known as 'back-chat' betwixt counsel and witness, although not materially important, was unsatisfying and undignified.

Despite the difficulty of extracting sufficient evidence from reluctant witnesses to justify further and more serious steps being taken, the authorities quietly pursued their investigations until the following spring. On 9 March 1920 the chief constable of Carmarthenshire, Mr Picton Philipps, embodied the accumulated results of his own and his subordinates' researches into the circumstances of Mrs Greenwood's death in a lengthy report to the Home Office. After detailing the facts regarding a death 'surrounded by mystery, falsehood, and, as it seems to me, culpable negligence and callousness', Mr Philipps requested an opinion on the propriety of exhuming Mrs Greenwood's body, 'either in the interests of justice, or, if that should happily not be so, then to relieve the husband of a terrible suspicion which will otherwise probably cling to him for life.' In consequence of this report the Director of Public Prosecutions was consulted, and decided that the facts should be sent to the coroner, Mr J. W. Nicholas, who would have the power to order exhumation and hold an inquest. Regret was expressed by the Home Office that this step had not been taken sooner. It was recommended that after the coroner had been communicated with an unobtrusive watch should be kept on Greenwood in case he attempted to leave the country.

The coroner, after considering the circumstances, was inclined to order an exhumation of the body, but expressed a doubt whether any very definite results would accrue, in view of the fact that death had taken place nine months before. On 16 April 1920 Mrs Greenwood's remains were exhumed from the grave in Kidwelly churchyard. Her family, the Bowaters, when the news became public property, were emphatic in their declaration that the movement for this step had not come from them, and they were as much horrified and surprised as anyone else. There had certainly been rumours of a possible exhumation long before it actually was an accomplished fact. Greenwood's caretaker told him on his return from his honeymoon that she had heard that Miss Bowater intended to have her sister's body exhumed, 'to see if she had been poisoned', but Mrs Groves was unable to remember her informant.

A post-mortem examination of Mrs Greenwood's remains was held in Kidwelly Town Hall on the morning of 16 April by Dr Alexander Dick, of Llanelly. Two other Llanelly doctors were present – Dr John Davies and Dr Dixon Smith – as well as Dr Griffiths, of Kidwelly. An inquest was opened and adjourned after formal evidence had been taken, and the following day certain organs removed from the body were sent in sealed jars for the purpose of analysis to Mr Webster, official analyst to the Home Office. He could discover no valvular disease, or other natural cause to account for the death, but found arsenic present in all the organs examined. The total amount was 18 milligrams, or rather more than one-quarter of a grain. Dr Willcox,[1] consulting medical adviser to the Home Office, a famous authority, also examined all the

---

[1] Later Sir William Willcox.

organs in the possession of Mr Webster, and came to similar conclusions.

On the Tuesday following the exhumation Greenwood met an acquaintance, Mr Smart, of Mountain View, Kidwelly, the husband of the lady in whom Nurse Jones had confided her doubts regarding Mrs Greenwood's death. The two men discussed the matter in the train to Llanelly. Greenwood remarked: 'They say that I was seen on the Town Bridge the night my wife's body was exhumed. That was not true. I was in bed fast asleep, and damn fast asleep too.' On a later date Greenwood said to Mr Smart: 'They are taking a long time over my case. I don't suppose they can find anything.' On 17 April, the day after the exhumation, Greenwood gave an interview to a representative of the *Daily Mail*. He described himself as 'a victim of village gossip, of village scandal', and complained that 'it all started from the fact that four months after my first wife's death I married again.' Greenwood gave the same newspaper another interview on 12 June, as well as the one to the *South Wales Daily Post*. He professed himself unable to understand how arsenic could have been found in his wife's body, but would not have been surprised had poison of some sort been discovered, owing to her habit of constantly taking medicines of every kind. He pooh-poohed the possibility of suicide, although he had previously suggested to the vicar that his wife might have 'taken something' herself. Another point which he stressed was the difficulty of obtaining arsenic. He would have had to sign the poison-book, and the transaction could easily have been traced to him. As a matter of fact, Greenwood had done so when buying Cooper's Weedicide twice in June 1917.

The adjourned inquest on the body of the late Mrs Greenwood was opened at 11 a.m. on Tuesday 15 June 1920. The proceedings occupied two days, being again held in the Town Hall, Kidwelly. By a grim coincidence, 16 June, the concluding day, was the first anniversary of the poor woman's death. Mr J. W. Nicholas, the coroner, presided, with Mr Seward Pearce, Assistant Director of Prosecutions, sitting near. Mrs Greenwood's brother and sister, Sir Thomas Vansittart

Bowater and Miss Bowater, were present. She was briefly examined with regard to Mrs Greenwood's money affairs, but was not called at the trial. Greenwood was represented by Mr Ludford, his solicitor. He had received a subpoena to attend, but, acting on Mr Ludford's advice, did not appear.

Eighteen witnesses were examined, one or two being re-called. The coroner's summing-up occupied about three-quarters of an hour, following which the jury – thirteen in number – retired. After an absence of thirty-five minutes, they requested a consultation with the coroner, and remained in private with him for a quarter of an hour. Soon afterwards they returned into Court, and handed in the following verdict in writing by their foreman, Mr George Jones:

We are unanimously of opinion that the death of the deceased, Mabel Greenwood, was caused by acute arsenical poisoning, as certified by Dr Willcox, and that the poison was administered by Harold Greenwood.

It throws a horrible searchlight on the prevailing feeling in Kidwelly towards the wretched Greenwood that there was a delighted demonstration in Court on hearing the verdict, and several people present clapped their hands.

In the meantime an almost unprecedented event had occurred. Shortly after the coroner had commenced his summing-up, by the orders of the chief constable, Police Sergeant Hodge Lewis and Police Constable W. J. Thomas left the Court, changed their uniforms for ordinary clothes, and went to Rumsey House. They asked for Greenwood, and directly he appeared seized him, and charged him on suspicion of having caused his wife's death by the administration of poison. He was taken at once to a cell in the local police station. Subsequent to the inquest verdict Greenwood was seen there by Inspector Haigh, who had first been sent down by Scotland Yard to make inquiries into the case at the beginning of June. On his arrival the C.I.D. man found immense local excitement and bad feeling, while everywhere the impression prevailed that Greenwood had poisoned his wife. The inspector interviewed all the persons whose statements had previously been taken by the local police, the great plurality of Joneses concerned proving exceedingly confusing to the stranger in the strange land. Inspector Haigh informed Greenwood that the coroner's jury had returned a verdict against him, and that he would be charged with the wilful murder of his wife by the administration of arsenic. Greenwood, who seemed 'concerned, but not agitated', asked the inspector what the precise wording of the jury's finding had been, and, on hearing it repeated, ejaculated, 'Oh, dear!' His removal to the police station had been accomplished comparatively unobserved, at a time when the streets were practically deserted owing to Kidwelly's attention being focused on the proceedings going on in the Town Hall. Directly news of Greenwood's arrest was known an immense crowd collected in the vicinity of the police station to watch the accused man's removal to Llanelly. Amid hisses and cheers — a horrible commentary on our so-called civilization and British notions of justice and fair play – Greenwood was bustled into a waiting motor and driven off.

At Llanelly police station the charge was read over to him, he was cautioned by Superintendent Jones, and replied that he understood. The following morning he was brought before the magistrates at Llanelly, formally charged with the wilful murder of his wife, and remanded for a week. There was another remand on 25 June, and, commencing on 1 July, a hearing before the magistrates which lasted for three days. The upshot was Greenwood's committal to the next Carmarthen Assizes to stand his trial on the above charge. He pleaded 'Not guilty', and reserved his defence. The large crowd assembled outside Llanelly Town Hall to watch his departure booed him vigorously.

5

From the outset the prosecution admittedly had a weak case. The strictest investigations into the relations of Harold Greenwood and Gladys Jones during the lifetime of Mabel Greenwood failed to discover the smallest tittle of admissible evidence to prove that there had been anything but an ordinary friendship between them. Mrs Groves, the caretaker of

Greenwood's office, alleged that Miss Jones was in the habit of visiting him there frequently. Asked at the inquest whether she had ever witnessed any familiarities between Greenwood and Miss Jones, Mrs Groves replied that she had seen him kissing her, and that Miss Jones did not appear to object. A smart cross-examination by Mr Ludford elicited the fact that this was *after* the death of Mrs Greenwood, and never before.

The caretaker told another story at the inquest of a visit by Mrs Greenwood to her husband's office on the Wednesday prior to her death. Mrs Groves knew that Miss Jones was with Greenwood, and accordingly informed Mrs Greenwood that he was out. When she spoke of the episode to Greenwood afterwards, and regretted having uttered an untruth, Greenwood said that it was quite all right. The incident was alleged to have happened on the same day, and much about the same time, that Greenwood took his wife for her first and only drive in the car, an event testified to by the between-maid, Powell, and Ben Williams, who worked in the garden.

The real reason for the indecent haste of Greenwood's second marriage, apart from the theory of the prosecution that it was due to passion for Gladys Jones, has never been explained. He did not deny that he and she had been extremely friendly over a period of many years, but asseverated that he was on equally intimate terms (employing the word in a harmless sense) with the other members of her family. He had never taken her for a drive without some of her relations accompanying them. Miss Jones worked in the *Mercury* office, and he was accustomed to see her when he lunched there. At the time of his proposal to her, which he alleged was due to his suddenly realizing that he was sufficiently fond of her to wish to marry her, Miss Jones was engaged to be married to an army man named Frank Russell. During the trial this unknown warrior was referred to as 'a lieutenant in India', but as a matter of fact he had just arrived in London from Bombay about the time of Greenwood's second marriage. At Bombay he had received his fiancée's letter, asking him to release her from their engagement, which had been entered into so far back as 1915, and wrote her a reproachful reply from a

London hospital, upbraiding her for her faithlessness, and reiterating his own loyalty. Miss Jones replied that she was to be married 'very early next week', and heard nothing further from her discarded lover.

The day of Greenwood's arrest Rumsey House was thoroughly searched, as well as the adjoining stables and outhouses. With the exception of three small bottles of liniment, labelled 'Poison', nothing else of this nature was discovered, or anything suspicious or incriminating. There were numerous letters, but none of these had any bearing on the case. In short, no purchase of poison was at any time traced to Greenwood, with the exception of weed-killer. This he had bought openly, had had delivered without any secrecy, and in fact never attempted to conceal the transaction. Malicious gossip and tattling spread and exaggerated small incidents such as the week-end visit of the Jones sisters, magnifying and misrepresenting them.

Greenwood was four and a half months in prison awaiting his trial at Carmarthen Assizes. Sir Edward Marshall Hall stressed this as a proof of the accused's innocence. A guilty man, counsel contended, would have moved to be tried earlier and elsewhere, afraid of local opinion prejudicing a local jury. During this time, while the slow machinery of the Law moved towards its appointed purpose, when the most unimportant people were being interviewed and examined by the police, no attempt was made on the part of the Crown authorities to approach Irene Greenwood. She had not been present at the inquest on her mother's body, either voluntarily or to give evidence. She was not asked to give evidence, or volunteered to do so, in spite of admitting in cross-examination at her father's trial that she knew that he might become involved in criminal proceedings. No statement of any kind was taken from her, with the exception of the one made to Mr Ludford.[1]

[1] At the trial Irene was asked, in cross-examination by Sir E. Marlay Samson, whether it was as a result of Mr Ludford's advice that she did not attend the inquest and state what she knew about her mother's death. Sir Edward Marshall Hall objected to the question, and the judge ruled that it had better not be put.

After her father's second marriage she had stayed away from Rumsey House until the following Christmas. She remained at Kidwelly with her father and stepmother until the end of May 1920, and then took a post as governess at Rendell. *Not until after the inquest* had she to consider what she drank at meals on the day of her mother's death, and she acknowledged having discussed the matter freely with her father when investigations into the first Mrs Greenwood's death were pending. The Crown's failure to call her was the defence's opportunity, a trump card kept until almost the last stages of the trial.

The Guildhall at Carmarthen, where the trial was to take place, proved to be totally inadequate accommodation for the large number of persons having no connexion with the case who were wishful to hear it. The Court was packed to suffocation each day, and those who found themselves unable to obtain admission to the hearing swelled the excited groups congregated outside. Among certain people who were sent empty away was a large number of so-called ladies, who occupied a prominent position in the best circles in London, and had applied for tickets of admission to the trial. Not since the Maybrick case had any poisoning mystery so stirred and captured the morbid imagination of the public, sated, it might have been thought, by four years' ghastly horrors and incessant deaths. Special and stringent arrangements were made to cope with the crowds and facilitate the arrival and departure of those whose presence was essential. Carmarthen itself had all its available accommodation booked up for weeks ahead. Sir Edward Marshall Hall only managed to secure a room in the principal hotel after some difficulty, and others concerned in the case, whose evidence at the trial was necessary, were obliged to seek quarters as far afield as Ferryside or Llanelly, seven and twenty-odd miles away respectively.

The trial opened on Tuesday 2 November. The calendar included three cases of alleged murder and one of alleged manslaughter, but interest in the fate of Harold Greenwood overshadowed everything else. Even the American press desired to be represented. The utmost strictness was observed in the guarding of the jury. Each day they were marched to and from their lodgings in the Central Hotel, as straitly policed as the prisoner himself. They sent in a unanimous request to be allowed to attend church on the Sunday which intervened during the seven days of the trial, but, after consideration, the petition was refused on the ground that some reference to the trial, or allusion to the case, might be made from the pulpit. It was probably regarded as adding insult to injury by these devotional and deeply conscientious Welshmen to be offered a charabanc drive instead – in mid-November! Mr Justice Shearman, the presiding judge, arrived at Carmarthen on the previous Friday. He was accompanied by Lady Shearman, who occupied a seat on the bench, and by his son, Mr Montague Shearman, who acted as judge's marshal. The prisoner was brought very early each morning from Carmarthen gaol, the scene of his eighteen weeks' incarceration, to the Guildhall, a few yards up a steep hill, but eager crowds assembled daily in the hope of catching a glimpse of him. His carriage, escorted by mounted police, was practically mobbed, and on more than one occasion there was a hostile demonstration and some booing.

Sir Edward Marlay Samson, K.C., and Mr Wilfrid Lewis (instructed by the Director of Public Prosecutions) appeared for the Crown. Sir Edward Marshall Hall, K.C., and Mr Trevor Hunter (instructed by Mr T. R. Ludford) defended Greenwood.[1] Mr Clark Williams (instructed by Mr Mervyn Paton) held a watching brief on behalf of an interested party, a firm of weed-killer manufacturers. On being asked whether he had any objection to any of the jurymen, after these had taken their seats in the jury-box and answered to their names, Greenwood, after consultation with his solicitor, Mr Ludford, instanced three, two of whom belonged to Llanelly and the third to Llandilo. Messrs Thomas Morgan, David Knoyle,

---

[1] In order to avoid any possible confusion when both the prosecuting and defending counsel were alike styled 'Sir Edward', the former was throughout the trial and in the press reports addressed, and referred to, by the title of 'Sir Marlay Samson'. I have adhered to this.

and Charles Simpson were accordingly informed that their services would not be required, and three substitutes were called into the box to take the oath. Strangely enough, there was not a single juror from Kidwelly.

In answer to the charge against him, Greenwood pleaded 'Not guilty'. Throughout the whole proceedings he sat cool and collected, smiling, and even laughing, on occasion, only very rarely displaying emotion, and at other times appearing thoroughly bored. When he moved from the dock to the witness-box, and his examination commenced, at first he spoke hardly above a whisper, but, according to one who was present in Court, became quite bold before his ordeal at Sir Edward Marlay Samson's hands was over. Greenwood's own legal advisers were reluctant to put him in the box. They anticipated that, voluble and irresponsible, he would make a bad witness in his own defence, but he did not damage his case in any way. The whole time that he was in the witness-box he remained comparatively cool and unruffled. He declined the judge's suggestion of a seat, and continued calm, serene, alert under the prosecuting counsel's searching fire of questions. His examination by the defence only lasted for a few minutes. To the vital question: 'Did you directly or indirectly administer or cause to be administered to your wife any arsenic at any time in your life?' Greenwood replied with a quiet but emphatic: 'I have not.' In answer to a further question: 'Had you anything to do with your wife's death?' he rejoined promptly: 'Nothing whatever.' His own explanations of certain episodes – the purchases of the dressing-bag and diamond ring, and the letter to Miss Griffiths – were credible enough. As the judge hinted, some of his actions might not have been wholly admirable, but that did not necessarily make him his wife's destroyer.

6

Before commencing his opening speech for the Crown, which occupied some two hours in its delivery, Sir Edward Marlay Samson requested that all the witnesses, including those liable to be called for the defence, should leave the Court, excepting the two experts, Dr Willcox and Mr Webster. When this had been done, counsel addressed the jury, and first outlined the three main points on which they must make up their minds. First, did Mabel Greenwood die of arsenical poisoning? If they agreed that she did, they must ask: Was the poison taken by herself, either voluntarily or accidentally, or was it wilfully administered? If they decided that this last was the case, they must ask: Did the prisoner give it to her? The Crown alleged that he had done so. They must ask what means, opportunities, and motives he had, and consider minutely his conduct before, during, and after his wife's fatal attack of illness. Counsel then sketched in outline the events centring round those sinister dates – 15 and 16 June 1919 – and particularly stressed Greenwood's purchases of Eureka weed-killer in February and April 1919. It contained 60 per cent of arsenic, was easily dissolved in water, and, if in red wine, its similar colour, likewise any taste, would be unnoticed. Thirty-six grains of the weed-killer amounted to half a teaspoonful, sufficient to cause death in one glass of wine.

As is inevitably the case in a trial for murder by alleged poisoning, the medical evidence was of paramount importance. The Crown alleged and sought to prove that Mabel Greenwood died from arsenical poisoning. The defence contended that she died from morphia poisoning, through an error on the part of Dr Griffiths, who administered pills containing a dose of the latter drug sufficient to cause death. Dr Griffiths, at the outset of his evidence, threw the defence off its prepared lines by acknowledging that the pills in question, which he had hitherto admitted contained half a grain of morphia, a dangerous dose, had contained instead half a grain of opium. There was 1/40th of a grain of morphia in each pill. Sir Edward Marshall Hall, on hearing this belated admission, which must of necessity entirely change the character of the defence, started the first of the famous 'scenes' for which the trial became notorious, and which called forth repeated rebukes from the bench.

Dr Griffiths's evidence was throughout hesitating and contradictory. The defence did not fail to use him as a scapegoat.

Sir Edward Marshall Hall went so far as to suggest openly that the doctor had by what the judge characterized as 'a colossal blunder' administered Fowler's solution of arsenic instead of bismuth to Mrs Greenwood, as bottles containing both stood side by side in his surgery. Mr Justice Shearman objected to this insinuation, tantamount, he pointed out, to an accusation of criminal negligence. Dr Griffiths had retired from practice before the trial, and a further point against him was his inability to produce his prescription book.

To prove their contention – that Mabel Greenwood died from arsenical poisoning – the Crown called the two experts who had examined the organs taken from the body. Mr Webster, who used the Reinsch test, and afterwards the modified Marsh test, in examining for traces of arsenic, stated that the amount found in milligrams in the organs submitted to him was – stomach, ·58 of a milligram, or ·009 of a grain; small intestine, omentum, and mesentery, 4·33 milligrams, or ·067 of a grain; large intestine, ·55 of a milligram, or ·008 of a grain; liver, 8·508 milligrams, or ·131 of a grain; spleen, ·40 of a milligram, or ·006 of a grain; two kidneys, 1·21 milligrams, or ·019 of a grain; uterus, ·75 of a milligram, or ·012 of a grain; rectum, ·39 of a milligram, or ·005 of a grain; heart, ·27 of a milligram, or ·004 of a grain; lungs, ·79 of a milligram, or ·012 of a grain; oesophagus, ·21 of a milligram, or ·003 of a grain; brain, ·09 of a milligram, or ·001 of a grain. The total amount was 18·07 milligrams, or ·278 of a grain, approximately a little over a quarter of a grain.

The witness tested for morphia among other alkaloids, but found none. He was asked to examine the organs for traces of poisoning generally, not arsenic in particular. By a process of elimination he arrived at the presence of arsenic. Results were negative as far as other poisons were concerned. Another method, by precipitation, and weighing the amount precipitated, gave exactly the same results as the two previous tests. The minimum fatal dose was 2 grains. It was possible that ten months after death no traces of morphia would be found.

Mr Webster examined Eureka weed-killer and estimated that it contained 55·6 per cent of arsenic. Four grains of weed-killer would correspond to $2\frac{1}{4}$ grains of arsenic. When, in the course of witness's experiments, weed-killer had been added to port wine, the colour of the wine was only slightly altered, and no difference in taste could be detected. Four grains of weed-killer added to an ordinary cup of tea produced the same results as to colour and taste as in the experiment with port wine.

Dr Willcox, who had given evidence for the Crown in the Seddons trial, when the cause of the victim's death was arsenical poisoning, and the same test – the Marsh – had been employed to ascertain the quantity of poison found in Miss Barrow's body,[1] was of opinion that Mabel Greenwood died from heart failure. The heart failure was caused by prolonged vomiting and diarrhoea, due to the effects of arsenic. He thought that the fatal dose must have been taken by the mouth at least nine hours before death; e.g., if death occurred at 3.30 a.m. on 16 June, the arsenic would have been taken before 6.30 p.m. on 15 June. Had the arsenic been taken in a solid form, some solid particles would have adhered to the mucous membrane of the stomach and intestine and have been visible (which was not the case), thus causing a higher amount to have been found on analysis. The arsenic, in Dr Willcox's opinion, was taken in soluble form, probably between 1.30 p.m. (the time of lunch) and 6 p.m. The pain round the heart of which Mrs Greenwood complained, according to her husband's statement, was probably stomach pain arising from the effects of arsenic. The muscles were not examined, but witness stated that these must have contained a considerable amount of arsenic. The vomiting and diarrhoea would account for the disappearance of a certain

In comparison with the Seddons case, the amounts of absorbed arsenic in the liver, spleen, and kidneys, the most important organs to consider, showed that the quantities of absorbed arsenic in the case of Mrs Greenwood corresponded to about three-quarters of those in the case of Miss Barrow. Thus: Mrs Greenwood – liver, 8·5 milligrams; Miss Barrow, 11·13 milligrams. Mrs Greenwood – spleen, ·4 milligram; Miss Barrow, ·44 milligram. Mrs Greenwood – kidneys, 1·21 milligrams; Miss Barrow, 1·9 milligrams. See *Trial of the Seddons*, edited by Filson Young, 'Notable British Trials Series'.

quantity of the poison from the system. Using the Seddons case as a basis of calculation, the amount present in the muscles would have been, taking three-quarters as the factor for absorbed arsenic, 50 milligrams. This would bring the total amount of arsenic present to 68·07 milligrams, i.e. just over 1 grain, and in addition arsenic would have been present in certain other organs which were not examined, such as the pancreas, skin, etc. Dr Willcox was convinced that a dose of at least 2 grains must have been swallowed by Mrs Greenwood within twenty-four hours of her death, which would have been a possible fatal dose for a woman. If her heart were weak, and her general state of health indifferent, she would have less resistance to poison, and a small dose would operate more rapidly and fatally in her case than in that of a robust person.[1]

For the defence Lieutenant-Colonel Toogood, toxicologist to the London County Council, gave as his opinion that Mrs Greenwood's death was due to morphia poisoning, following an acute attack of gastro-enteritis set up by swallowing gooseberry skins. Diarrhoea would be the earliest symptom, whereas in a case of arsenical poisoning vomiting was more likely to commence first. Under the circumstances witness would not have expected to find traces of morphia in the intestines so long after death as ten months. A lengthy, persistent, and thorough cross-examination of this witness by Sir Edward Marlay Samson elicited a good many facts which tended to weaken the effect of Dr Toogood's evidence on the jury's minds. He admitted that the suggestion of arsenic being accidentally absorbed by inhalation was only made by him a day or two previously, that he was not an analytical chemist, had had no experience in calculating amounts by the Marsh test,

---

[1] It is a well-known characteristic of poisoners to 'mak' siccar' by giving their victims an extravagantly large dose, as witness the cases of Mrs Armstrong, Mrs Crippen, and Miss Barrow. The Crown never attempted to explain how Greenwood, who was no toxicologist, poisoned the bottle of burgundy with an accuracy and skill that would have been required by an expert in order to ensure that each glass of wine should contain two grains of arsenic, the minimum fatal dose.

and therefore was in no position to challenge the figures given by the Crown experts.

Dr William Griffiths, of Swansea, contended for the defence that the finding of a quarter of a grain of arsenic in the viscera of a dead body was not conclusive evidence that it had been the cause of death. A living body could, and often did, contain $2\frac{1}{2}$ grains of arsenic without any injurious effect to the person's health. The witness was of opinion that Mrs Greenwood died from morphia poisoning, her death from this cause being contributed to by the state of her heart and generally impaired health.

Eleventh-hour theories on the part of the defence to account for the small quantity of arsenic found in the body were:

That it had been absorbed by inhalation when Mrs Greenwood was walking in a part of the garden where weed-killer had been sprayed on the paths.

That it had been taken in glucose.

That Dr Griffiths had accidentally administered Fowler's solution of arsenic instead of bismuth.

That during gardening operations the gooseberry skins had been sprayed with weed-killer containing arsenic.[1]

7

No definite conclusion was ever arrived at as to what this unfortunate woman really died of. The question of whether her husband had poisoned her was settled by the jury's verdict, but the actual cause of her death remains in dispute to this hour. She was admittedly, as proved by the evidence of several independent witnesses, in failing health for some time. She had eaten an indigestible meal on a hot day after over-exerting herself the previous afternoon. Her heart may have ceased quietly to perform its functions owing to the strain put upon it through a gastric attack. The defence's theory of morphia poisoning was more or less upset by Dr Griffiths's unexpected admission that he had not given her morphia. On the other

[1] This theory was quite untenable owing to the fact of the gooseberry tart having been eaten by other people in the house who experienced no ill-effects afterwards.

hand, it was never cleared up exactly what he did give her. She relapsed into coma, followed by death, shortly after taking the pills. For the Crown theory of death by arsenical poisoning, while her symptoms were those associated with the taking of arsenic, they were also the ordinary symptoms of internal disorder caused by unsuitable food. She suffered from vomiting and purging, but not to an extent to alarm either the doctor, her husband, her friend, or her daughter. The nurse confessed to feeling concerned about these symptoms – but on account of the state of the patient's heart.[1] She was a devotee of patent medicines, and the question of what she was in the habit of taking, apart from Dr Griffiths's prescriptions, was scarcely touched upon by the authorities who were inquiring into her death.

A great crime is sometimes easier to condone and understand than an error of taste. Harold Greenwood would in all probability never have found himself in the dock on the capital charge had it not been for the haste attending his second marriage. The inference was that he had not loved his first wife when he replaced her so speedily. From not loving her it was only a step to the suggestion that he was tired of being tied to an invalidish woman, and had sought his freedom. Kidwelly gossip tried and condemned him months before that long ordeal at Carmarthen. As chorus to the main tragedy, village cackle, the exchange of theories and ideas, growing wilder and more inaccurate at each repetition, the misdating of letters, conversations, and confidences played their dangerous parts. It is ironical that a woman whom everyone liked should have been the centre of so much that was ugly and distressing and untrue.

The evidence of one of the chief witnesses for the Crown – the parlourmaid, Hannah Maggie Williams – was well summed up by *The Times* in its leading article on the case

[1] Nurse Jones stated: 'I would have treated the case much more seriously if the doctor had not said that she had been like that many times before.' Dr Griffiths stated that he was accustomed to treat Mrs Greenwood for bilious and gastric attacks, to which she was very subject and that her fatal illness commenced in precisely the same way as these.

as 'hesitating and indefinite'. It should, however, be remembered that the girl was more accustomed to Welsh than
English, that Sir Edward Marshall Hall's manner in cross-
examining the Crown witnesses was such as to call down repeated requests from the judge that he would refrain from
'shouting at', 'bullying', and 'pitching into' them, that she
was being questioned as to events which had taken place
nearly eighteen months previously. Her own admission, 'I
cannot remember everything', when she was taxed with in-
accuracy or contradiction of previous statements, was probably the stark truth. She left Rumsey House on the Tuesday
following Mrs Greenwood's funeral, on the morning of which
several people in the house maintained that they saw her
under the influence of drink. Mrs Greenwood told the cook
that she had given Hannah Williams notice for coming in late
at night. The servant denied this, saying that her aunt
required her for haymaking, and she had given notice for
her niece to Mrs Greenwood. On the other hand, Benjamin
Williams, the odd-job gardener, stated that the girl had asked
him to request Mrs Greenwood to keep her, as she was one of
a large family and did not want to lose a good place. Since her
departure from Rumsey House, either voluntarily or because
Greenwood, after his wife's death, did not retain her services,
she had been employed as general servant and nurse by a Mrs
Morris, to whose house in Alstread Street, Kidwelly, she went
on 3 July 1919. Sir Edward Marshall Hall, alluding to her
appearance in the witness-box, referred to her as 'poor, little,
frightened thing', charmingly oblivious of the fact that his
own method of cross-examination was enough to alarm the
stoutest-hearted. To the end she adhered with stubborn per-
sistence to her story that Greenwood had spent at least half
an hour in the china pantry before lunch on the fatal Sunday,
and that she had not known of his going there to wash his
hands as a regular practice.

Last of all, from the tangle of lies, misrepresentations,
gossip, evil-speaking, and the frantic twisting of the truth by
jealous or ignorant women, we come to the figure of Irene
Greenwood. Her position was singular and pathetic. Her

mother's death and the speedy advent of a stepmother deprived her of a home. Her father was responsible for the latter event, if not for the former, so that her feelings towards him were hardly likely to make her anxious to perjure herself on his account. As regards her relations with both her parents, Hannah Williams stated: 'So far as I could judge, Miss Irene was on equally as good terms with her mother as she was with her father.' Miss Phillips was questioned by both counsel for the Crown and for the defence on this point. In answer to Sir Edward Marlay Samson's query: 'Did you form any opinion as to Irene's attitude towards her mother?' the witness replied: 'I do not know what to say. I do not think there was quite as much affection as between some mothers and daughters. I do not think she was specially fond of her mother.' In reply to Sir Edward Marshall Hall, Miss Phillips said that Irene did not show much affection to her mother, but on the night of Mrs Greenwood's death she was 'very good to her'. Irene's relations with her father are best described in her own words, deeply pathetic in the light of after-events. 'Daddy was always good to us. We were always together.'

As Sir Edward Marshall Hall pointed out grimly to the jury, Greenwood, whether condemned or acquitted, was a ruined man. Counsel sought to play upon the feelings of the twelve arbiters in his client's fate by a moving reference to Greenwood's children. Should he be found guilty and hanged for the murder of their mother, their fate was to be overshadowed all their lives by his crime. Irene Greenwood brought the case to an end by her declaration upon oath that she drank twice of wine on the fatal Sunday from the bottle alleged to have contained the poison. Sir Edward Marlay Samson, after her evidence, if accepted as true, had shattered the Crown theory as to how the poison was administered, made a further suggestion that wine was not the only liquid drunk by Mrs Greenwood within twelve hours of her death. She had taken tea, brandy, and medicine, any one of which might have been the vehicle that contained the poisonous weed-killer.

Miss Greenwood was the last witness called for the defence. At the conclusion of her evidence the judge said that he hoped the case might finish on Monday, and the Court accordingly adjourned until 10 o'clock on that morning. The chief points for the jury to consider, Mr Justice Shearman added, were: Was there arsenic in the body? Was the accused intentionally responsible for introducing it there? If the jury thought that he was not, there was an end of the case. If they did think it, the next question to be asked was: Did the arsenic produce death? If it did, it was murder; if not, it was attempted murder. The judge did not know if the prosecution had considered that. Sir Edward Marshall Hall replied that the defence contended that Greenwood never administered arsenic at all.

Public interest in the case had increased rather than diminished as the trial proceeded. On Monday 8 November the crowds both outside and inside the Guildhall were greater than on any of the preceding days. The contrast which all along had been marked between the prosecuting and defending counsel appeared even more significant in the concluding speech of each. Sir Edward Marlay Samson had remained calm, confident, speaking in a cool, dignified, unruffled way every time, whether he addressed a witness, the jury, or the bench. Only once throughout the hearing did he betray the smallest trace of irritability at the repeated interruptions from the other side. The judge administered the mildest of oblique rebukes by reminding the learned counsel that his lordship had already told everybody in the case not to get excited. This was a liberal inclusion of the white sheep with the black, the only person who had required and received the admonition incessantly being Sir Edward Marshall Hall. Sir Edward Marlay Samson rejoined solemnly, 'I don't think I ever get excited, my lord.'

Sir Edward Marshall Hall, on the other hand, played to the gallery for all the case was worth. His dramatic appeals to the jury, his constant reminder in cross-examining the unhappy Crown witnesses that 'Mr Greenwood is here for his life', 'I am defending a man on trial for his life', his encounters, frequent and heated, with the judge, his violent

manner, excitable and intimidating, at every contested point
or contrary opinion, were all bound to have their effect on
any towards whom they were directed. His final speech to the
jury lasted for three hours and a quarter. He was alternately
passionate and pleading, his utterance rapid, but his matter
concise, logical, and closely reasoned. The speech was delivered in circumstances of physical discomfort which prevented Greenwood's advocate remaining in Court to hear Sir
Edward Marlay Samson. The latter spoke with a low-toned
quiet that was strikingly different from the fiery oratory of his
opponent. His last address to the jury occupied over three
hours. It was concluded in almost complete darkness, the
November night brooding outside, two gas-jets flickering inside, affording inadequate illumination, the whole effect
adding to the tension of the circumstances.

A vast amount was made afterwards of the defending
counsel's state of health, his immense effort to do justice to his
client – a member of his own profession – while suffering great
physical pain. It was not generally known at the time, but the
burden on the shoulders of Sir Edward Marlay Samson was
even heavier. Though the fact only crept into a few of the
local newspapers, he was far from well, and, in addition to
this handicap, found himself placed in the very unusual position of having to open the case for the Crown in another
murder trial, the 'Cross Hands' tragedy, while the jury in the
Greenwood one were still out deliberating on their verdict.
Sir Edward's handling of the Crown case in the latter, scrupulously fair, moderate, and impartial, was in keeping with the
great traditions of the English Bar, and added largely to his
reputation. He was out to find the truth, not to hunt down
Greenwood. In these trying and tangled circumstances it is
scarcely surprising that so eminent a counsel forgot the provisions of the Criminal Evidence Act, and in his last address
to the jury commented on the defence's not having placed
Gladys Greenwood in the witness-box in order to substantiate her husband's statement as to their relations prior
to the marriage. Sir Edward desired to withdraw the observation next day, although, curiously enough, it had escaped the

notice of the learned judge and counsel present at the time.[1]

Mr Justice Shearman was commendably fair throughout. At the close of Crown counsel's address he spoke a few words to the jury before the Court adjourned until the next morning. They must avoid side-issues, and concentrate wholly upon the guilt or innocence of the prisoner. They must not allow any personal dislike of him to bias their judgement. They must not let their verdict be influenced by popular opinion or what people would like. These few grave sentences, delivered in the unlighted Court, with the November dusk thickening, were deeply impressive. Afterwards an adjournment was made in complete darkness. The summing-up the following morning was in the direction of an acquittal, though his lordship scrupulously refrained from biasing the jury. They retired to consider their verdict at twenty minutes past 1 on Tuesday 9 November. At seven minutes to 4 they returned, bringing a verdict of 'Not guilty'. Greenwood was formally discharged, the jury's decision having been received in Court with some cheering, instantly suppressed.[2]

[1] During the trial of John Alexander Dickman at Newcastle Assizes in July 1910, Mr Tindal Atkinson, K.C., who led for the Crown, in his final address to the jury commented upon the prisoner's failure to call his wife as a witness with reference to certain stains on a garment which Dickman alleged she had cleaned. Lord Coleridge, the presiding judge, in his summing-up alluded to counsel's slip, and desired the jury to banish it from their minds, and not to allow it in any way to influence their verdict. The foreman replied that, so far from this being the case, the matter referred to had not been mentioned during their deliberations. The Lord Chief Justice in the Court of Criminal Appeal stated: 'With regard to the point based on the comment made as to the not calling Mrs Dickman to speak to the stains on the coat, it must be remembered that it had been withdrawn from the jury, and they indeed stated that they had not even spoken about it, so that it was impossible for the Court to support the contention that there was a mistrial. It was an accidental slip, such as must often occur, and its effect, if any, was removed before the verdict was given.' (*Trial of John Alexander Dickman*, edited by S. O. Rowan-Hamilton, 'Notable British Trials Series'.)

[2] Mr. Greenwood's nervous system seems to have been nearly as unimpaired as that of the late Miss Madeleine Smith after passing through a similar ordeal. The day following his acquittal he entertained the representative of a local newspaper to lunch at Rumsey House, and joked about the absence of burgundy from the table!

A mistaken impression prevailed, and found its way into several of the newspapers, that Mr Justice Shearman stated that he agreed with the jury's finding. The learned judge said nothing of the kind, and was merely replying to a question by a juryman as to whether he and his colleagues could be exempted from further service for a period of years.

Next morning the leading London and provincial dailies, as well as a host of lesser journals, devoted long articles to the Greenwood case. The tone of most of the newspapers was satisfaction at the outcome of the trial, congratulations upon the vindication of an innocent and much-maligned individual, coupled with sharp and, in some instances, unfair criticism of the Crown's handling of the case. One influential organ openly wondered that the acquitted man had ever been put on his trial with such flimsy grounds for the accusation. This universal outburst of journalistic jubilation would have been considerably modified had a certain fact then been made public. This was the weighty addition to the jury's finding of 'Not guilty' of a supplementary and written verdict. It had been the intention of their foreman, Mr E. Willis, to state whether or not the jury found the prisoner guilty of the crime with which he stood charged. The foreman having replied to the question, 'Not guilty', did not amplify the spoken verdict, but a paper containing a fuller statement was handed by him up to the judge. It ran as follows:

'We are satisfied on the evidence in this case that a dangerous dose of arsenic was administered to Mabel Greenwood on Sunday 15 June 1919, but we are not satisfied that this was the immediate cause of death.

'The evidence before us is insufficient, and does not conclusively satisfy us as to how, and by whom, the arsenic was administered. We therefore return a verdict of "Not guilty".'[1]

Upon close examination, the verdict will be seen to be just

[1] An almost identical verdict was returned at the trial of Adelaide Bartlett in 1886 on a charge of poisoning her husband with liquid chloroform, with the addition that the jury considered that grave suspicion attached to the prisoner. (*Trial of Adelaide Bartlett*, edited by Sir John Hall, 'Notable British Trials Series'.)

and impartial. Undoubtedly arsenic was found in Mrs Greenwood's body, but whether she had come to her death exclu-
sively through its agency must always remain a matter for
controversy. That somebody inside Rumsey House certainly
administered a dose of arsenic to her, probably within twelve
hours of her end, is an undisputed fact, but the precise means
by which she was induced to swallow the poison continues in
doubt, as well as whether she actually died through its sole
operation. So much contradictory evidence was brought forward in connexion with the pills alleged to have been given
by Dr Griffiths, and the charge that they were harmful to a
person in Mrs Greenwood's state was to some extent sub-
stantiated by the medical experts for the defence. The appalling possibility of the accidental substitution by the same hand
of Fowler's solution of arsenic instead of bismuth could not be
overlooked. Nevertheless, the above verdict very considerably
takes away the satisfaction of a complete and thorough acquittal. In effect it implies that Mrs Greenwood was poisoned
by an unnamed person – her husband purposely, Dr Griffiths
accidentally, being the only individuals possible – through
means impossible to locate, and that, though her actual
death may have been occasioned otherwise (i.e. by the
morphia pills), she would undoubtedly have died through
arsenical poisoning, but definite proof was lacking that she
actually did.

Mr Justice Shearman did not disclose the written verdict,
although it was manifestly the intention of the jury that it
should be made public. Its existence came to the knowledge
of counsel for the Crown, and the following morning an application was made in private to the judge that this might be
done. The judge declined to accede to the request, and the
matter being subsequently brought to the notice of Sir Archibald Bodkin, he communicated with Mr Justice Shearman
with a view to the publication of this written verdict, but the
judge again refused his consent. It is now made public in
accordance with the original intention of the jury in the case,
and with the permission and approval of their foreman, Sir
Edward Marlay Samson, and Sir Archibald Bodkin.

In the Armstrong case Sir Henry Curtis Be..., fended Armstrong, was so confident of an acqui..., client that he left the Court during the closing scenes, a..., turned, fully expecting to meet Armstrong a free man. In stead, he was greeted by the cries of the newsboys calling the verdict in the Hereford streets. Sir Edward Marshall Hall, who had been in a state of health that to some extent excuses his irritability throughout the Greenwood trial, was not present at the conclusion, and heard the verdict from a porter when he was awaiting the London train at Cardiff Station. In connexion with Sir Edward's absence from Court on the last day of Greenwood's trial, a story has been circulated that his client refused to pay a 'refresher' for this on the ground that the counsel had omitted to attend. Both counsel and client are dead, but the facts about the unpaid 'refresher' are briefly as follows, stated on the authority of Mr Ludford, Greenwood's solicitor:

Sir Edward Marshall Hall undertook the defence of Greenwood on the undermentioned terms: Brief, 200 guineas, plus 100 special, and 50 guineas a day refresher. The trial, commenced on Tuesday 2 November 1920 and terminated on the following Tuesday, six refreshers, with consultations came to £759 15s., and this was promptly paid. A special visit to Carmarthen by Sir Edward Marshall Hall, who considered that a personal consultation with his client before the trial was vitally necessary, cost £67 10s., and is included in the above figure.

After the acquittal of Greenwood, a suggestion was made by Marshall Hall's clerk, that, in view of the way Greenwood had been met over the brief fee, the strain on Sir Edward, and that he had to refuse all briefs during the trial, an additional sum might be paid as a Sunday refresher and amended refreshers. The matter subsequently dropped, but may possibly have been the foundation for the story of the unpaid refresher. Greenwood, not unnaturally, thought it unfair and unheard-of for counsel to ask for extra or additional fees after the verdict. He was, in any case, hardly in a position to supply these.

and his financial circum-
...m[1] offered him by an enter-
...f his acquittal, he would write
...per.

9

...after the conclusion of the Green-
...ublic's appetite for sensationalism was
... y another case which presented extra-
ordi...   ...eatures. Herbert Rowse Armstrong,[2] like
Greenw...   a country solicitor, practising in a South
Wales coun... djacent to Carmarthenshire. The position in
life of each was very much akin. Armstrong was tried for an
identical crime by exactly the same means – the murder of
his wife by arsenical poisoning, the poison being obtained
from weed-killer. The setting of the Armstrong tragedy was
almost parallel with the Greenwood mystery, both taking
place in a small village where everybody's affairs were known
to his neighbour. Armstrong, whose guilt was clearly brought
home to him, owed it to Greenwood's acquittal that in his
own case the sword of justice so long delayed its fall. The
Home Office, whose attention had been directed by a sharp-
witted doctor to certain suspicious features in connexion with
Mrs Armstrong's death, hesitated to arrest her husband until
every link in the chain of circumstantial evidence was firm
between their fingers. The Crown authorities had been adversely criticized for their handling of the Greenwood case,
notably for putting a man in the dock on the capital charge
with such slender grounds for the accusation. They were not
anxious to become a laughing-stock through a second igno-
minious blunder. Had it not been for Armstrong's abortive
attempt to poison a fellow-solicitor by the same means, thus
arousing Dr Hincks's suspicions, his secret destruction of his
unfortunate wife would probably never have been detected.

The circumstances leading up to the two trials were almost

[1] £3600.
[2] *Trial of Herbert Rowse Armstrong*, edited by Filson Young, 'Notable
British Trials Series'.

identical, but the protagonists differed widely in their characters and conduct. Armstrong was cool, crafty, calculating, and, up to a point, successful. The motive for the crime in his case was neither monetary nor sexual. There was some small financial benefit accruing to him through Mrs Armstrong's death, but he had no entanglement with another woman beyond a vague friendship with a lady who gave evidence at his trial and was meditating marrying him. Armstrong went smoothly on his way, a widower with young children, until his success with one crime overpersuaded him to essay a second on the same lines. Another curiously similar feature of his case to Greenwood's was the important part played by a country practitioner in each. Dr Hincks showed a courageous and commendable spirit in first suspecting and later bringing the criminal to justice. Dr Griffiths had no suspicion that Mrs Greenwood's death was other than a natural one, and afforded a convenient scapegoat when the blame for it came to be discussed.

The medical evidence at the two trials was the chief feature of both. In each the Crown sought to prove death by arsenical poisoning. The body of Mrs Armstrong, exhumed ten months after death, was found to contain over $3\frac{1}{2}$ grains of arsenic, and evidence that she had swallowed at least 5 grains of the poison within twenty-four hours of death. Mrs Greenwood's body, also buried ten months, only contained a little over a quarter of a grain of arsenic. Mrs Armstrong, until her husband started his diabolical scheme of slowly poisoning her, was a comparatively healthy woman. Mrs Greenwood, for months prior to her death, had been ailing and invalidish. Mrs Armstrong had taken medicines that contained a small amount of arsenic. None of Dr Griffiths's prescriptions for Mrs Greenwood had at any time contained it. The defence in the Armstrong case was suicide. It was not attempted to deny, save by an eleventh-hour theory of the defence, speedily shown to be fantastic and valueless, that Mrs Armstrong had died of arsenical poisoning, but the defence strove to prove that she had taken the poison intentionally herself. This was revealed as a physical impossibility, seeing that for several days prior to her death she could neither leave her bed nor feed herself. In Mrs Greenwood's case the more ingenious defence was urged that her death was due to morphia poisoning through the carelessness of Dr Griffiths, who administered two pills containing the drug. When Dr Griffiths exploded this theory by a belated admission in the witness-box that the pills under discussion had not been morphia pills, but opium, the defence still stuck to its guns. Medical experts called and examined swore that to the best of their belief and knowledge Mrs Greenwood had died from morphia poisoning, notwithstanding the absence of any traces of the drug from the organs analysed. Mrs Armstrong's case was a comparatively straightforward one compared with Mrs Greenwood's. From the first the medical experts on both sides were in entire agreement as to the cause of death. It was arsenical poisoning, without controversy or possibility of doubt. In Mrs Greenwood's case the presence of a minute quantity of arsenic in the organs was not denied by either side, but each battled fiercely over the question of its being sufficient or insufficient to have caused death. The Crown doctors contended that it was, and had in fact done so. The medical men called for the defence argued that a fatal dose had not been swallowed, and that Sir Edward Marshall Hall's theories of absorption by inhaling or swallowing in glucose were not impossible or untenable to account for the presence of even so small an amount as a quarter of a grain. The conclusion of the Armstrong case left the public mind satisfied that justice had been done. The end of the Greenwood trial found most people puzzled, bewildered, disappointed, and annoyed. Greenwood was condemned for marrying again with what looked like indecorous haste as much as for his wife's mysterious end. Each trial, interesting from a pathological, physiological, medical, and social point of view, showed more than one disquieting X-ray glimpse into the sordidness of our human nature. As usually happens with a murder, the victim in both cases was a shadowy figure around whose poor ghost hovered the ugly realities of her survivor's and destroyer's subsequent acts. Mrs Armstrong was admittedly peculiar and trying. Mrs Greenwood was much liked and universally regretted by her circle of friends. The martyrdom of the one at her husband's hands lasted for months in a manner reminiscent of the case of Mrs Pritchard, and culminated in days and nights of agony only comparable to the sufferings of the wretched victim in the Seddons case. Mrs Greenwood's short illness was so far free from dangerous or disquieting symptoms that four hours before she died her daughter went to bed at her mother's suggestion, and her friend, apparently reassured, returned home.

There is much in the Greenwood case that can never be brought to light here. Did Mrs Greenwood die of arsenical poisoning, morphia poisoning, or from natural causes? Who was responsible for the first rumour that her easily-consoled husband's had been the hand that dealt death? Which spoke the truth on oath – Irene Greenwood, who swore that she drank burgundy at lunch and supper, or Miss Phillips, who swore that there was no wine on the supper-table? Were the loss of over £600 a year, the companionship of a considerate and affectionate wife, the awful risk of the gallows, worth contemplating for the charms of a woman of past thirty, a lifelong acquaintance, without money or expectations? It was argued in the case of Dr Pritchard that he had no motive for murdering his wife [1], yet murder may be committed without apparent motive, as instanced by Herbert Rowse Armstrong.

It is possible that had the Greenwood case been tried in Scotland the verdict would have been 'Not proven'. Despite the jury's finding, local believers in Harold Greenwood's guilt remained, like the unconvinced lady in the rhyme, 'of the same opinion still'. Guilty or innocent, the mind shrinks from contemplating the fate which followed him. He suffered outlawry, ostracism, exile from everything that he had hitherto known and enjoyed. The words of his counsel touching his social and professional ruin, whatever the outcome of the trial, became singularly true. The other figures of the story who had come under the fierce searchlight of publicity went back to

[1] *Trial of Dr Pritchard*, edited by William Roughead, 'Notable British Trials Series'.

obscurity, and stayed in obscurity. The chief actor in the brief drama vanished, following an abortive attempt to take up his old life. Twice after his acquittal the name of Harold Greenwood appeared again in the newspapers. In March 1922 he was plaintiff in a successful libel action which he took against a firm of waxworks proprietors who exhibited him in effigy. Eight years and two months from his sensational trial a brief paragraph in a few daily journals announced the death on 17 January 1929, at a little-known Herefordshire village, of a man of fifty-four who, dogged by poverty, notoriety, and ill-health, had lived there under the name of Pilkington. Harold Greenwood, whose fame was once on everybody's lips, had made his last bow and exit from a world that had offered him little and deprived him of much. If innocent, his was a more than Greek fate.

William Joyce

· 1945 ·

BY

J. W. HALL

I

IN a sense this is written for posterity, for to his contemporaries in Great Britain William Joyce – better known by his nickname of 'Lord Haw-Haw' – needs no introduction.

On 3 September 1939 Great Britain and France declared war on Germany. On 18 September, William Joyce, the holder of a British passport, and believed by the British authorities (and possibly by himself) to be a British subject, entered the German Broadcasting Service. Between 18 September 1939 and 30 April 1945 he broadcast regularly in English from German stations, especially Zeesen, Hamburg, and Bremen. There can hardly be anyone in Great Britain who had access to a wireless set during that period who did not at some time tune in, deliberately or by accident, to that irritating voice which proclaimed 'This is Jairmany calling', and proceeded to prophesy – sometimes accurately – the unpleasant things that Hitler and his cronies had in store for us.

Joyce's distinctive accent was a common topic of discussion. There were even those who insulted our senior University by alleging that it was an 'Oxford accent'. But this was an accent such as Balliol had never conceived, nor Magdalen heard; indeed, as an Oxonian, I am prepared to assert that if (which is not admitted) there be such a thing as an Oxford accent, that accent is not – thank Heaven – the accent of William Joyce, which may have been some sort of hybrid between a Yankee twang and an Irish brogue.

William Joyce, as was proved at the trial, was born on 24 April 1906 at 1377 Herkimer Street, Brooklyn, New York,

73

the son of Michael Francis Joyce and his wife, Gertrude Emily Brooke, formerly of Shaw, Lancashire, whom he had married at All Saints Church, New York, on 2 May 1905. Michael Joyce was born in 1869 or 1870 (his age was given as thirty-six on William's birth certificate) at Ballinrobe, Mayo, Ireland. In 1888 he went to the United States; on 22 July 1892 he filed in the Court of Common Pleas of New Jersey a declaration of his intention to become a citizen of the United States of America 'and to renounce forever all allegiance and fidelity to any and every foreign prince, potentate, state, and sovereignty whatever, and particularly to the Queen of the United Kingdom of Great Britain and Ireland, whose subject he has heretofore been.' On 25 October 1894 this declaration of intention was followed by a petition for naturalization, accompanied by a declaration on oath renouncing all foreign allegiance in the same terms as above, and Michael Joyce thereupon became a naturalized American citizen. It followed that when William was born in New York in April 1906 he was a natural-born American. In 1909 the Joyce family returned to Ireland, and between that year and 1921 they lived at various addresses, first in County Mayo and later in Galway. In 1917 Mrs Joyce visited England and was required to register as an alien at her native place, Shaw.

In December 1921 William Joyce came to England, being then fifteen. His parents, with the rest of their family, followed in 1922, and settled in England; apparently, coming from Ireland, they were assumed to be British subjects, for there is, as far as I have seen, no record of any aliens registration at this time. It may be that this was the origin of the confusion as to nationality. Be that as it may, in that same year, 1922, William Joyce passed the London matriculation, and began to study science at the Battersea Polytechnic. In the following year he took up English language and literature, and history at Birkbeck College, where he studied for four years, and graduated in 1927.

On 21 October 1922, soon after his matriculation, Joyce formally applied for enrolment in the University of London O.T.C. In a preliminary letter, dated 9 August 1922, he says,

'It is my intention, if possible, to study with a view to being nominated by the University for a commission in the Regular Army. I have served with the irregular forces of the Crown, in an intelligence capacity, against the Irish guerrillas. ... I have a knowledge of the rudiments of Musketry, Bayonet Fighting, and Squad Drill. I must now mention a point which I hope will not give rise to difficulties. I was born in America, but of British parents. I left America when two years of age, have not returned since, and do not propose to return. I was informed, at the Brigade Headquarters of the district in which I was stationed in Ireland, that I possess the same rights and privileges as I would if of natural British birth. I can obtain testimonials as to my loyalty to the Crown. I am in no way connected with the United States of America. ... As a young man of pure British descent, some of whose forefathers have held high positions in the British Army, I have always been desirous of devoting what little capability and energy I may possess to the country which I love so dearly.' The University of London O.T.C. being a unit strictly limited by the War Office to British subjects of pure European descent, the adjutant, on receipt of Joyce's formal application for enrolment, wrote to his father on 23 October 1922: 'He says you were never naturalized as an American. Perhaps, therefore, you would confirm this point, when I shall be able to proceed with his enrolment and registration.' Michael Joyce replied on 26 October:

'With regard to my son William. He was born in America. I was born in Ireland. His mother was born in England. We are all British and not American citizens.' So William Joyce was duly enrolled, and served till 1926.

Meanwhile, from 1923 to 1925 he was a member of the British Fascists, a body whose activities at that time were largely anti-Communist. In the course of one affray between Fascists and Communists Joyce himself was slashed in the face with a razor, which left him scarred for life. On 24 April 1927 he came of age, and a week later married Hazel Kathleen Barr at Chelsea Register Office; that marriage was dissolved in 1936. In 1928 he did a year's post-graduate course in philology. From 1928 to 1930 he spoke for and assisted the Conservative party, and from 1931 to 1933 he studied psychology at King's College, London. From all of which it will be seen that by the time he embarked on the broadcasts for which he was tried, William Joyce was a man of very high education well qualified for the task he undertook.

On 4 July 1933 he applied for a British passport. On the application form he described himself as a British subject by birth, 'having been born at Rutledge Terrace, Galway, Ireland.' The application was verified by an official of a bank (against whose good faith no suggestion has at any time been made). This rather suggests that the present system of verification is of little value: it is certainly a nuisance to those who belong to the limited classes entitled to verify, who are constantly being put in the position of offending their acquaintances or risking the making of serious statements on inadequate evidence. And what real value is it as a safeguard? If one of His Majesty's judges, or an intimate friend at the Bar, came to me and said: 'I'm going abroad: do you mind verifying my passport?' I should no doubt say: 'By all means.' But even in these circumstances I am, in most cases, acting on inference rather than knowledge. What I *know* is that my friend has for a number of years practised at the Bar, or held a judicial office: that he speaks English like a Briton, and, possibly, that he was educated at a British school or University. From which, I *infer* that he is a British subject – an inference probably correct in at least ninety-nine cases out of 100. But one very seldom sees one's friends' birth certificates, and, if one meets them for the first time in adult life, often knows nothing about their parentage. In the hundredth case the inference can easily be mistaken. During the war of 1914-18 there were two ladies, later personally known to me as connexions of my wife, for whom I should have had not the slightest hesitation in verifying a passport application. All through the first Great War they lived in England as Englishwomen, doing war work, and I am sure as loyal as any two women could be. After the war they wished to go abroad, and applied for a passport. To their horror they were told: 'It appears from the facts stated that you are, and always have been, German subjects.' What had happened was that they were the daughters of an Englishwoman married to a German, who, at the time of their birth, was British consul at a town in South America. They were brought back to England in childhood, after their father's death, and had always erroneously assumed that, having been born in a British consulate, they were British subjects (as they would have been if it had been a British *embassy*). If I remember rightly, they were given some sort of temporary document till they could be naturalized.

The list of persons entitled to verify passports is 'a member or official of any banking firm established in the United Kingdom, or a Mayor, Magistrate, Provost, Justice of the Peace, Minister of Religion, Barrister-at-Law, Notary, Solicitor, Physician, Surgeon, &c.'. That '&c.' in the circumstances is delicious. What on earth does it mean? And what would happen to a person who stated his qualification as '&c.'? In these democratic days it is difficult to see the reason for so narrow and, if one may say so, so snobbish a list. One might have supposed that a man's employer would be far more reliable as a sponsor than a doctor, parson, or bank official, who sees him only occasionally, and for a limited and special purpose.

But, compared with some documents which one is asked to vouch for, a passport application is a model of sound sense. During the war I was staying in a hotel in Scotland for some weeks. A fellow guest, whom I did not for a moment doubt, asked me to sign an application for permission to enter a 'protected area' to visit her brother who was the local laird. I said: 'Well, I don't doubt for a moment that you are who and what you claim to be, but three weeks' hotel acquaintance is hardly enough to justify me in signing you up as a fit and proper person to enter a protected area in war-time: still, let me see exactly what has to be certified.' She produced the form, and all I was asked to state was that 'I have no reason to doubt the truth of the foregoing particulars', or words to that effect. I told her that I did not mind signing that, as it did not pledge me to any personal or affirmative knowledge. But what earthly use it was from a security point of view I have never discovered. But I award the prize for idiocy to the form which I was asked to sign for someone who had lost clothing coupons or ration book (I forget which). I had solemnly to declare – under fearsome penalties for false declarations – that I had put to the applicant the question 'Have you lost your coupons?', and that I had received the answer 'Yes'!

Is it unreasonable to suggest that the system of 'verification' of applications – including passport applications – needs overhaul or abolition?

At all events, a passport was duly issued to Joyce, valid for five years; it was renewed for one year in pursuance of an application dated 24 September 1938, and for a further period of one year from 1 July 1939 in pursuance of an application dated 24 August 1939 only ten days before the outbreak of war. That renewal became a matter of crucial importance at his trial.

Meanwhile, from 1933 to 1937 he was a member of Sir Oswald Mosley's 'British Union of Fascists'. In December 1934, with Sir Oswald Mosley and others, he was charged before Mr Justice Branson and a jury at Lewes Assizes with riotous assembly at Worthing. The defendants were acquitted. On 13 February 1937, his first marriage having been dissolved in the previous year, he married Margaret Cairns White at the Kensington Register Office.

In March of the same year he formed his own organization, the 'National Socialist League'. I am informed by friends in Bristol that this body had an office in Park Street, Bristol, with a shop at which one could buy, without restriction, such useful and necessary articles as rubber truncheons and daggers. One of these daggers is now in my possession, having been acquired by my friend for some perfectly innocent and lawful purpose. During the career of the National Socialist League, Joyce was twice charged before Metropolitan Magistrates with assault, but on both occasions the charges were dismissed. In September 1937 he wrote *National Socialism Now*, and he also wrote articles and pamphlets in support of Fascism.

The final renewal of his passport having been granted on 24 August 1939, on the 27th Joyce ordered the National Socialist League to be dissolved, and at some date before the actual outbreak of war he went with his wife to Germany, and a fortnight later he started the broadcast propaganda which ultimately brought him to the dock. The events affecting Joyce between September 1939 and his arrest on 28 May 1945 can be briefly stated. In September 1940 he was granted German nationality, and on 12 April 1941 a German military passport was issued to him. On 26 June 1942 he was appointed chief commentator on the German Radio for the English Group, and on 1 September 1944 the Kriegsverdienstkreuz 1st Class (a civilian award) was conferred on him by Hitler. On 3 November 1944 a German passport was issued to him in the name of Wilhelm Hansen – the acquisition of passports showed signs of becoming a habit; possibly by that time the progress of the Allies in the west suggested the advisability of building up an *alias*, as William Joyce had every reason to think that it would be bad for his health to fall into British hands. The certificate, issued on 21 December 1944, that he was a member of the Volkssturm may have had a similar object, but if so, why the reversion to his own name? It may be that lack of man-power compelled everyone, including foreign broadcasters – and he was now a German citizen – to enrol in the Volkssturm. Be that as it may, it is not without interest to note that 'Wilhelm Hansen' was said to have been born on 11 March 1906, in Galway, Ireland, while on the Volkssturm certificate the date and place of birth are correctly stated. On 30 April 1945 Joyce delivered his last identified broadcast. On 28 May 1945 he encountered two British officers near Flensburg on the Danish frontier, one of whom shot him in the leg, and they arrested him. I trust it does not sound cynical to say that if the officer had aimed higher much trouble would have been saved.

Both Joyce's parents had died in England during the war: his father, Michael Joyce, on 19 February 1941, and his mother, Gertrude Emily Joyce, on 15 September 1944. In 1940 Joyce wrote and published in Germany a book,

Twilight over Europe, of which 100,000 copies in German and English editions were sold on the Continent. It has never been published in England or obtainable here.

Such, in barest outline, was the career of the prisoner down to his arrest. We may now consider more closely the nature of the treasonable acts which brought him to the dock.

2

When Joyce first began to broadcast from Germany, just a fortnight after the outbreak of war, the British authorities, it is believed, were not a little perturbed as to the possible effect on morale, and they were far from displeased when a journalist almost immediately christened him 'Lord Haw-Haw', and the name stuck. Usually the inventor of popular nicknames is unidentifiable, but the 'onlie begetter' of Lord Haw-Haw was undoubtedly Mr Jonah Barrington, then of the *Daily Express*, who kindly gave me his own account of how he came to invent the name.

He was working at that time on the collation of foreign broadcasts at a wireless receiving station in Surrey, and had come across Joyce's broadcasts several times, and realized that they had a certain 'nuisance value'. It occurred to him that the most effective counter was ridicule, and he wrote an article about these broadcasts in which he referred to the broadcaster as 'Lord Haw-Haw', and gave an imaginary pen-picture of him as a brainless idiot of the type of 'Bertie Wooster' in Mr P. G. Wodehouse's books. The name caught on; it was taken up by the press generally, and Mr Barrington records with joy that on 17 October 1939 the French newspaper, *Paris-Midi*, in a burst of enthusiastic inexactitude, reported that there was a new radio traitor called 'Lord Ah! Oh!' whose real name was Jonah Barrington!

Thenceforward, it is probably true to say, William Joyce's hope of exercising any real influence on British morale was at an end. From being a sinister bogey-man, he had to many people, if not to most, become a figure of fun, about whom comedians sang songs on the wireless. The Western Brothers, for instance, had a song called 'Lord Haw-Haw the

Humbug of Hamburg', which was one of many in similar vein.

Early in 1940 the listener-research department of the B.B.C. prepared a report, at the request of the Ministry of Information, on the effect of Joyce's propaganda in this country. It will be remembered that at that date the war was still in the 'phoney' stage, before the invasion of Norway and Holland, and that many of Joyce's broadcasts were directed to attempts to make people dissatisfied with conditions at home, and to comparing them unfavourably with life under the Nazi régime in Germany. Curiously enough, this was the peak period of listening to Joyce, which fell to insignificant proportions when the 'Phoney war' ended, and never revived. The report covers most of the period in respect of which Joyce was convicted.

Before receiving this official report, I had made personal inquiries (for what they are worth) among the particular section of the community with which I happened to be mainly in contact – the legal profession, members of my club, and so forth – and the answers showed several different reactions to Lord Haw-Haw. My own, which apparently was not a very common one, was: 'By listening to Lord Haw-Haw I am doing precisely what the enemy wants me to do. They do not put him on the air for fun, or with any goodwill to this country, but in the hope that people will listen, and be filled with "alarm and despondency". I should not believe him, anyway, so why gratify the enemy by listening?' And I never did listen, unless I got him accidentally in tuning in to something else. Others took a different view: 'Oh, I always tune in to Haw-Haw and have a good laugh. He's the funniest turn on the air. One can't take him seriously.' Yet others said: 'It is disquieting to find how much information he seems able to get, and some of his forecasts seem to have been unpleasantly true.' On the whole, my impression was – and it is gratifying to find it is in agreement with the official report – that those who regarded him as a joke, if a joke in a very bad taste, probably outnumbered those who paid him serious attention. He was, no doubt, responsible for a certain amount of distress to persons residing, or having relatives and friends residing, in the places he mentioned as intended targets, but since his purpose was undoubtedly the more serious one of causing alarm and despondency among the population generally, he must go down to history as not merely a knave, but an unsuccessful knave. His influence overseas seems to have been still more negligible, even where it can be said to have existed at all.

One may perhaps sum up the general British attitude to Joyce's broadcasts in the words: 'If our people ever catch Lord Haw-Haw, he'll "get it in the neck".' Probably thousands of people used this slang expression without giving a thought to its grim and precise accuracy in the case of William Joyce.

3

For if the substance of Joyce's broadcasts was regarded by many people as a joke, the fact that he should deliver them was not. Treason is an ugly thing, especially in time of war, and a traitor does not redeem his treachery because his methods make him a laughing-stock – though actually his technique of building an elaborate structure of prophecy of allied disaster on a foundation of quarter-truths was a dangerous one and skilfully worked out, if only he could have induced sufficient people to take him seriously.

Hence there was no doubt whatever that if Joyce – being, as everyone then believed, a British subject – fell into British hands he would stand his trial for treason by 'adhering to the King's enemies'. That was also the crime of Sir Roger Casement[1] in the war of 1914–18, and it is almost inevitable that one should compare and contrast the two cases. Both turned on questions of law; in neither were the main facts seriously in controversy: nevertheless, the contrast soon becomes more striking than the resemblance.

Casement was tried at Bar, in the King's Bench Division, before a Court of three judges and a jury, under the old and highly technical procedure in the cases of treason. This pro-

[1] See *Trial of Sir Roger Casement*, edited by G. H. Knott, 'Notable British Trials Series'.

cedure bristled with formalities, such as the delivery to the prisoner, ten days at least before the trial, of a copy of the indictment, a list of the witnesses, and a copy of the jury panel. These things may have been necessary safeguards in periods of our history when treason sometimes meant little more than finding oneself on the wrong side politically; they are merely troublesome snares for the prosecution in days when judges are, happily, above suspicion, and the packing of juries an impossibility. But the case of Joyce came under a new act, the Treason Act, 1945, a Statute nominally purely procedural, to assimilate the procedure on a trial for any form of treason in all respects to that on a trial for murder. This had already been done in the case of treason consisting of a direct attempt on the life of the Sovereign by the Treason Act, 1800.

The new act is a very clear example of 'legislation by reference'. One might have supposed that all that was necessary was to say that: 'The procedure in all cases of treason and misprision of treason (whether alleged to have been committed before or after the passing of this Act) shall be the same as in trials for murder', and to repeal the old Acts prescribing special procedure, including the Act of 1800, which would now be covered by the general provision. That is far too simple for Parliamentary draftsmen. Sec. 1 of the New Act begins: 'The Treason Act, 1800' – so the first four words necessitate reference to a Statute nearly 150 years old; then, with unusual generosity, we are told in general terms what the Treason Act, 1800, is about – '(which assimilates the procedure in certain cases of treason and misprision of treason to the procedure in cases of murder) shall apply in all cases of treason and misprision of treason whether alleged to have been committed before or after the passing of this Act.' In other words, the Act of 1800 is treated as (though not called) the 'principal Act', and the practitioner or Court must turn to it to find out *precisely* what the new Act effects. He has, even then, to read it subject to five separate repeals of specific words, and to a saving clause in sec. 2, sub-sec. (2) of the new Act, the effect of which is completely unintelligible without further research into the provisions of two still more ancient

Statutes of 1695 and 1708 respectively. This saving clause is said to be 'for the removal of doubt', which could, one imagines, never have arisen if the Act of 1800 had simply been repealed and re-enacted in the wider terms now desired. That there may be cases where 'legislation by reference' is unavoidable or even convenient I am not concerned to deny, but to complicate a completely simple matter by enacting something which no mortal can possibly understand without going back 250 years through the Statute Book shocks the conscience of the ordinary person.

There is, however, a more serious criticism of the new Act. It was introduced into the House of Lords as a purely procedural Statute [1] merely designed to eliminate archaic provisions in treason trials, among which was mentioned, quite incidentally, the necessity for two witnesses. The possible importance of this seems to have escaped attention, though Lord Maugham did comment on the possible danger of abolishing the rule that no evidence should be given of overt acts not charged in the indictment. Under sec. 2 of the Treason Act, 1695, it was necessary to have at least two witnesses, either both to the same overt act, or one to one overt act and the other to another overt act of the same kind of treason. The Treason Act, 1800, had abolished that safeguard in cases falling within it, namely attempts on the life of the Sovereign; and now sec. 2, sub-sec. (1) of the Treason Act, 1945, provides that: 'The enactments set out in the Schedule to this Act are hereby repealed in so far as they extend to matters of procedure in cases of treason or misprision of treason, that is to say, to the extent specified in the third column of that Schedule.' Among the Acts so repealed is the Treason Act, 1695, except secs. 5 and 6. So the protection afforded to the accused by sec. 2 of the Act of 1695 is taken away – probably,

---

[1] See *Hansard* (H.L.), 30 May 1945, vol. 136, col. 265: 'Its provisions are absolutely confined to matters of procedure, and it does not make any change whatsoever in the law as to what constitutes treason.' That is strictly accurate, if an important change in the law of evidence is correctly described as a 'matter of procedure'. If so, all the law of evidence is 'procedure'.

even without sec. 2, sub-sec. (1) of the Act of 1945, that would have resulted from the application of the Act of 1800. In the Joyce case, *one witness only*, Detective-Inspector Hunt, connected Joyce directly with the broadcasts. If the Act of 1695 had been in force, possibly other witnesses might have been available, but that is not self-evident, for he was not definitely identified by the B.B.C. till 2 August 1940, after the last date alleged in count 3. Admitting that the line between matters of procedure and matters of substance is sometimes a narrow one, to include a statutory requirement of corroboration in the former category is rather startling.

The main issue in the Casement case was whether a person could be convicted of treason in respect of acts committed outside the King's dominions. That case definitely settled the law on that point, and it was no longer open to Joyce's counsel. But Casement was a British subject, and the first question in the present case was: 'Is Joyce a British subject?' That question of mixed fact and law was decided in his favour, and two further questions remained which were the important issues in the trial. These questions were:

1. Can any British Court try an alien for a crime committed abroad (with the sole exception of piracy, which by the *jus gentium* has always been justiciable anywhere, on the basis that a pirate is an enemy of the human race, to be eliminated by whoever has the good fortune to catch him)?

2. Assuming that there was jurisdiction to try him at all, did the fact that Joyce had applied for and obtained a British passport impose on him a duty of allegiance during its currency even when he was outside the British dominions? The determination of this question involved a consideration of the condition in which an alien may owe allegiance to the British Crown, and the circumstances which may put an end to such temporary or local allegiance.

On these questions Mr Justice Tucker ruled against Joyce, after which the verdict of the jury on the question whether he had, in fact, assisted the enemy, was inevitable, for no attempt was or could have been made to deny the facts.

The Joyce case is essentially one of legal interest. *Rex* v.

William Joyce will certainly rank among the leading cases on that branch of the law of treason which deals with the doctrine of allegiance, and it will probably be found of historical as well as legal importance as the first occasion on which the House of Lords, in its judicial capacity, has pronounced on certain statements of the law based on a somewhat mysterious resolution of the judges in 1707, in the reign of Queen Anne.

4

Joyce was brought to England on 16 June, and on 18 June he was charged before the Chief Magistrate, Sir Bertrand Watson, at Bow Street. The terms of the charge were as follows:

'William Joyce is charged for that he in the County of London,[1] within the Metropolitan Police District and within the jurisdiction of the Central Criminal Court, committed High Treason between the 2nd day of September, 1939, and the 29th day of May, 1945, in that he, being a person owing allegiance to His Majesty the King, adhered to the King's enemies elsewhere than in the King's realm; to wit, in the German realm, contrary to the Treason Act, 1351.'

After formal evidence of arrest, he was remanded to 25 June. On that occasion the Crown was represented by Mr L. A. Byrne, Senior Prosecuting Counsel to the Treasury (now Mr Justice Byrne), and Mr H. A. K. Morgan, of the Department of the Director of Public Prosecutions, while Mr C. B. V. Head, of the firm of Ludlow & Co., solicitors, appeared for Joyce. Joyce reserved his defence, and after a further formal remand to avoid committal to the current session of the Central Criminal Court, which would have been inconvenient for want of time to prepare the case, he was, on 28 June 1945, committed to the July Session.

At the July Session of the Central Criminal Court, Mr Derek Curtis-Bennett, K.C., applied for the case to be sent over to the next session. He told Mr Justice Charles that, look-

---

[1] The curious allegation that treason committed 'in the German realm' was committed in the County of London, etc., is due to the statutory provisions as to venue in the case of treason committed abroad in the Treason Act, 1543, 35 Hen. VIII, ch. 6.

ing at the indictment, the first fact for the Crown to prove was that Joyce was a person owing allegiance to our lord the King. There had been investigations in the United States as to the nationality, not only of Joyce, but of his father, and the defence had documents from the State of New Jersey concerning a man who might or might not prove to be Joyce's father. It was necessary that someone should go to the United States to see the original documents and signatures, and it might be necessary for the latter to be seen by persons who knew the handwriting of Joyce's father, so that sworn evidence in an admissible form might be before the Court. That would take time, and could not be done in that session. One matter absolutely vital in the case was Joyce's nationality. There was also a record of the birth of William Joyce in New York in 1906, and it would be the submission of the defence that if Joyce was born in the United States he could not owe allegiance to the British Crown.

MR JUSTICE CHARLES. – 'I express no view about it at all.'

MR BYRNE (for the prosecution). – 'We do not desire to put any obstacles in the way of the defence. It is our desire to render any assistance of which we are capable.'

MR JUSTICE CHARLES. – 'There being no opposition by the Crown, I am prepared to accede to the request. This case will be adjourned until the September Session, 11th September.'

At the September Session the presiding judge was Mr Justice Tucker, who fixed 17 September for the opening of the trial. On that day Joyce was arraigned, and pleaded not guilty to an indictment containing three counts. The first count charged that being a person owing allegiance to our lord the King he adhered to the King's enemies elsewhere than in the King's realm, by broadcasting between 18 September 1939 and 29 May 1945; the second, that being a person owing allegiance to our lord the King he adhered to the King's enemies elsewhere than in the King's realm by purporting to become naturalized in Germany. During the trial these two counts were amended by substituting 'being a British subject owing allegiance' for 'being a person owing allegiance', thereby emphasizing that in these counts the prosecution were relying on British nationality. The evidence of Joyce's American nationality being, as Mr Justice Tucker said, 'really overwhelming', the Attorney-General intimated that he was not going to invite the jury to say that he was British, and therefore the jury were directed to return formal verdicts of 'Not guilty' on those counts. The real issue was fought out on the third count, which alleged that Joyce being a person owing allegiance to our lord the King adhered to the King's enemies elsewhere than within the realm by broadcasting between 18 September 1939 and 2 July 1940. The latter was the date on which Joyce's British passport expired. It will be more convenient to deal separately with the important legal questions involved, the nature of which has already been indicated, and to say here that Mr Justice Tucker ruled as a matter of law that Joyce did owe allegiance to the British Crown, and left to the jury the question whether he had adhered to the King's enemies. To that there could be only one answer, and Joyce, on 19 September 1945, was convicted and sentenced to death.

On 27 September he gave notice of appeal to the Court of Criminal Appeal against his conviction,[1] on four grounds:

1. The Court wrongly assumed jurisdiction to try an alien for an offence against British law committed in a foreign country.

2. The learned judge was wrong in law in holding, and misdirected the jury in directing them, that the appellant owed allegiance to His Majesty the King during the period from 18 September 1939 to 2 July 1940.

3. There was no evidence that the renewal of the appellant's passport afforded him or was capable of affording him any protection, or

---

[1] It is a 'vulgar error', beloved of the more popular organs of the press, and occasionally perpetrated even by the B.B.C., to describe a prisoner as appealing 'against the sentence of death', which, being fixed by law, cannot be appealed against. This is carefully provided by the Criminal Appeal Act, 1907, which refers to 'appeal against sentence (not being a sentence fixed by aw)'. The appeal in capital cases is, and must be, against conviction. In practice, leave, when necessary, is always granted in capital cases.

that the appellant ever availed himself or had any intention of availing himself of any such protection.

4. If (contrary to the appellant's contention) there was any such evidence, the issue was one for the jury, and the learned judge failed to direct them thereon.

The appeal was heard before the Lord Chief Justice (Viscount Caldecote), Mr Justice Humphreys, and Mr Justice Lynskey on 30 and 31 October and 1 November 1945. After reserving judgement till 7 November, the Court dismissed the appeal. The Criminal Appeal Act provides that one judgement of the Court shall be delivered, and this was given by the Lord Chief Justice, but its language makes it clear that the decision was unanimous.

No further appeal could be brought unless the Attorney-General was prepared to certify that the decision 'involved a point of law of exceptional public importance, and that it was desirable in the public interest that a further appeal should be brought.' On 16 November Sir Hartley Shawcross, Attorney-General, issued his certificate to that effect.

The appeal was heard by the House of Lords on 10 to 13 December, the noble and learned Lords sitting being the Lord Chancellor (Lord Jowitt) and Lords Macmillan, Wright, Simonds, and Porter. On 18 December they announced their decision dismissing the appeal (Lord Porter dissenting), and intimated that they would give their reasons at a later date, which they did on 1 February 1946.

5

It may be useful to the reader to give some account of the law relating to nationality, of the history of passports, and of the conception of allegiance.

At common law, nationality depended on place of birth – a person born within the King's dominions was a subject, a person born outside them was an alien. On this simple doctrine various statutory modifications were grafted, of which the most important was the rule that the children and grandchildren (but not remoter issue), wherever born, of a natural-born British subject, were also British subjects, provided that

the father had not before the date of the birth divested himself
of British nationality. Before 1870, when the Naturalization
Act was passed, a British subject could not divest himself of
British nationality. Such divesting could only happen, if at
all, by operation of law, e.g. by outlawry.

Thus, if Michael Joyce, the prisoner's father, being a British subject, had gone to America and William Joyce had been
born there before his father acquired American citizenship,
he would have been a British subject by birth. But as soon as
it was proved that Michael Joyce completed the formalities
of naturalization in the United States in 1894, while William
Joyce was not born till 24 April 1906, it became clear that
William was an American and not a British subject.

As regards persons born since 1 January 1915, British
nationality has been governed by the British Nationality and
Status of Aliens Act, 1914, which defines natural-born British
subjects in sec. 1, sub-sec. (1) as follows:

The following persons shall be deemed to be natural-born British
subjects, namely:

(*a*) Any person born within His Majesty's dominions and allegiance; and

(*b*) Any person born out of His Majesty's dominions whose father
was a British subject at the time of that person's birth and either was
born within His Majesty's allegiance or was a person to whom a
certificate of naturalization had been granted; and

(*c*) Any person born on board a British ship, whether in foreign
territorial waters or not.

Provided that the child of a British subject whether that child was
born before or after the passing of this Act shall be deemed to have
been born within His Majesty's allegiance if born in a place where by
treaty, capitulation, grant, usage, sufferance, or other lawful means,
His Majesty exercises jurisdiction over British subjects.

(This proviso would cover persons born in British em-
bassies and legations abroad.)

The reader will notice the recurrence of the expression
'born within His Majesty's allegiance', and much turned at
the trial of William Joyce on the meaning of allegiance. Until
this case was decided, any lawyer called on to explain what
was meant by 'allegiance' would probably have considered

that he had given a correct definition if he had defined it as the duty of loyalty and faithfulness owed to a Sovereign by a person within his protection, and had gone on to say that allegiance might be of two kinds: (1) natural and permanent, which is the allegiance owed to the Sovereign by his own subjects at all times, and in all places, so long as the relation of subject and Sovereign subsists. It is because of this natural and permanent allegiance that a British subject can be guilty of treason even outside the British Empire. (2) The second kind of allegiance is local and temporary, being that owed to a Sovereign by an alien so long as he remains within the dominions of the Sovereign and under his protection. Until the Joyce case it was supposed that such allegiance automatically terminated when the alien left the realm. That must now be recognized as subject to qualification where any alien has, whether by mistake or fraud, applied for and obtained a British passport.[1]

The reason for the temporary and local allegiance of an alien is clear: no country can be expected to admit foreigners within its borders except on the terms that while they enjoy its hospitality they will conduct themselves in accordance with its laws, and refrain from activities subversive of its security or political institutions. Hence it is clear that a man may be subject at the same time to two allegiances. For instance, a British subject who goes on business or pleasure to the United States does not lose, or even suspend, his allegiance to the British Crown, but he has in addition a temporary allegiance to the American Constitution. He must not plot against America, but neither must he engage in activities which would be treason in Britain. This overriding natural allegiance is recognized in the principle of international law by which a subject of a belligerent in enemy-occupied territory may not be required to bear arms against his own

[1] It was never established, nor in these proceedings was it material, whether Joyce in applying for the passport, or for its renewal, was mistaken or fraudulent in stating his nationality. It may be said that if he honestly believed himself to be British, it makes his treason all the worse, since he was morally as well as legally a traitor to 'the country he loved so dearly'.

country. So far as ordinary law is concerned, the alien is subject to the law of the country where he is temporarily residing, to the exclusion of the law of his own country; thus the Englishman in Switzerland may, if he will, add to the pleasure of drinking a glass of beer in the middle of the afternoon by thinking of his thirsty compatriots at home with two hours to wait before opening time.

It will be noticed that in defining allegiance I have brought it repeatedly into relation with the word 'protection'. They are, indeed, correlatives. It was said by Blackstone, and quoted by the Attorney-General in opening the Joyce case, that so long as the Prince affords protection to his subjects, so long that subject owes a debt of allegiance to the Prince. And long before Blackstone in *Calvin's* case (1608), 7 Co. Rep. Ia; 77 E.R. 377, Lord Coke refers to the maxim '*Protectio trahit subjectionem et subjectio protectionem*', and much of the Crown's argument in the present case was based on the proposition that by deliberately applying for and obtaining a British passport, Joyce had placed himself under the protection of the Crown, and had thereby undertaken the correlative duty of allegiance so long as the right to claim the protection of the passport continued.

Up to a point, both sides in the Joyce trial agreed on the effect of the authorities. In Foster's Crown Law (1762 [1]), p. 183, sec. 1, it is stated: 'With regard to natural born subjects there can be no doubt. They owe allegiance to the Crown at all times and in all places. That is what we call natural allegiance in contradistinction to that which is local. The duty of allegiance, whether natural or local, is founded in the relation the person standeth in to the Crown and in the privileges he deriveth from that relation. Local allegiance is founded in the protection a foreigner enjoyeth for his person, his family or effects during his residence here, and it ceaseth whenever he withdraweth with his family and effects.' And on p. 185, sec. 4, he says: 'And if such alien seeking the protection of the

---

[1] 1762 s the date of the first edition of Foster. The edition used at the trial was the third, of 1809, but there appears to be no material change in text or pagination.

Crown and having a family and effects here should during a war with his native country go thither and there adhere to the King's enemies for purposes of hostility, he might be dealt with as a traitor. For he came and settled here under the protection of the Crown, and though his person was removed for a time his effects and family continued still under the same protection. This rule was laid down by all the judges assembled at the Queen's command, 12 January 1707. It is to be observed that the judges in the resolution last cited laid a considerable stress on the Queen's declaration of war against France and Spain, whereby she took into her protection the persons and estates of the subjects of those Crowns residing here and demeaning themselves dutifully and not corresponding with the enemy. King William and Queen Mary did the same in their declaration of war against France, and so did his present Majesty (George III). These declarations did in fact put Frenchmen residing here and demeaning themselves dutifully, even in time of war, upon the foot of aliens coming hither by licence of safe conduct. They enabled them to acquire personal chattels and to maintain actions for the recovery of their personal rights in as full a manner as aliens may. But as I said before all aliens enemy residing here under the protection of the Crown, though possibly not favoured as the persons last mentioned, yet they in case they commit crimes which in a subject would amount to treason may be dealt with as traitors. For their persons are under the protection of the law, and in consequence of that protection they owe a local temporary allegiance to the Crown.' That resolution of the judges was also referred to in East's Pleas of the Crown (1903) but in somewhat different terms; the original is apparently not extant, nor are the circumstances in which it was passed known.

The Crown sought to rely upon it as authority that in some circumstances an alien could be prosecuted for treason committed outside the realm, if he was still receiving the protection of the Crown for his family and effects. In the present case Joyce had not left his family and effects in England – for 'family' clearly must be limited to wife and children over whom he can be presumed to exercise some control, and does not include parents and brother and sisters who are in no way responsible to him. But in the Attorney-General's picturesque phrase, by obtaining a British passport he had 'enveloped himself in the Union Jack' and put himself in a position to claim British protection. That protection involved the corresponding duty of allegiance. By broadcasting for the enemy Joyce acted in breach of that duty, and was thereby guilty of treason, for which he could be tried and executed in this country. Such, in the briefest outline, was the case for the prosecution. Against it the defence urged (in addition to the argument that there was no jurisdiction at all to try an alien for a crime committed abroad) that a resolution of the judges had no binding authority as such; it did not appear that it was a decision in any case then before a Court. In any event, it did not support the Crown's contention, for the exception suggested in the case of the alien leaving his family and effects was due – if it was the law, which, in the submission of the defence, it was not – to his still receiving protection *within the realm*. The protection necessary to attract the duty of allegiance was the protection of the law, and it could arise only where the British law ran, that was to say, within the King's dominions. It must, in other words, be *de jure* protection, and not mere *de facto* protection; not that there was any evidence that Joyce had ever in fact used his British passport to claim protection from any British authority anywhere.

A passport, it was submitted, was not a document granting any right to protection: it was merely recognition of the status of the holder as a British national, and a request to foreign governments to give the holder such rights as flowed from that status. Like other documents certifying status, it was not conclusive, but could be displaced by proof that the status did not in fact exist, and was then a mere nullity. Just as two persons going through a form of marriage were entitled to obtain an official certificate of marriage, so a British subject intending to go abroad could, and in most cases nowadays must, obtain a British passport. The rights and duties of the spouses did not flow from the certificate, but from the relation of husband and wife; and the rights and duties of the traveller did not flow from the passport but from his British nationality. The marriage certificate could be displaced by proof that the marriage was in fact bigamous on the part of one of the spouses, or that they were within the prohibited degrees; so the passport could be displaced by proof that it had been issued to an alien whether he had obtained it fraudulently or under an honest mistake as to his true national status.

Moreover, it was submitted, to say that Joyce, having wrongly obtained a British passport, thenceforth owed allegiance, even though he proved that he was in fact an alien, was the introduction into our law of 'crime by estoppel'. He could not, in a criminal case, be debarred from setting up the defence that he was an alien because he had, for the purpose of obtaining the passport, previously alleged that he was British. (For the benefit of the lay reader, it may be explained that 'estoppel' is a rule of evidence whereby, if a man has made representations as to a matter of fact, on the faith of which someone else has altered his position, the maker of the representation will not be allowed, in *civil* proceedings, to rely on the true facts – in so far as they differ from his representation – against the person who has so altered his position. But this doctrine has never found a place in *criminal* proceedings, in which a defendant can always rely on any defence open to him, notwithstanding previous contradictory statements, which may, of course, be material for cross-examination.)

The *Shorter Oxford English Dictionary* attributes the word 'passport' to the beginning of the sixteenth century. It seems originally to have been a licence to leave the realm, which was otherwise prohibited at common law, possibly because it deprived the King of a man's military service. This sense, with the analogous sense of a licence to enter or pass through a country, is said to be obsolete from the early seventeenth century. The definition given of the modern sense, dating from 1536, is 'a document issued by competent authority, granting permission to the person specified in it to travel, and authenticating his right to protection.' It will be noted that the passport is only said to *authenticate*, not to *confer* the right to protection. The first mention of passports in the Statute Book is in 1548, 2 Ed. VI, c.2, sec. 10, where it is applied to what would now be called a soldier's leave-pass.

There appears to be no steady or consistent development of the system of passports. They seem to have been required or not required of individuals according to the state of contemporary politics in various countries. In *Reg.* v. *Bernard* (1858), 8 St. Trials (N.S.) 887, Orsini was stated to have travelled in France and Belgium under a false passport, six years old, issued by the British Foreign Office under the name of Allsop. Sixty years later, before the war of 1914–18, passports were not necessary for visiting most European countries other than Russia and Turkey, but they were not infrequently carried as a convenient means of identification, and an assistance in claiming the help, in case of need, of diplomatic or consular representatives. Since the first world war they are generally necessary for travel, and British regulations state that 'British subjects travelling to foreign countries must be in possession of valid passports bearing, when required, the visa of the consular representatives of the country or countries to be visited.'

In 1887 Lord Salisbury sent a circular asking British representatives abroad to supply information as to the laws of their respective countries regarding the admission of aliens as residents. The result, published in Parliamentary Papers, 1887, No. 81, contains factual information, but no general statement as to the nature of a passport. But from the various replies, it appears that a passport was regarded as a document required by the country in which the traveller found himself as a formal reference, as a safeguard to that state. In Austria-Hungary the state authorities could grant a traveller a provisional passport, if his own was not in order, provided that he was not a suspicious character. So at that time a British subject might lawfully have entered Austria, with not a British, but an Austrian passport.

In 1872 the British Government apparently regarded it as an inconvenience that British subjects should be required to carry passports, and made representations to France with a view to their abolition. The French Government gave two reasons for retaining them: (1) Security to France. (2) They were a valuable source of revenue which she could not at the moment afford to forgo. There was no suggestion that the passport was a document ensuring the holder British protection; it was rather represented as an unreasonable requirement of the French Government, resented by the British Government, and acting as a deterrent to travel. As a result of this correspondence passports were abolished between Britain and France, but the right of a British subject in France to claim protection cannot have been diminished or affected, which seems rather to support the view that the passport is merely evidence of rights, not their source.

Of judicial authority on passports there is very little. Apart from *Reg.* v. *Bernard (supra)*, in *Rex* v. *Brailsford and M'Culloch*, [1905] 2 K.B. 730, a conspiracy to obtain a false passport for use in Russia was involved. The gravamen of the offence, as set out in the indictment, was the endangering of the relations between this country and Russia, not a wrongful claiming of protection, and in his summing-up Lord Alverstone, the Lord Chief Justice, thus defined a passport: 'It is a document, issued in the name of a Sovereign, on the responsibility of a Minister of the Crown, to a named individual, intended to be presented to the governments of foreign nations and to be used for that individual's protection as a British subject in foreign countries, and it depends for its validity upon the fact that the Foreign Office, in an official document, vouches the respectability of the person named. Passports have been known and recognized as official documents for more than three centuries, and, in the event of war breaking out, become documents which may be necessary for the protection of the bearer, if the subject of a neutral state, as against the officials of the belligerents, and in time of peace, in some countries, as in Russia, they are required to be carried by all travellers.' There appears to be no more recent judicial criticism or amplification of that definition, which does suggest that the protection of the bearer is the object of a passport, but not that the right to protection springs from the passport, which seems to have been a novel doctrine in the present case, though one which found favour in all three Courts, and must therefore be accepted as the law.

6

The reasons for their lordships' decision were delivered on 1 February 1946, nearly a month after Joyce's execution. It is perhaps worthy of passing comment that the Home Secretary, before allowing the law to take its course, did not think it necessary to wait and see whether any passages in their lordships' opinions might afford some ground for the exercise of clemency. It may well be that they would not have done so, and that delay would merely have been a prolongation of Joyce's ordeal.

The Lord Chancellor said that the question of law, of far-reaching importance, was whether an alien who had been resident within the realm could be held guilty and convicted in this country of high treason for acts committed by him outside the realm.

The Statute of 1351 was wide enough to cover any man anywhere: 'If *a man* do levy war', etc. But the question whether the act was treasonable depended on the relation in which the actor stood to the King to whose enemies he adhered. Attention had naturally been concentrated on the question of allegiance. To say that an act was treasonable if the actor owed allegiance, and not treasonable if he did not, left undecided the question by whom allegiance was owed. New considerations might demand a reconsideration of the scope of the principle. It was not an extension of a penal law to apply its principles to circumstances unforeseen at the time of its enactment, so long as the case was fairly brought within its language.

It was implicit in the argument for the appellant that, however brief his absence from the realm, he could not during that absence, in any circumstances, by giving aid and comfort to the King's enemies outside the realm, be guilty of a treasonable act. That statement was not only at variance with the law, but was inconsistent with authority which could not be disregarded. The passage in Foster's Crown Law (already cited) had been repeated without challenge by numerous authors of the highest authority, nor had it been challenged in any judicial authority.

In the present case there was no question of vicarious protection. But was there not such protection still afforded the appellant by the Sovereign as to require his continued allegiance? It would be strangely inconsistent with the robust and vigorous common sense of the common law to suppose that an alien quitting his residence in this country, and adhering and giving aid to the King's enemies abroad, could do so with impunity.

The appellant had long resided here, but he (the Lord Chancellor) made no assumption one way or the other about his intention to return, and treated as immaterial the fact that he made a false statement as to his status. When he first made it, it might be that he thought it was true.

The possession of a passport by a non-British subject gave him rights and imposed on the Sovereign obligations which would otherwise not be given or imposed. He was enabled to obtain in a foreign country the protection extended to British subjects. The question was whether by the receipt of the passport he extended his duty of allegiance beyond the moment when he left the shores of this country. As one owing allegiance he sought and obtained the protection of the King for himself while abroad.

The argument that, since the protection of the law could not be given outside the realm to an alien, he could not, outside the realm, owe any duty had no substance. At the time when the common law established between Sovereign and resident alien the reciprocal duties of allegiance and protection, it was to the personal power of the Sovereign rather than to the law of England that the alien looked. It was not therefore an answer to the Sovereign's claim to fidelity from an alien without the realm who held a British passport that there could not be extended to him the protection of the law. He was of opinion that so long as an alien held the passport he was, within the meaning of the Statute, a man who, if he adhered to the King's enemies in the realm or elsewhere, committed an act of treason.

He did not dissent from the general proposition that an alien could withdraw his allegiance on leaving the realm. But there was no suggestion that the appellant had surrendered his passport, or done any other overt act to withdraw from his allegiance, unless, indeed, reliance was placed on the act of treason itself, which in his opinion could not be done. Such an act was not inconsistent with the appellant still availing himself of the passport in other countries, and even in Germany.

With regard to the question of jurisdiction, a proper regard of the State for its own security required that all who committed the crime of treason, whether within or without the realm, should be amenable to its laws. There was no principle of comity to the contrary.

It was further urged for the appellant that there was no evidence that the renewal of his passport afforded him, or was capable of affording him, any protection, or that he ever availed himself or had any intention of availing himself of any such protection; and that if there was any such evidence the issue was one for the jury, and that the judge had failed to direct them thereon. That point also failed.

Lords Macmillan, Wright, and Simonds concurred with the Lord Chancellor.

Lord Porter dissented. He agreed that the renewal of the passport on 24 August 1939 was evidence from which a jury might have inferred that he retained that document for use after 18 September 1939, when he was first proved to have adhered to the enemy. If an alien was under British protection he occupied the same position when abroad as he would occupy if he were a British subject. But the question of continued allegiance depended on the circumstances of the case, and was a matter for the jury. In the present case a jury properly directed might well have considered that the allegiance had been terminated. He would have allowed the appeal.

It will be observed from the above summary that their lordships have expressly decided that a passport is not merely an evidential document, but one which gives rights and imposes duties; and that an alien in possession of a passport may be tried here for crimes committed abroad. Those matters may well be thought amply sufficient to justify the Attorney-General in granting his certificate. Even so, it is easy to underestimate the significance and importance of the Joyce case. *Directly*, its importance may well be small, for only in the infinitesimal number of cases in which an alien obtains, by fraud or mistake, a British passport, and then goes abroad and commits treason, can it be directly in point. A British subject is covered by his general duty of allegiance, and the passport is immaterial.

But *indirectly*, the case may well prove of vast importance. It has introduced into our jurisprudence, for the first time, the doctrine that a British Court has, in certain circumstances, the right to try an alien for a crime committed abroad. It does not need much imagination to see that, unless those circumstances are very precisely and narrowly defined, this may be the thin edge of a very large wedge indeed.

Secondly, it has introduced, or at least declared, the doctrine that the holder of a British passport *ipso facto* owes allegiance to the British Crown. This may have far-reaching repercussions in British mandated territories, and among 'British protected' persons, where persons who are not British subjects may be entitled to hold British passports.

It is also possible to envisage a perfectly honest person being involved in a conflict of allegiance where it is completely impossible for him to avoid committing treason! Suppose, for instance, that Joyce, instead of being American, had been German by birth, but had lived here and honestly believed himself to be British, and went abroad with a British passport. On the outbreak of war he is claimed as a German subject, liable to military service. If he obeys, he is (under this decision) liable to be hanged by the British; if he refuses, he will certainly be shot by the Germans.

The decision is no longer open to argument: the reasoning

underlying it is a legitimate subject of legal discussion, and it would be untrue to pretend that it meets with unanimous acceptance among lawyers, many of whom thought the appeal would succeed.

7

On 3 January 1946 William Joyce was hanged at Wandsworth, the Home Secretary, Mr J. Chuter Ede, having intimated a few days earlier that he was unable to find any reason which would justify him in interfering with the course of law. A morbid-minded crowd of some 300 persons gathered outside the gaol, and according to the evening papers police had to control the crowd which surged forward to read the official notice that the execution had been carried out. Two men, it was reported, had travelled from Glasgow to be present. But the most scandalous aspect was the presence of young children brought by their parents.

The statutory inquest produced the inevitable verdict. One may be pardoned for some scepticism as to the value of these formal inquiries after an execution; we have never read of one which failed to record that the execution was carried out expeditiously and without a hitch. There is no reason to doubt that everything possible is done, and was done in this case, to ensure the minimum of suffering to the victim, but there are some grim stories in the history of executions, even in modern times, and there is considerable reason to doubt whether, if a hitch did occur, the regulations would permit any news of it to reach the outer world via the coroner and his jury. When Major Wallace Blake was tried in 1926 for a breach of the Official Secrets Act, by disclosing details of a recent execution in a newspaper article, an official of the Home Office was cross-examined as to the instructions issued on 10 January 1925 by Sir Ernley Blackwell, K.C.B., Permanent Legal Under-Secretary to the Home Office, to Prison Governors with regard to their conduct at executions, and the form of their evidence at inquests, which was to be confined to as few words as possible, e.g. 'it was carried out expeditiously and without a hitch.' If pressed for details, 'the Governor should say he cannot give them as he did not time the proceedings, but "a very short interval elapsed", or some general expression of opinion to the same effect.' Questions were asked in the House of Commons by Mr Pethick-Lawrence as to these instructions, but the Home Secretary (Sir W. Joynson Hicks) said: 'It is undesirable to give the exact terms of the instructions ... the less said at the inquest either by Governors or anyone else, the better.' (See Hansard, 23 June 1927, vol. 207, No. 85, cols. 2022-2023.) One is left sharing Mr Pethick-Lawrence's doubts whether it can possibly be proper to give a witness instructions as to the form and content of the evidence he is to give *on oath* before a judicial tribunal entitled to hear 'the truth, the whole truth, and nothing but the truth.' Whether any alteration has been made in the instructions since 1926 it is impossible for a private individual to know: the regularity with which the phrase 'expeditiously and without a hitch' occurs in the reports of these melancholy occasions suggests that it is improbable.

At an inquest at Lincoln Prison on a man executed on 4 January 1928, the Governor's answer to the question how long elapsed between Pierrepont entering the cell and the drop was: 'I am not allowed to say anything except that a very short interval elapsed.'

The Coroner. – 'Are you allowed to say how long the body remained hanging?' – 'No, sir, I am not.'

Perhaps one day a jury will have the courage to return a verdict, 'That the deceased met his death by judicial hanging, but the jury have not been allowed to receive sufficient evidence to enable them to say whether the execution was properly carried out.'

In writing this I wish to make it emphatically clear that I am not for one moment suggesting that anyone concerned with the execution of Joyce failed to carry out his duty with complete propriety. My criticism is directed at the system, not at individuals or individual cases. One cannot help wondering whether the American system of summoning a certain number of respectable and responsible citizens (not the type who voluntarily gather outside the gaol to stare at a sheet of paper) as witnesses of the execution is not a greater safeguard, provided that they are not muzzled if there is anything that should be disclosed in the public interest.

For Joyce's crime one can have no sympathy whatever. Though in law an alien, he had lived many years in England, had deliberately served in the O.T.C., and had referred to her as 'the country I love so dearly'. But the question remains, for many thoughtful people: What useful purpose have we served by hanging Joyce, or John Amery about a fortnight earlier? Treason, it is true, is the greatest of crimes, but there are degrees even in treason, and the crime of treason by broadcasting propaganda is hardly comparable to that of treachery in the field. On the day after Joyce's execution a man named Schurch was hanged at Pentonville. He had been convicted on nine charges of giving information to the enemy, and of desertion with intent to join the enemy. Still less, one might have thought. was Joyce's crime, detestable though it was, deserving of the same punishment as the mass murders and torture of prisoners of which the Belsen criminals were convicted.

If it be said, 'There would have been a public outcry if Joyce had been reprieved', my answer would be that the first function of a legal system is to substitute the reasoned and dispassionate judgement of the law for the clamour of popular prejudice. It may, however, be doubted whether there would have been any popular clamour, for much to my surprise I have found, with a universal reprobation of Joyce's conduct, a very considerable feeling, shared by lawyers and laymen, servicemen and civilians, that (with the utmost respect to the eight out of nine learned judges) the decision was wrong, and that an unmeritorious case has made bad law. The feeling is not so much that Joyce, having been convicted, should have been reprieved, but that he should not have been convicted.

Ley and Smith

· 1947 ·

BY

F. TENNYSON JESSE

ON 29 November 1946 the body of a murdered man was found in a chalk pit near Woldingham in Surrey. Round the man's neck was a loose cord tied with a half-hitch, so that it only had to be pulled slightly upwards to strangle him. On the neck of the corpse was a deep mark which might have been made by such a cord, had it been so employed. The body was that of John Mudie, a barman employed at the Reigate Hill Hotel. His murderers had been careless enough to leave his visiting card in his pocket.

In spring and summer the place is screened by the thick leafy green of the trees that grow so profusely in Surrey. But there is no evergreen, not so much as one holly-bush. The chalk pit is extremely slippery and grass slopes rise perpendicularly on either side. There was nothing in November to conceal Mudie's body except bare twigs and good luck. The trees were free of any leaf and the shallow grave at the end of a sort of corridor of bushes looked like the remains of an army latrine. The army had camped in these parts, as it had all over England before the end of the war. The trench seemed to have been dug much earlier than 1946 with a spade; it was deepened in the middle, probably with the pickaxe brought by the murderers. It was about a foot and a half across and a foot deep, neither long nor deep enough to cover a body. Yet it was in this ill-disguised spot that the body of Jack Mudie was found.

A Mr Walter Coombs who lived at Woldingham happened to be passing by after his work for the day was over, and saw something that he guessed to be the body of a man. He did not go up to it or touch it; he went home and called his father, who accompanied him back to the chalk pit. Neither man altered the position of the body; the older man raised one of the trouser legs in order to see the flesh and to make sure it was a dead man lying there. The chalk pit is not in winter the haunt of picnickers or of lovers. One approaches it by a sharp turning off a good secondary road. Mr Coombs and his son went to the Surrey Joint Police Force [1] at Oxted, and P.C. Hearn went back with them, arriving at about 4.45 p.m. The body was lying upon its right side but with the feet sticking out over the end of the trench or grave. It was clothed in a blue chalk-stripe suit of what is known as the 'Demob.' type. An over-coat was twisted over the dead man's head, inside out. A rope was wound twice outside the overcoat. The rope was tied by two loose half-hitches, not very tightly. One end of the rope went under the body and the shorter end of the rope came from the neck under the left arm and was tied with another half-hitch.

P.C. Hearn untied the forearm first and then the rope from the man's neck, the rope in which there were the two half-hitches. He was then able to pull off the overcoat, and he noticed that the rope continued round the man's neck and that there was a piece of rag lying there that smelt of polish. This rag was still wet at the time that the police officer found it. It may have been merely wet with rain; it had been raining heavily and all the ground round the base of the chalk pit was inches deep in mud. Yet the soles of Mudie's shoes were clean, so he could not have walked to the place where his body was found. He must have been carried. This is a most important point, for a pickaxe was lying near by, a pickaxe that, like the french polisher's rag, was eventually traced to a house in Beaufort Gardens, S.W.

P.C. Hearn at once informed his superior officer, Detective-Sergeant Cox, of the discovery of the body.

Here the fates began to take a hand in the murder. On 27 November 1946 two landscape gardeners on their way home from work at a nearby property were bicycling along

[1] Since 1 April 1947 the Surrey Constabulary.

Slines Oak Road. These men were a Mr Clifford Tamplin
and a Mr Frederick Smith, and as the road rises sharply by
the chalk pit they had descended from their bicycles and were
walking up the hill. To their surprise, for on a November evening it was a place where few would like to linger, they saw a
car inside the entrance of the chalk pit parallel to the main
road.

It is a great mistake to imagine that a countryman notices
nothing. He notices far more than a townsman, about whose
head circumstances seem to be perpetually whirling. It was
an event for Tamplin and Smith to see such an unlikely thing
as a car on the lip of the desolate chalk pit and they paused
for a moment. They might not have paid any more attention
if they had not seen a man who was farther up a steep bank
beyond the car — a man who, at sight of them, at once ran
down, jumped in the car, and, reversing with some difficulty
in the thick mud round the chalk pit, got on to the road and
drove away. Clifford Tamplin and Frederick Smith were
honest witnesses and they never pretended to have agreed
upon the index letters of the car number; it was dusk of a
November evening, and the time for observation was short.
But they were so certain that they had seen a car at that deserted spot on 27 November, that when they heard a body
had been found there on the 30th, they at once, being good
citizens, informed the police of the incident.

They both agreed that the car bore the number 101 and as
it drove quickly past them they saw that it was a dark saloon.
They were not quite sure of the make – one of them thought
it was a Ford.

These two witnesses not only could not agree about the
index letters of the car, but at an identification parade later
on each chose a different man as the driver thereof. One chose
Lawrence John Smith, a foreman joiner, who was working
for a Mr Ley at 5 Beaufort Gardens, London, S.W. Identification is one of the worst forms of evidence. One realizes this,
remembering the cases of Oscar Slater and of Adolf Beck, also
the not unhumorous incident when one of the witnesses at
the 'Moat Farm' trial identified the criminal, first among the

jury, and then proceeded to choose the Shire Hall keeper.

But what is important about the matter of Frederick Smith and Clifford Tamplin noticing this dark saloon car, the number of which was 101, was the fact that they noticed it on the day before Mudie was murdered. Now, one Lawrence John Smith had hired a car for a week; it was a dark Ford saloon of which the number was 101. For some inexplicable reason – since it is impossible to look inside a man's brain – somebody or other had driven such a car to that deserted chalk pit on Wednesday 27 November 1946. Nothing shook these two honest men, the landscape gardeners, in cross-examination. They might perhaps have forgotten the whole affair if the man, whoever he was, had not run so quickly down the dangerous and greasy slope to the car, jumped into it, reversed with difficulty owing to the sticky mud, and driven off. It is, to say the least, a coincidence that a man drives to the lip of an abandoned chalk pit, and that a dead body should have been deposited there the next evening. What is there to conclude except that whoever had gone to the chalk pit driving such a car had gone for the purpose of finding a quiet and unfrequented spot? In summer either of two reasons, both normal, for which a quiet spot is sought might have obtained, but not in winter.

There is no getting away from the fact that the body of Jack Mudie was found in that chalk pit on Saturday evening 30 November. There is no getting away from the fact that he was decoyed up to London on Thursday 28 November. There is no getting away from the fact that a dark saloon car, No. 101, was there on the Wednesday evening, and John Lawrence Smith had hired just such a car on the Monday of that week. For the murder of Mudie, Thomas Ley, John Lawrence Smith, and John William Buckingham, an army deserter, were arrested.

Buckingham turned 'King's evidence', but Ley and Smith were found guilty on the clearest possible evidence and sentenced to death. This sentence was confirmed by the Court of Criminal Appeal.

Ley was the brain, if such it can be called, which designed

the whole affair. Smith was the hand which at least helped to carry it out. There is a curious weakness in the people of England which causes them to dislike, when the brain which designed the crime has been found to be insane, hanging the man who obeyed the primary directions. It seems to me, a mere layman, that anyone who is prepared to commit a felony in which there is at least danger of death to the victim should be executed, as long as there is capital punishment in England. A man who is capable of putting in deadly danger another human being, and therefore assisting in the actual murder of that human being, is just as guilty whether his employer be sane or a paranoiac. Smith was none the less guilty because Ley went to Broadmoor, a most comfortable spot, where a man of means can have a private room if there be one unoccupied, can have a batman if there be a fellow prisoner willing to serve him (and it is amazing what snobs are to be found among criminal lunatics), and, save for the sunken walls – which he cannot see – in that lovely garden, believe himself to be in a comfortable country house. Ley was sent to Broadmoor on 5 May 1947. He died there of a seizure on 24 July 1947. Anyone who cared for him must be glad that he is out of his misery. The taxpayer will naturally feel, and quite rightly, a certain relief.

Ley is supposed to have been the richest prisoner ever sent to the Criminal Lunatic Asylum. But the fact that Ley was a rich man had only helped him in his career of dishonesty, it had nothing to do with his reprieve. I merely mention this because in some other countries justice can be bought. In Great Britain no judge can be bought with money, nor yet by ' a ribbon, star or garter ... a great man's smile, a seat in Parliament, a tap upon the shoulder from a courtly sword, a place, a party or a thriving lie. ...' Mr Pecksniff thought these things might have been worth acceptance by any man making his way up, but even Mr Pecksniff would have known that justice is not for sale in what has been called this 'land of hypocrites' of which Mr Pecksniff is himself the supreme example. Dickens knew better than to make Mr Pecksniff fall into such an error.

The story first told about what was known as 'The Chalk

Pit Murder' was an extremely curious one, and it remained curious until the end. The leading character, if one may so describe him, was Thomas John Ley.

Smith, 'Snug the Joiner', was an ordinary enough little man to look at. It was suggested he had ambitions to change his way of life, to go out to South Africa, or to buy a business of his own. He was a quiet lodger at the house where he had a room at Dulwich.

Ley had held an important Government position in Australia in former days. He had been the Hon. Thomas Ley, Minister of Justice of New South Wales. He was born in England and had gone out to Australia at the age of eight. He began life selling newspapers in the correct romantic manner, then became a junior clerk and stenographer to one of the most respectable and oldest firms of solicitors in Sydney. Yet although he became a partner he was never particularly liked. He married and had a family. In the early twenties of this century he became interested in politics and stood for the local state electorate of Kogarah, a Sydney suburb that is partly industrial and partly 'white collar'. His firm did not like any partner of theirs taking an active part in politics, so the partnership was dissolved and he joined with another solicitor, but the firm did more company promoting than law work. Ley organized a team whose effort was to sweep the Hurstville municipal poll, and push through his policy of rating unimproved land values. This was fairly good going for a young man in his twenties.

In 1917, at the age of thirty-six, on a policy of electoral reform and more Australian participation in the war, he captured Hurstville. Then he broke with his leader, became unofficial head of the Progressives (equivalent to the Conservatives over here) and won his seat again with a big majority. He had formed the coalition that defeated the Dooley Government in 1922, and had come within an ace of leadership, when he was made Minister of Justice. He filled this important office successfully, and showed a sense of values. He handled the Marriage Amendment Bill and the Liquor Bill, and, as he entered his forties, he competed with

Hughes as the dominant figure in Australian politics. It is one of the most curious facts of this case that Ley was quite a good Minister of Justice, although while holding this responsible office he unloaded some disreputable shares upon one of his colleagues. He was nominated for the federal electorate of Barton, which included his own state electorate.

Now we come to one of the most odd matters connected with Ley. A certain man put up against him announced that he was withdrawing from the contest and, whether truly or not, the word went round that he was withdrawing because Ley had paid him to do so. Nevertheless, he did stand, but Ley was elected, though a little later the accusation was made that Ley had offered a bribe, and a political agitation, not unnaturally, took place.

The High Court of Australia, which deals with matters affecting the Federal House, was to make an inquiry. The man whom Ley was supposed to have paid never turned up at the inquiry, and the case lapsed for lack of evidence. The usual rumours ran around New South Wales. Some people said that Ley's political opponent had been paid by Ley to leave Australia. Certainly no trace of him has ever been found. Other people said that Ley had tried his hand at murder – and tried it very successfully.

It must be admitted that Ley was most unfortunate in the fate of his friends. He had a business association with a Mr Goldstein, whose lifeless body was recovered shortly after dawn on 3 September 1928 from the foot of Coogie cliffs. One Mr Puddifoot, sentenced to three years' imprisonment in September 1923 for the manslaughter of a boy whom he had criminally assaulted, was released on Ley's order nineteen months later. Ley may, owing to the curious workings of his mind, have taken a fancy to shorten Puddifoot's sentence. There is no proof of any guilt on the part of Ley in any of these deaths, and coincidences occur in real life of which no one would dare to write in fiction.

Most of Ley's co-members of the Cabinet are now dead, but those still alive seem to remember him as a 'smarmy' sort of individual, although they admitted he administered his department well. The great thing to remember about Ley is that few people liked him. True, he was a teetotaller, even an ardent one; he was nicknamed 'Lemonade Ley', which may have accounted for some of the dislike he met, but although he did well in politics, was hail-fellow-well-met and what might be called a good sort, he still was not liked. That he did well in politics is not surprising; doing well in politics is not necessarily to be beloved, and when the head of the Government went on a trip to Europe, Ley thought he was going to be Deputy Premier. He was only left in his former position, and left Australia, probably for that country's good, to go to the Riviera and to England. His share-pushing in Australia had not been looked upon favourably.

Before Ley left Australia, a friend of his went to England, and when she came back, so rumour has it – and I am merely quoting Australian rumours – she showed a very important member of the National Party a letter from her husband telling her that the wife of the man who had disappeared and the wife's sister had both come to Ley's house to demand news of him and had refused to leave, and that Ley had finally had to call the police to cause them to be evicted from the drawing-room. It is very probable that the man who had disappeared was in some matrimonial or financial trouble and that he might have accepted money to leave the country and escape his home obligations. That, however, since the murder of Mudie, has not been the common opinion in New South Wales. The absurd notion remains that it is easier to bury a body in the great spaces of Australia than in little England. But such notions remain in the realm of speculation.

An interesting point is that a large framed photograph of Ley hangs in the Justice Department together with all the other holders of the office of Minister of Justice. When the Chalk Pit Case 'broke' various people approached the Minister in office and asked him to have it removed, but he said it must remain as part of the historical sequence, in which he was perfectly right. It would be of interest to know whether a footnote will be placed below it to say that this particular Minister of Justice died in Broadmoor.

Ley was a man whom you or I might have met at dinner and considered pleasant, educated, full of knowledge, though perhaps a little pompous. Yet because under his smooth exterior Ley was mad, Jack Mudie is dead. Ley was a vain old man, he was corrupt. He had never found anything in life he could not buy. And for an entirely idiotic, foolish jealousy he bought Jack Mudie's death. He bought it as plainly and clearly as though he had lived in some dictator state, as plainly and clearly as though he had been a member of the Council of Ten in Venice and had wished an enemy to be removed. He did this in modern England, because he found tools to his hand whose price was slightly higher because of modern economics. He did this while he spoke amiably to his fellow men and women, while he took taxi-cabs and omnibuses, while he ate in popular restaurants, while he played gin-rummy with his ex-mistress, while he went to and fro on his lawful occasions. It was as though a shadow man had lived amongst us, a man whom no one would have dreamed of suspecting of anything ill, but a man, nevertheless, whose heart was the heart of his great prototype, Cain. Unlike Cain, he had a bank balance, and therefore it must have seemed to him that the urgencies by which he was impelled were easier to arrange.

He was mistaken, but that does not alter the fact that through his arteries, making his strange heart beat, his strange brain think, ran that same envious blood which actuated the earliest of murderers. The blood of Cain runs through the veins of every one of us. It doubtless ran through those of Abel, although Cain got his blow in first. There is no one of us who at one time or another has not wished another human being dead. Even in love 'deep as a well' there lurks the seed of hatred, which may come to the bloom in love's very waters.

There may seem to us no question of what sane human beings call love in Ley's case, but hatred can grow even without love. Ley, competent, gifted, and rich, was so bemused by these qualities that he thought he could choose between the good way and the bad way. He chose the bad way deliberately. He could buy it as he had bought everything else. Abel was fortunate to be the murderee and not the murderer. But there is a very fine hair-line between the two.

There are many of us who have a certain amount of sympathy with Cain; he was (and I do not for a moment put this forward as a cause for sympathy) a vegetarian, but at least his pathetic little offering to the Almighty was made from the vegetables that he grew. Abel started right in with the idea of blood sacrifices, and 'brought of the firstlings of his flock and of the fat thereof. And the Lord had respect unto Abel and to his offering. But unto Cain and to his offering he had not respect.' When Cain lost his temper and slew Abel he started a long line of descendants against whom not only God's hand but Man's hand is for ever raised. The voice of our brother's blood cries from the ground; if thoughts were deeds, we should all bear the brand of Cain. He wandered forth saying that his punishment was greater than he could bear, although the Lord had been merciful and had a mark set upon him to prevent anyone who met him from killing him. There is a certain resemblance between this and the difficulty which ex-prisoners have in getting an honest job of work. Nevertheless, we have to remember that Abel was not a killer save of innocent sheep, and that Cain was a killer of his brother.

Ley's sheep were shareholders whom he had cheated, and from this exercise, not unknown to many of our great men to-day who have happened to have had luck, he graduated to killing. Cain, perhaps annoyed with the blood-thirstiness of Abel, became himself the prototype of all killers. At least we can say that Cain knew what he was doing. Ley's plots, Ley's killing were as stupid and baseless as that of the carrot fly in the vegetable garden. And the activities of the carrot fly at least benefit the fly, though not the carrot or what is nowadays called the 'consumer'.

We come now to the most interesting matter that there is to be found in this tangled story. What was it that brought together three such different men as the Hon. Thomas Ley, ex-Minister for Justice of New South Wales; Smith, a foreman joiner; Buckingham, a deserter who turned King's evidence; and Jack Mudie, an ordinary harmless young man whose bad luck it was that he should have been picked upon for a kidnapping that ended in death?

The answer is to be found in that strange character, Ley. To Smith two or three hundred pounds was a fortune. We all have our temptation point, and Smith's was set very low – he came into it simply because of Ley's nature. He lived no fantasy life such as Ley lived, such as every murderer in essence must live, whether he be mad or not. Smith was merely a greedy, hard-bitten little man who was willing to engage in an act of violence for money.

Ley, an insanely jealous man, had had for some twenty years a mistress, Mrs Brook, who was at the time of Mudie's death sixty-six years of age. Ley had met her and befriended her in Australia. She was a widow, her husband having died untimely from being stung by bees. She became his mistress, and when he left Australia she came to England with her daughter. For some ten years before the trial there had been no question of any sexual intercourse between them, but she acted as his housekeeper. There is no doubt she was afraid of Ley, though not too afraid to be an honest if reluctant witness at the trial.

Mrs Brook's daughter married in England a respectable young man, son of an ex-golf-club steward called Barron. The young Barrons took a flat at the house of a Mrs Evans in Homefield Road, near Wimbledon Common. Young Mrs Barron fell ill and had to go into hospital for an operation. At Ley's own suggestion, Mrs Brook went to Mrs Evans's house to look after her son-in-law and to be near her daughter.

Mrs Evans, whose house was a grey brick Victorian villa which she let out in rooms, was in herself a most unusual person as well as having been an excellent witness. Her chief interest in life was music, and she played beautifully. Her lodgers, amongst whom was Jack Mudie, were men who went out to work, so she was enabled to give most of her time to the practice of her art. Young Mrs Barron when in health was no trouble, as she looked after her own flat. There is no doubt about Mrs Evans's opinion both of Mudie and of Ley. Of Mudie, she said he was a harmless decent young man, anxious to get on in the hotel world, and pleased when he got his job at the Reigate Hill Hotel. He had been barman at the 'Dog and Fox' at Wimbledon, and doubtless thought he was stepping up in the world when he went from its human warmth to the studied refinement of the Reigate Hill Hotel. Mudie was kindly and thoughtful. He did not forget his land-lady and came up twice to have tea with her. His bed-sitting-room in Wimbledon, painted a pale sea-green with a divan bed, looked out on trees. He was companionable and evi-dently treated Mrs Evans as a friend – which she was. When she had a severe attack of rheumatism he used to bring her tea and run her errands. Mrs Evans did many things for him, such as a young man living on his own cannot do for himself, keep-ing his room tidy, seeing to his washing and all the rest of the tiresome matters which have become more and more difficult since the war has ceased. 'Jack Mudie looked very like Bing Crosby,' Mrs Evans remarked nostalgically.

Of Mr Ley, Mrs Evans had an equally positive opinion. He was enormously fat at the time he came to see her and he sat overflowing one of the armchairs in her living-room, and not only made all the coarse remarks which were attributed to him by the Crown, but made them with an unpleasant leer. She took a dislike to him which she naturally saw no reason to change.

On his second visit to Homefield Road to see Mrs Brook, Ley seized Mrs Evans and gave her a resounding kiss, an attention which somewhat startled poor Mrs Evans, and which she would have preferred to have done without. He also produced two pound notes and said: 'This is for the Cause.' He knew that Mrs Evans was interested in institu-tions for the blind and gave piano recitals at two of them in the neighbourhood. She duly sent £1 to each, saying what at the time she thought was true – that the money came from 'a gentleman who was interested in the Cause.' Yet Mrs Evans, as people who let flats have to be, was a shrewd judge of char-acter. None of the young men who lived in her house, she was certain, was wishful to approach old Mrs Brook with any fell intent, and indeed did not do so. Knowing Jack Mudie's ambitions, Mrs Evans naturally thought when Ley said to her that he would like to help the young man that he meant to get him on in the hotel world. She did not at that time realize that the bluebottle suspicions of Ley, settling first here and then there, had finally decided that poor Jack Mudie was the best resting-place.

Mr Romer, another lodger, a respectable married man who went home to his wife and children for the week-ends, was not called as a witness: he, like the dead Mudie, had nothing to do with Mrs Brook. And young Mr Barron certainly had no notion of assaulting his aged mother-in-law. Yet at one time Ley had settled on Mr Romer as the villain in the case and wanted to arrange a meeting with him. Romer replied courteously that he would be delighted to see Ley, but accompanied by his two brothers – who happened to be good boxers. Nothing more came of that approach from Ley.

At the time that Ley had picked on young Mr Barron a curious incident occurred. Mr Barron senior was rung up at his office by his son, who said that Mrs Brook had invited him to tea at 5 Beaufort Gardens, the house which Ley was converting into flats and where he lived. Young Barron added: 'It can't have been Mrs Brook; it must have been her maid, she spoke in a most uneducated voice', and he therefore asked his father's advice as to what to do. Mr Barron senior said: 'Don't touch it with the end of a barge pole', or words to that effect, and later on the son telephoned to say he had taken his advice. When Mr Barron senior asked Mrs Brook whether she had indeed sent such an invitation, she replied indignantly that she was not living at Beaufort Gardens but at a room in West Cromwell Road, and that she had no knowledge whatever of the affair.

Young Mr Barron was more fortunate than poor Jack Mudie, for at 5 Beaufort Gardens Ley was lying in wait with some physically powerful friends ready to attack Mrs Brook's son-in-law had he in all innocence arrived for tea.

While Mrs Brook was staying at Wimbledon to be near her sick daughter she met Mudie once. Mrs Evans introduced them, when Mrs Brook was sweeping the stairs from her daughter's flat and Mudie happened to come out of his room. Mrs Evans made some remark about Mudie being a bachelor, and Mrs Brook replied jokingly: 'Well, he won't be one long with such beautiful blue eyes.' And that was the whole of the relationship between Mrs Brook and young Mudie. Mrs Brook had suffered much. She could not marry Ley, who was married already; she was a widow; she may at one time have been attractive; she became afraid of Ley, too afraid even to leave him.

So there we are back again at our first question: Why did Ley have this jealous obsession about an old woman with whom he had ceased to have sexual relations? We are all, as we know, born the slaves of our genes, we are more or less the servants of our glands. Ley was at one time, to judge by his photographs, enormously fat; when the present writer saw him in Court he was normal in size, distinguished-looking, white-haired. This does not mean that he was innocent of killing a fellow human being, but it does mean that something was terribly wrong with his physical outfit, and when one says 'physical' one means mental as well, for body and mind are so tied up together that it is quite impossible for the layman (and extremely dangerous for the expert) to say which influences the other the more. This does not deter the experts, who seldom fail to be sure of their judgements (and to disagree).

Ley had accused Mrs Brook of an adulterous relationship with her own son-in-law, and with the unfortunate Mudie who had met her once upon the stairs. Beset with suspicions, Ley went to the Royal Hotel, Woburn Place, the London hotel where his wife always stayed on her visits from Australia, and addressed Mr Minden, the hall porter, in those curious words: 'Do you know a man with a car who can look after himself and keep his mouth shut?'

Now, Buckingham was a friend of Minden's, and Minden had frequently rung him up when a hire car was necessary for clients staying at the Royal Hotel. Therefore he replied that he thought he did know such a man. According to Minden, Ley then said to him: 'My wife sends her compliments and says she is not coming back to England.' Since she had been resident in the hotel, off and on, for some years, Minden was naturally not surprised when Ley put something in his hand. After Ley had gone, Minden found that the envelope contained ten one pound notes. Minden had waited on Mrs Ley for a very long time, had sent ten trunks of hers to Australia, and assumed that the present was from Mrs Ley although it came from her husband. Mr Ley, incidentally, had never stayed at the hotel, though he came there nearly every day to see his wife. At all events it was obvious that Mr Ley was a lavish spender, and Minden saw no reason why his friend Buckingham should not get any money that was going.

Buckingham telephoned the number and spoke to Ley, arranging to meet him at the Royal Hotel the following evening. This appointment was carried out. Ley told Buckingham about two ladies who were being blackmailed by a man who had seduced them. He was cautious, and did not at that time give the names of the ladies. He merely said he would introduce Buckingham to another man who knew about the case. This man was Lawrence John Smith, the foreman joiner at 5 Beaufort Gardens, the somewhat derelict house where Ley lived in a certain degree of squalor, and which he was converting into flats.

Thus the fantastic series of meetings began between Buckingham, Smith, and Ley. The following evening Ley introduced Smith to Buckingham at the Royal Hotel. Ley went away, leaving Buckingham and Smith together. According to Buckingham's evidence, Smith said that he knew, through working at 5 Beaufort Gardens, that Ley had got into contact with a young lady who had been seduced by a man. Pressed by the Lord Chief Justice at the trial, Buckingham enlarged upon this slight statement and admitted that Lawrence Smith had told him that Ley had got into contact with two ladies who had been blackmailed, that they were mother and daughter, the mother having been seduced as well as the daughter, and that a certain man was blackmailing both women. This extraordinary affair appeared to have taken place at Wimbledon, but at the time no particular address was given to Buckingham. Ley had already said to Buckingham that he wanted to 'get something on this man' and Smith corroborated this statement. How Buckingham, a total stranger, was to 'get something on' this mythical man was not mentioned, nor did the fantastic suggestion seem to strike Buckingham as odd.

The word 'legal' played a great part in this trial. Mr Minden had asked Ley at the first meeting whether the affair was legal; since Ley was a solicitor, he concluded it was. Everyone seemed to know that it was a queer business, but that if it was 'legal' it would be all right. Mrs Bruce, a friend of Buckingham's, when asked to decoy Mudie up to London from Reigate, asked whether the affair were 'legal'. There is a strange half world, by which I do not mean the equivalent of the French *demi-monde*, which exists throughout England, where men and women may be bought for matters that are just within the law, and so, 'Is it legal?' are the first words that spring to their lips.

The plot rapidly progressed, and it must have become obvious to Buckingham father, to Buckingham son, who was also engaged in the affair, who helped his father in the car-hire service and was a witness for the Crown, and to Mrs Bruce and Smith that it was not 'legal' to kidnap a man, gag him, and tie him up.

At a later stage, after the first meetings of this strange trio, Ley, Buckingham, and Smith, Ley told Buckingham that he had had to 'fetch' Mrs Brook from Wimbledon at 2.30 on the morning of 19 June. He took her away in a hired Daimler in a state of distress.

The Lord Chief Justice extracted from Buckingham that Ley had spoken to him about money, that he had said he would get a year's salary if he did what he was told. These golden dreams floated round the Royal Hotel, and to Buckingham and Smith they bore the veritable stamp of Eldorado. Monies, and big monies, were paid both to Buckingham and to Smith, but the end of Jack Mudie was an ill-dug grave in a chalk pit, that of Smith in a convict prison, and that of Ley himself in Broadmoor. There is an old legend common to most countries, of fairy gold that turns to dead leaves, and it may be said that this legend was true of everyone concerned in this case.

After Mrs Brook had been 'fetched' at that fantastic hour in the morning from Wimbledon by Ley, she went to live in a room in West Cromwell Road. Nevertheless, though Ley was perfectly aware of this fact, he still brooded over his jealousy of Mudie. He began an absurd correspondence with the young man.

Ley was a director of many companies, and one of these was Connaught Properties, Ltd. Mrs Brook was a co-director and her signature, therefore, had to appear with his when cheques were needed by the company. Three cheques were needed, according to Ley, and there is no reason to doubt this, for the payment of salaries in the month of June.

Ley, who had himself taken Mrs Brook away from Wimbledon, yet sent the three cheques which required her signature to young Mudie at Homefield Road. He sent them with a covering letter in which he said:

DEAR SIR,

Mrs Brook telephoned last afternoon that she was going to the country about some arrangements in regard to the convalescence of her daughter who is still in hospital, and, as we want some cheques signed and returned to us not later than Friday next, we asked for her instructions. She directed us to send the cheques to her in your care, with a request that if she did not reach Homefield Road by 4 p.m. on Thursday, to ask you to be good enough to seal up the enclosed envelope and post it to her new flat at 5 Beaufort Gardens, London, S.W.7., so that we can send on Friday morning by taxi and obtain them. We enclose stamped addressed envelope addressed to her, and marked as she directed 'Strictly Private', her instructions being that we were not to open the envelope on any account until she returned on Friday morning. Thanking you in anticipation for your help in the matter. We are, yours faithfully,

(Sgd.) G. H. BAKER, p.p. Secretary.

Most of this letter was a lie. Mrs Brook had no flat at 5 Beaufort Gardens. That was where Ley was living. She was living in the room in West Cromwell Road whither he had taken her. She knew nothing about the sending of the cheques to Mudie and had given no instructions whatsoever.

What Ley hoped was that if by any incredible chance Mrs Brook had signed the cheques, that would be proof that she was 'carrying on' with Mudie. But the bewildered Mudie could make neither head nor tail of the affair, had no notion why Ley should have written to him, why he should be asked to give cheques to Mrs Brook to be endorsed, but he was a sensible young man and he took these cheques to Mr Barron senior, the father-in-law of Mrs Brook's daughter. Mr Barron, whose head was screwed on, if one may allow oneself the expression, extremely well, took the cheques to the office of Connaught Properties, Ltd, and insisted on getting a receipt for them. Ley, who was by then so obsessed by jealousy that he could not tell a hawk from a handsaw, when he did not at once receive the cheques back, told his solicitors to write to Mudie demanding their return, and two letters from these solicitors were found in Mudie's room at the Reigate Hill Hotel whither he had gone as barman. Ley then went down to the Reigate Hill Hotel and saw Mudie, who told him what he had done with the cheques, namely that he had handed them to Mr Barron. Ley insisted on taking Mudie all the way to Wimbledon to see if Mr Barron could verify this story. Naturally, Mr Barron did verify it. Ley's own account to Mr Barron was that he had sent the cheques to Mr Mudie as 'a bit of private detective work on his own.' There is no action of Ley's in this fantastic story for which there could have been any motive whatsoever. When Ley went down to the Reigate Hill Hotel it was, as far as we know, the only time he ever met Mudie. Mrs Brook had only met Mudie once on the stairs at the house of Mrs Evans.

The trial was so extraordinary, so beyond reason, that, speaking for myself, I should not have been surprised if everyone in court had turned, as they did in *Alice in Wonderland*, into a pack of cards, and Alice, who in this case might have been any one of the jurors, the talented counsel, or, more likely still, the Lord Chief Justice, would have beaten them away, quoting the immortal words: 'Why, they're nothing but a pack of cards.'

We have Ley, a man who had risen to a high position in

Australia, worrying himself about whether an old lady was having an affair with any one of three young men, one of whom was her own son-in-law, and the other two were almost unaware of Mrs Brook's existence.

Ley was obsessed with sex. He may have been impotent, and this may have caused his mind to dwell more and more upon the subject. Yet his obsession was such that it caused him to go to the infinite trouble and pains of suborning Smith, the joiner, the Buckinghams, and, through them, Mrs Bruce; of spending large sums of money to get a young man who was a total stranger up to his own house in London where he could murder him. And of these incredible series of events he could, or would, only say that he knew nothing. The man who died was innocuous, and had nothing to do with the strange outfit represented first by Ley and then by Smith and Buckingham, an outfit in which Mrs Brook, her son-in-law, and – for we may be sure she did not escape from suffering – Mrs Brook's daughter were all innocently involved. Mrs Bruce, Buckingham's friend, may have merely thought that she was asked to help in a chivalrous enterprise. Two women were being blackmailed, and of all crimes blackmail is the most evil. There can never have been so many people who had nothing to do with each other, whose lives and status in life were so entirely different, brought together for no reason whatsoever save a total lack of reason. As a rule it is the motive of a murder that makes it interesting. It is the total lack of motive in this tangled tale which makes it of supreme interest.

Buckingham's first scheme to get Mudie to London was that he should go with his son to the Reigate Hill Hotel, pretend to be drunk, and that Mudie, as barman of the hotel, should be asked to assist him into his car. They could then manoeuvre Mudie inside the car and drive off with him. Ley was not so mad that he did not see that this was a dangerous proposition. Jack Mudie was young and vigorous, and might have struggled and called for help. Buckingham then suggested that his friend Mrs Bruce, a visiting cook, should go down to the Reigate Hill Hotel, pose as a lady of means, and make friends with Mudie and ask him if he would come up

and act as barman at a cocktail party she was giving. She
went down and did make Mudie's acquaintance. Mudie said
that he would like to make a little extra money, and Thursday
would be the best day for him as it was his half-day off.

Therefore, on Thursday 28 November 1946 two cars set
off for the Reigate Hotel. One was a Wolseley belonging to
Buckingham; one was a dark saloon Ford, numbered 101,
which Smith had hired at the beginning of the week from a
garage in Beauchamp Place. Jack Mudie was waiting for Mrs
Bruce and young Buckingham, whom he thought was her
chauffeur.

The cars went back to London, Mudie and Mrs Bruce
being driven by young Buckingham in the Wolseley, while
the Ford saloon, with the elder Buckingham and Smith in it,
went on ahead and arrived at the front door of 5 Beaufort
Gardens. Mudie was driven to the back door, Mrs Bruce got
out of the car and gave a Yale key to young Buckingham. He
opened the door. She went in. Mudie followed her. Mrs Bruce
then made a pretence of wishing to speak to her chauffeur
and left the house, closing the door behind her. Mudie was
then seized upon by Buckingham senior and Smith, and
Mrs Bruce and Buckingham junior went to the 'Crown and
Sceptre' and had a drink, which they must have badly needed.
They were joined about five minutes after by Buckingham
senior, but not by Smith.

In most cases of murder one can truly say that even when
murderers are sane they are never normal. The fantasy world
guides them; it is to them the real world, as real as an exhibi-
tion may appear to a child. Yet it is but lath and plaster and
paint. In this fantasy world Ley lived. Now, this does not
apply to Smith, who had no fantasy world but who merely
wanted money to go to South Africa. In this he differs from
Ley. There is not, there cannot be, the smallest doubt that
Smith knew that he was engaged in an affair which was, to
say the least of it, criminal, or that he was engaged in an affair
which might bring death to Mudie. It is possible that he did
not realize the very sensible old British Law that anyone who
undertakes to play a part in a major felony that may endanger

life is guilty of murder if the victim die, even though he die by accident.

It is an extremely good law as long as capital punishment exists at all in the land. No one can possibly have made that expedition to the Reigate Hill Hotel, have seized upon Mudie in 5 Beaufort Gardens and helped to tie him up without knowing that he was committing a felony. It is of no importance whether Ley or Smith killed Mudie. The one was the brain, the other the tool, but let us hope there are few of us who would be the tool in such a plan. Smith, according to his landlady, was a decent sensible fellow, but there is no doubt that he carried out the task assigned him by Ley of bringing up Mudie to London to be a cocktail mixer at a mythical party. Whose was the hand matters not. What matters is that if a man be prepared to undertake a dangerous and unlawful affair and death result, it is murder.

As Buckingham, of whom not much can be said in favour, turned King's evidence, there is nothing more to be observed except the Lord Chief Justice's clear direction to the jury that anyone would have expected these two men, Buckingham and Smith, who had come into large sums of money for men of their position, to have celebrated that night. Smith did not. Buckingham, whose lady friend, Mrs Bruce, played Delilah to the unconscious Samson of poor Mudie, was not an intelligent witness, but she and Buckingham and Smith agreed in various matters. They all, for instance – and this is a most important point – swore that Buckingham went off with Mrs Bruce to do a round of public-houses and that Smith never turned up. Not only that, but Smith had said to Buckingham, 'I'm driving to Leicester to-night in my car.' Why did he say that when he was not driving to Leicester until the following night?

The Lord Chief Justice, with great firmness, and, if I may be allowed to say, acumen, at once noticed this point against Smith. True, the defence had brought in Smith's landlady to say he had taken a bath on Thursday night 28 November, and was in bed about 11 o'clock, but even she could not say he had gone to Leicester on Thursday. Her evidence was honest, but it still placed Smith at Dulwich. But what was Smith doing between – let us say – ten minutes to 7 in the evening, when he had been left with Ley and the pinioned and gagged Mudie, and the time that he went back to his lodgings in Dulwich? He may, of course, after having committed the crime – for kidnapping and assaulting a man by tying him up against his will are both crimes – have just gone out into the night and had a drink here or a drink there entirely by himself, and then slowly found his way back to his lodgings. But – and although negative evidence is poor evidence – there also is nothing to show what he did between 7 and half-past 10 that night. Taking the time – not summer-time nor what I have heard called 'God's time', but simply a matter of hours – it is quite possible that Buckingham, having played his part, went off with Mrs Bruce to have a drink, leaving Smith with Ley and Mudie. And there was sufficient space in whatever time there was to drive a dead body to the chalk pit and get back to Dulwich. There is nothing to show that Ley and Smith could not at once have put the body into the hired car (101) and taken it down and tossed it into that chalk pit, which, as we know, had been explored by some man, whether Smith or another, a day earlier, in a car of which the registration number was 101 and which was a dark saloon. There is a point where coincidence ceases to be coincidence and becomes a terrible pattern of facts.

Ley was undoubtedly the killer – with his mind if not with his hands. He had lived for many years not only a life, both in Australia and in England, of financial dishonesty, but had also lived a fantasy life as regards Mrs Brook. No one who saw Mrs Brook would have considered her guilty for one moment of anything save being afraid of Ley. She was not a young woman, she was not the sort of woman of whom some would have said: 'Yes, I know she is sixty-six, but she is so smart and so elegant one would take her for not more than fifty.' She was quite frankly sixty-six. She obviously suffered when giving her evidence; she had obviously been terrorized by Ley for very many years. It appears that in his curious fashion he was faithful to her; every night of his life when he was not giving Smith dinner he took Mrs Brook out to dinner. In a hundred years' time people will say: 'How wicked to have convicted Ley, he was obviously mad.' But he was not mad under the M'Naghten Rules, he was merely obsessed. He did not plead, as he should have, 'Guilty but Insane'. He was a man of fantasy, and he moved in fields of fantasy. Rich, old, vain, dishonest, he had never found anything he could not buy. He had bought Buckingham and Smith, as he had bought anything else he wanted during his career. He probably believed that he was telling the truth, and there is no more dangerous witness than the man who thinks he is telling the truth in the face of all the evidence against him. That is to say, dangerous to himself but not to the prosecution. Ley had throughout his life (and he had quite a good brain) believed he could, in common parlance, 'get away with it'. He had always got away with it, though not always with a clean garment as regarded his company-promoting activities. If a company promoter were forced to wear a white robe, or even a grey one, Ley's would have been found to have been extremely dirty.

What then was his motive in wishing Mudie killed?

Now, it is surely unnecessary to say that it is no part of the Crown's duty to prove motive, just as it is no part of the duty of the prisoner's counsel to prove his innocence. We come back, then, to the only question that really matters: 'What was Ley's motive in murdering that decent and ordinary young man, Jack Mudie?'

Ley was insanely jealous of Mrs Brook. She may have been swept off her feet by that attractive big shot the Hon. Thomas Ley. What we do know is that he persuaded her to allow him to become her lover, and that she was afraid of him.

There was an extremely good speech once made, probably the best speech ever made by anyone on the face of this earth (and I am not forgetting Gettysburg), by someone who said: 'He that is without sin among you, let him first cast a stone.' There I think we can leave Mrs Brook, though her desire to be inconspicuous was not helped by her leaving the Old Bailey in a large hired Rolls Royce. Indeed, this unfortunate choice of a vehicle drew upon her much more notice than she would have suffered had she employed a humble omnibus or even a taxi-cab.

Sir Walter Monckton had the most difficult part when he defended Ley. His client denied absolutely that he had ever known Mudie or had anything to do with him. He presented a blanket innocence. He looked distinguished, he spoke quietly. He had lost his vast adipose deposit. He simply said in the witness-box that he had never heard of Mudie, never met him, that (like Pranzini of unholy memory) he was '*pour rien dans cette affaire.*'

It would have been a most extraordinary coincidence if Smith and Buckingham and Mrs Bruce had agreed, as they did agree, to bring the unfortunate Mudie to 5 Beaufort Gardens, if they had not heard about him from Ley. They had nothing against him; indeed who had anything against him? We must accept the fact that Ley's glands or his mind, whichever way one looks at it, had made him insanely jealous of an elderly woman, and that he suspected man after man in his quest for vengeance. We can accept that fact, as indeed we are bound to accept it on the highest medical authority, that Ley was a paranoiac. We are not bound to accept the same of Smith. Many of us want to go to South Africa. Many of us would like to live there. But to accept £500 for committing a criminal act – and to kidnap a man and to tie him up forms a criminal act – is, I trust, beyond most of us.

Smith in evidence said that his wages were £7 10s. a week, and that he also had a lodging allowance amounting to £1, and a travelling allowance. He had served in the Royal Air Force during the war and had a gratuity of £32-odd when he came out. He said that he had thought about going to South Africa and also to New Zealand.

He admitted that Buckingham's first scheme which involved the question of pretending to be drunk had been turned down by Ley, but that Buckingham's second scheme of decoying Mudie up to Beaufort Gardens was accepted. He admitted that Ley had told him that he wanted Mudie left at Beaufort Gardens tied and gagged. Therefore he knew that the bringing of the innocent Mudie up to Beaufort Gardens involved a dangerous and unlawful act. He admitted that Ley had two bundles of bank-notes which he had asked him to count. That he did, and found the bundles contained £200 each. He added that Ley had said: 'This is here for you when you bring Mudie in. You will be able to collect your money and go right away.' He admitted that he met Mrs Bruce through Buckingham senior, that until then he had never met her, and that he had never met Mudie at all and had no grievance against him. He admitted that he bought a clothes-line early on in the day that Mudie was murdered. It was a clothes-line exactly similar to that with which Mudie was bound. He admitted that when the workmen went away in the evenings from 5 Beaufort Gardens the doors of the basement and the front area were locked and bolted so that it would be impossible for anyone to get in, unless he were let in or had a key. He admitted that when Mudie came in through the back door he grabbed him round the waist while Buckingham put a rug over his head. He told a different story from Buckingham in that he said when Buckingham was 'jumping' Mudie along the passage, the former stumbled and fell upon Mudie. He said that he had arranged with Buckingham that after they had delivered Mudie according to contract they would go to the 'Crown and Sceptre' in Brompton Road and have a drink.

This part of the programme was not carried out. Smith's story of why he stayed behind was that Ley told him that 'his end had slipped up; that he would like me to hang on for a moment or two. That he was having somebody come there to help him to get a statement.'

Smith insisted that by this he took Ley to mean that he wanted him to hang on – the use of the word 'hang' was most unfortunate. After Mudie had been tied up, according to Smith, Ley said: 'There is no need for Buckingham to stay. Let him push off.' Ley then handed Smith an envelope saying: 'Put this in your pocket. I've got Buckingham's here.' Smith continued: 'I told Buckingham that Ley wanted me to hold on as his people hadn't turned up. I told him that I didn't want to, as I had made arrangements with Buckingham to go and have a drink afterwards. I heard the car pull up at the back door and we again took up our positions.'

Smith did not deny that he saw Ley give Buckingham his envelope, that he took his own, that he let Buckingham out of the back door. From there on his story as given in examination-in-chief was that Ley had said to him his friends were arriving, that he, Smith, had heard steps so he went out of the door in the front area while Ley went up the stairs to the front door. Smith also said that he went and had a look at the 'Crown and Sceptre' to see if Buckingham's car was there, which it was not. He then went to the public-house nearest his own lodgings, and went home. He swore that he went home at about a quarter to ten or ten o'clock, when he took a bath and went to bed in Dulwich, not in Leicester. He did not go there for the week-end until the next day, when he went in the hire-car with the number 101. Smith swore that he had no part in taking Mudie's body to Woldingham, that he had not been there on the day before the murder. So whatever car was seen at the chalk pit, although its number happened to be 101 and it was a dark saloon, it cannot have been his hire-car.

Smith's evidence was peppered with the two terrible words 'actually' and 'definitely'. When asked whether the car at the chalk pit on the 27th had been his, he said 'Definitely not'. When asked what he was going to do with the car he had hired on the previous Monday he said, 'Nothing particular at all, actually,' and added, 'I was definitely going to Leicester for the week-end.' He persisted that he was using his car for his work until he wanted it for the week-end, but 'There was a bus, definitely.' It seems curious that he should have hired a car when there was a bus to take him to his work. He denied that Ley lent him the money and insisted that he had enough money himself, though he had to admit that he knew that a large sum of money was coming from Ley.

The Lord Chief Justice pounced:

'Were you hiring this car,' asked the learned judge, 'for the purpose of effecting what Ley wanted you to do?' Smith replied: 'No, not actually at all.'

However, Smith had to admit that he had not used the car on the Monday and Tuesday of the week he had hired it, but had kept it in a garage in Goose Green. He also said that during the day of Wednesday 27 November the car stood outside 5 Beaufort Gardens; and there remained the insuperable difficulty of the fact that he left the car outside his lodgings on the nights of Wednesday 27th and Thursday 28th, with no corroboration as to the time he had parked it there. On the late afternoon of Wednesday the 27th a car with the number 101 was seen at the chalk pit, and on the Thursday Mudie's body was deposited in the chalk pit.

Smith said that he was quite aware that in hiring the car he had 'definitely' signed his name to a document which had the number of the car upon it. He returned the car to the hire-service from which it came on the Monday when he came back from Leicester, the day he saw Ley again, at Beaufort Gardens, 2 December. Smith swore that all Ley said to him was that everything had gone off quite all right and that Mudie had been 'dropped' at Wimbledon. He did not, apparently, have the curiosity to ask by whom he had been dropped – or exactly where. The subconscious is a curious thing, and Wimbledon was the last place that Smith, for his own sake, ought to have mentioned, but he knew that that was where Mudie had been living before he went to the Reigate Hill Hotel.

He went on to tell a story of wishing to buy a car, but being unable to afford to, which is not unnatural considering his wages, Ley offered him the money to buy one and lent him £300 on 4 December. Smith, however, did not buy any car, although he says he made one or two inquiries. But he was keener on going abroad than anything else, and so, according to his own statement, came to the conclusion that he would not need a car. He opened an account with Ley's cheque for £300, but on 9 December took the money out and paid it back to Ley through Miss Ingleson, Ley's secretary.

Mr Curtis Bennett, defending Smith, asked: 'What did you say to him?' and Smith replied: 'I told him I had no use for the money and thanked him for it and I was thinking of going abroad and did not need the money.'

Mr Curtis Bennett pressed the matter further: 'I suppose the suggestion was that you were paid that £300 for being a further party to the murder of Mudie? Any truth in that?'

'None whatever,' replied Smith firmly.

'Were you a party to a murder plot at the price of £200 or the price of £500 or any other price?'

'Never.'

'When,' said Mr Curtis Bennett, 'I said £500, I was adding the £300 on to the £200. Was your idea to go abroad and avoid the consequences of this?'

'Definitely not,' replied Smith.

'Is all you have told us true?'

'Definitely,' said Smith, using his favourite word.

Mr Curtis Bennett did the best he could for Smith, and it was a very good best, and on the whole he did not have quite such a difficult job as Sir Walter Monckton did in trying to put over Ley's blanket defence of innocence, but the whole affair was very much like the three-cornered duel in *Midshipman Easy*. Since there were two prisoners, it meant that the counsel of each prisoner could discredit his learned friend's client, and added to that were Mr Anthony Hawke and his junior for the prosecution.

Smith never denied, and Mr Curtis Bennett made a great point of this, that he was 'definitely' responsible for getting Mudie to Beaufort Gardens. Naturally Sir Walter, who was appearing for Ley, suggested to Smith that it was quite untrue that Ley had anything to do with the affair at all. Our sympathies can be with Sir Walter; he could not plead 'Guilty but Insane' because his client refused to do so.

The cross-examination of Smith by Mr Anthony Hawke was deadly:

'Did you know Mudie at all?' – 'Not at all.'

'Had you any interest in Mudie?' – 'None whatever.'

'Did you know until you were told that he was at the Reigate Hill Hotel?' – 'I did not know anything about him until told by Mr Ley.'

'Did Buckingham?' – 'As far as I know, no.'

Definitely and actually, that was apparently all that Smith knew, and though his evidence did not quite chime with Buckingham's, it was not the complete ignorance that Ley presented.

Now, when Smith gave this evidence, Ley had already given his. It was not very interesting, for it consisted of a denial of everything. Ley, so he swore, had not been in the house that night. He had dined at the Cumberland and spent the evening playing gin-rummy with Mrs Brook in her room in West Cromwell Road. He had never mentioned Mudie to either Smith or Buckingham. This blanket denial did not aid Sir Walter Monckton, who had to do his best for a client who lied quite steadily and blandly, whereas Smith did confess to certain things such as the kidnapping and tying up of Mudie, in both of which matters he was confirmed by Buckingham.

There was one delightful little sentence in Ley's evidence. He described how, when he had gone down to see Mrs Brook at the flat of her daughter in Mrs Evans's house on one occasion, a certain incident had occurred; this was on 8 June. 'I arrived at the house rather early,' said Ley, 'and walked in with someone who was opening the door and was under the impression that I was going to give her some surprise that she would welcome. When I got to the top of the hall I heard her voice and another man's voice, both of whom seemed to be very happy, and she was calling him "Arthur". I went down stairs and closed the door because I was quite satisfied from what I had heard that I was not wanted, and I pushed the bell, ringing the electric bell in the flat. Mrs Brook put her head out of the window and she looked transfigured, very white, and she said she was boiling an egg.'

This exquisite *non sequitur* deserves to be remembered. The transfiguration of physical passion being explained away by the boiling of an egg is one that surely only the brain of a madman could conceive, but at least it has the quality of being unique. The passion is, quite rightly, denied by Mrs Brook. The egg remains in suspension. But it is a very decorative rococo detail, delightful in its unreality.

The circumstance that would have hanged both Ley and Smith, if Ley had not been proved by three of the best doctors in lunacy we possess to be a paranoiac, was chiefly that fatal car numbered 101. The next matter was Ley's absurd correspondence with young Mudie about the signature to cheques by Mrs Brook, and the third was the paying out of large sums of money to Buckingham and Smith. It may also be argued, and very reasonably, that Ley's blanket defence of complete innocence did him no good at all. It was proved beyond a doubt that he had told Smith about Mudie, and that he had engaged through Minden, the porter of the Royal Hotel, the hire-car owner, Buckingham. It was proved beyond a doubt that Buckingham and Smith, young Buckingham and Mrs Bruce took part in the decoying of Mudie up to London. None of them, save for Ley, would ever have joined in a foul and dangerous conspiracy. Yet Ley persisted that he had never mentioned the name of Mudie to any one of them, and that he knew nothing about it! Why, then, did Buckingham senior, Buckingham junior, Bruce, and Smith all conspire to bring Mudie up to 5 Beaufort Gardens? You may have one coincidence, but three or four or five are too many.

There never was a crime more stupidly conceived or more badly executed, except that it did bring about the death of Mudie, which was Ley's aim.

Buckingham senior, Buckingham junior, and Mrs Bruce were all involved in the case. Buckingham, terrified when he found that murder had been done, went with Mrs Bruce to Scotland Yard. Smith did no such thing. There are many people willing to commit what we might call a little illegal act who are, quite rightly, especially in England, terrified of a murder charge, and there is no doubt that the Buckinghams and Mrs Bruce were horrified when they heard of the discovery of Jack Mudie's body. They all three, about a fortnight after the murder, when the crime was bruited abroad in the papers, told of their share in it, though naturally not admitting that they had guessed the greatest crime of all had been contemplated when they played their parts and took their money. Indeed, why should any one of them have thought anything except that the rich Ley was telling the truth when he said Mudie was blackmailing the two women and that he wanted a signed confession? To entice a man, to tie him up and gag him – yes. But murder is something so terribly apart, so far from the life even of a Buckingham, that one may well imagine it chills the heart and stimulates the conscience, which latter may be described as a lively sense of self-preservation.

One of the most interesting points in the trial was when the Lord Chief Justice disallowed expenses in the case of Mrs Bruce, Buckingham senior, Buckingham junior, and the hostile witness, Miss Ingleson, who was Ley's secretary. There is not the smallest suggestion that these people took the notorious blunt instrument and hit Mudie on the head with it. But there is far more than the suggestion, there is the certainty, that Smith connived at bringing Mudie up to the flat in Beaufort Gardens, that Mrs Bruce did the same (perhaps thinking the whole thing was not serious), and that Buckingham helped, afterwards turning King's evidence. This last is an established fact. The hostile witness was the personal secretary of Ley who was quite obviously determined not to incriminate him further than was possible. It is clear that if the oath is of any consequence whatsoever to the witness, the truth, the whole truth, and nothing but the truth should be told. The fact that the Lord Chief Justice disallowed expenses in these four cases needs no comment.

No account of the 'Chalk Pit Case' is complete without a description of Cruikshank, one of the most extraordinary witnesses ever seen in any Court of Law. It is easy for those who know nothing of the anxiety of defending a man for his life to cavil at the decision made by Sir Walter Monckton to call Robert John Cruikshank, but those who knew the issues involved, the terrible weakness of the defence, that absurd blanket innocence of Ley, will sympathize with Sir Walter Monckton.

Cruikshank, according to his own account, was a married man with two children. He was a man of many occupations. He had been a steward on board a ship, he had worked in war factories, he had been a clerk. After he was discharged from this last occupation as redundant – and redundant seems a mild word to use in connexion with Mr Cruikshank – he tried to get back to Australia where he had been once before. Eventually he found himself living with his children in a hotel in Berne, in Switzerland.

Cruikshank came by air from Berne on the afternoon of 28 November. He could not say how he got a passage, but merely that the plane in which he travelled was to the best of his belief an unauthorized plane. He declared that he did not know the name of the man who took him over, and that he was merely coming to bring over a parcel; in other words, that he was engaged in smuggling between Switzerland and London. He swore that he did not know where he landed in England or who met him in a car and drove him into London to hand over his packet. According to his story, one thing was certain, he was in Berne at 4 o'clock on the Thursday afternoon and that he was there again at 7 o'clock on the Friday morning. At about 8 o'clock on the evening of Thursday 28 November, Cruikshank (according to his own account), having a few hours to spare before catching another plane (also presumably unauthorized) back to Switzerland, decided to call upon Ley. He had heard of Ley some time before, in some bar, as a rich man who might help him to get back to Australia. He went to 5 Beaufort Gardens, up to the front door, and hammered at it with his hand. He got no answer, and went down the area steps to the basement door. This he found open.

Again he hammered with his fist. He again got no answer. He wondered whether if the house were empty there might not be an opportunity for him to commit a felony. He pushed the door open and went in. He swore that he did not see any lights in the house from the time he arrived to the time he left. He went through the basement, and finally found himself in a small room. He tried to get a light from his lighter; he merely succeeded in getting a flicker, but what he saw appeared to him to be somebody in a chair, somebody who was tied up. He stood for a couple of moments there and heard 'some sort of a moan or grunt'. He went across to the person tied in the chair, felt some ropes, and started pulling at them. He was not sure where the ropes were, they were round the legs and there were some round the top part of the body. According to his own account, he just pulled at them in a sort of frenzy. He noticed that the man had some sort of gag round his mouth, but made no attempt to pull it off. Cruikshank's own account was:

'Well, I was just trying to collect my thoughts. I was thinking all sorts of things. I was thinking about probably somebody upstairs who was going to come down and beat me up. I thought it was the caretaker, all sorts of thoughts entered my mind, and some sort of noise happened. I don't know whether it was a car, whether it was a hot-water pipe. I have got no idea at all ... my nerve just snapped and I got out of the place as quickly as I could. ... There is one sentence in my statement which might make other people believe otherwise, but never at any time did I think this man was in danger of death. ... I want you to understand that at the time this occurrence happened I was already worried. I had lost my home; I had lost my money; my children were in Switzerland. ... I cannot describe clearly what happened afterwards. I got out of the place and made my way to Sloane Square. ...'

Sir Walter Monckton asked him: 'Tell me, did you tell anybody about this at the time?' Cruikshank replied: 'No ... but one thing you have got to bear in mind with everything I say is that in 1938 I have been informed ... I believe there was a warrant out against me by the police in London, something to do with getting rid of furniture before I had sold it. ... That was one of the reasons that I have been hesitant in this matter. I can only say that I have never made any secret of the fact that I've got a criminal record. ... I just told my wife I knew something about the case. On several occasions I read about it. My trouble is I must contradict something which you have got in writing, which is I was frightened I had killed the man. Well, in a sense that is true and in another it isn't. I didn't know I had killed him and yet there was ...'

Again came one of the bleak queries from the Lord Chief Justice:

'Are you coming here to confess to killing this man?'

'Oh no,' said Cruikshank, 'but if there was a possibility, if he was bound in such a way ... I can't say how it was done.'

'Well,' continued the Lord Chief Justice, 'you said you pulled some ropes on his arms. That wouldn't kill him.'

From his own evidence that same evening, Cruikshank appears to have taken his plane, authorized or unauthorized, back to Berne. Cruikshank was a quarrelsome witness. He contradicted himself as such witnesses do, and eventually said that he could not swear that Mudie was alive, but that he had formed that opinion. He made a mock valiant effort at playing the hero when he said: 'I have never made a secret of it, I haven't got a good record, my word is nothing. I am just an outcast, I have had convictions. I didn't want to get mixed up in it, it is nothing to me what happens in this case. By coming forward I have brought upon myself suspicions of being bribed and corrupted. I have an impossible story to tell, I have got no story to tell, I have got no witnesses, I have put myself in great danger by going into this box.'

In his summing-up the Lord Chief Justice said: 'With regard to Cruikshank, that man, whom we know as an ex-convict, came and told you his story which you may or may not believe to have any truth in it at all. It is not uncommon, you know, that people of bad character come and tell these various stories. ... It is not for me to express any opinion as to the wisdom of his being called, but you know he tells you he saw a man sitting bound in the room and he saw him with the aid of a cigarette lighter which he had got in his pocket and he said he fumbled with the cords. Well, supposing he did, how could that have mattered? ... Members of the jury, you probably have formed your own opinion about it, but I should have thought you had not very far to seek. If an ex-convict of that description sees a man in trouble, who, according to the evidence, has been willing to give £300 to one, £200 to another, might he not have thought that if he, finding that man in trouble, comes forward and tells some story that might help him afterwards, he might also be a recipient of this man's bounty?'

There, I think, we can leave Mr Cruikshank, always with the qualifying remark that he was the most fantastic witness that this writer has ever heard trying to put over a story in the witness-box of any Court in the world.

Let us, now we have read the whole story, think for a minute about the personalities involved in this terrible affair.

It may well be asked why the trial of Ley and Smith should be of such great interest in the history of English criminal law, since as a rule it is the relationship of the murdered person to the murderer that gives human interest to any trial on the capital charge. The ' Chalk Pit Trial' is of interest, as I have said, exactly because of this lack of reason and also because of a strong Lord Chief Justice and the brilliance of counsel both for the Crown and the Defence. Ley was a man who as far as could be discovered was perfectly certain that he could succeed in whatever he did. He had a good brain, and yet he put up that absurd defence of complete ignorance. It is easy to say that his brain had degenerated, but we still have the fact that from his early youth he had used his brain for making money in an illicit manner, and so come to believe that there was nothing he could not buy. He was an ardent teetotaller, probably because his egoism did not need any aggrandizement; he was the great 'I am'. He was a man who could always succeed, whether it were with company promoting, with legal or illegal proceedings, or with stocks, and yet there was within him that tainted spot which encouraged him to continue with whatever his business of the moment might be. It was the tainted spot that grew bigger than the man himself. It is easy to say that he was mad, that he was a paranoiac, and both these things are true. It will probably be a hundred years before mankind has begun to find out very early in a child's existence that this tainted spot exists.

That Ley was an egoist goes without saying. A murderer is always an egoist, and no fraudulent company director really thinks he can possibly fail; he is the clever man, the man who always imposes himself upon society, the man who even when he has not been liked has been believed. Few fraudulent company directors commit murder. Few murderers have the intelligence to be fraudulent company directors. Ley must have known within himself that he had the gifts both of taking money and taking life, and when at last justice caught up with him he probably felt himself a much aggrieved man. A double criminal such as was Ley is extremely rare. We get the multiple killer, we get the clever fraud, but the two things in conjunction are seldom found.

Smith was more normal than Ley. He was greedy and heartless and avid of money. Unluckily Ley had a deep purse. Buckingham was not a scrupulous man and proved to have deserted after Dunkirk. Mrs Bruce retired into obscurity for all we know. Mrs Brook retired from the world to a house that Ley had bought her in a London suburb, with her daughter and son-in-law and the son-in-law's parents.

It would seem incredible, were it not true, that all these people, the guilty and the innocent, should have come together in the fatal knot of death about someone who was completely guiltless and never knew what it was all about.

Now we come to the innocent bewildered murdered man – 'the forgotten man', for once a man is dead it is in his murderers the public are interested.

Jack Mudie was exceptionally unlucky not only in the fact that he was murdered but in the even more terrible circumstance that he was murdered for nothing – and that he was unsuspecting. The mind of a distorted man had seized upon him for a victim. This man had money enough to employ tools. It is easy but horrible to imagine Jack Mudie's feelings when he went on a dark night into the back way of 5 Beaufort Gardens. Mrs Bruce went on ahead of him and called him to come in. She said she had to have a word with the driver and went out. Mudie then had a rug thrown over his head, he was trussed up, pulled, or, as they said, 'jumped' along the passage by Buckingham and Smith and met his death in the chair of a little room that was used as an office. He must have been terribly bewildered as to what it was all about. He knew nothing about Ley except from the curious affair of the cheques.

He knew nothing about the Buckinghams or Smith. He was merely asked to make a little extra money by shaking the drinks at a cocktail party. This meant nothing to him whatever until it meant his death. Strong young men are not easily killed, and it is – in the true sense of the word – awful to imagine Jack Mudie sitting trussed up in that chair with a gag in his mouth, terrified as any man in his position would have been terrified, awaiting the hand of the strangler. The hand of the strangler came, and poor Jack Mudie, that decent, ordinary fellow, left 5 Beaufort Gardens as a corpse, though he had come into it as a young, strong, vital man. If there is anything to add to the terror of being murdered, one can surely say that there is the terror of being murdered when one cannot imagine why.

He had come to London in all good faith, he was called in at the back door and at once assaulted, bound up, and eventually strangled. If he had any last thoughts, they must have been of the most bemused. Whether he saw Ley or not we do not know; the rug was taken from off his head, the gag was thrust into his mouth, and he then was killed by the rope round his neck pulled with 'a certain degree of suspension'. Hanging, except at official hands, is not a merciful business. A man who is hanged in England dies because his neck is broken, generally at the third cervical. But poor Jack Mudie sat in the chair unable to cry out, still wondering what it was all about, and killed slowly by a rope from 'a slight degree of suspension'. True, the murderer who is hanged suffers the torments of the damned during his time of waiting, and the torments consist of knowing that a term has been set to his natural life. This was not Jack Mudie's fear. His fear must have been that of someone caught up in a nightmare who knew nothing but who yet must have realized that he was in deadly danger. He must have known from the moment that he was 'jumped' along the corridor with the rug over his head and the ropes about him that there was something very strange afoot. Nobody employs a barman to shake cocktails and treats him in this manner. Therefore this strangeness must have struck the poor young man's heart with a sense of doom. He had wandered into a nightmare and the nightmare was coming true. There is the terrible innocence of death on his face when it was photographed in the chalk pit.

Thus the sorry story comes to an end, a stupid story, a wicked story, and a mad story. Nothing can bring Jack Mudie back to life; his murderers have been fortunate. Many innocent people in the case have been unfortunate in that they were inextricably connected with it. Jack Mudie was not an important person, but he had just as much right to live as the greatest amongst us. Through no fault of his own he lost that right – and indeed his very unimportance points the moral though it may not adorn the tale.

There is no one, not even a criminal, who has not the right to the protection of the law and the right to be treated decently by society, just as there is no one, not even a professional prostitute, who has not the right to choose with whom she wishes to spend the night. It is just as possible to rape a prostitute as to rape an innocent woman. The right of choice, the right to be an individual is, or at least so we have thought in in England, a right that we all share.

Dr Pritchard

· 1865 ·

BY

WILLIAM ROUGHEAD

IN the notable series of evil and forbidding portraits which forms our national picture-gallery of crime, the sinister presentment of Dr Pritchard is entitled to an eminent place. Comprehensive as that collection, unhappily, is, it exhibits no more infamous example of unfeeling cruelty, masked by crafty dissimulation, in the relentless pursuit of a deadly purpose. The secret poisoner is the most dangerous of malefactors; and he is specially to be dreaded when, as here, he prosecutes his subtle design in the twofold disguise of loving relative and assiduous physician. The relation that existed between the perpetrator and his hapless victims – the one his wife, the other her mother – the affectionate terms upon which they lived; the terrible suffering, which, in the case of the former, it was part of his nefarious scheme to produce and continue during long and painful weeks; and the fact that these two confiding women, in their dire necessity, relied for help upon the very hand that was mercilessly raised against their lives, combine to make this offence one of the blackest recorded in the annals of crime.

The case of Dr Pritchard, while lacking those elements of romance and mystery which give to that of Madeleine Smith its unique attraction, affords a psychological problem of much interest, and presents many curious and striking features to the student of criminal anthropology. No other trial of the period – excepting the celebrated Rugeley case, with which it has many points in common, suggesting that Pritchard had studied and improved upon the experience of Palmer – excited more widespread attention, not only among members

143

of the medical profession, but also of the general public throughout the United Kingdom. 'The scene of the double tragedy', in the words of the Lord Justice-Clerk, 'is all confined within the four walls of the dwelling-house in Sauchiehall Street', and though less than a century has elapsed since the curtain fell upon that sorry drama of domestic treachery and sin, yet only in the darkest times of medieval intrigue, when poisoning was reduced to a fine art and practised as a lucrative profession, can we find a parallel to the monstrous nature of its plot and the cynical hypocrisy of its guilty author.

Edward William Pritchard was the son of John White Pritchard, a captain in the Royal Navy, and was born at Southsea, Hampshire, on 6 December 1825. After going through the usual preliminary education, he was apprenticed, in September 1840, to Messrs Edward John and Charles Henry Scott, surgeons of considerable practice in Portsmouth. During his apprenticeship, it is stated that he diligently studied the elementary branches of his profession and conducted himself with propriety. There is considerable uncertainty with regard to the next step in his career. One account states that, on completing his apprenticeship, he proceeded to London, and entered on his hospital studies at King's College in October 1843; but the officials of that institution denied that there was any foundation for the statement, which appears to have been based on the entry relating to Dr Pritchard in the *Medical Directory*, which, in turn, probably depended on his own veracious authority. A contemporary writer remarks: 'Whatever the extent of his medical education, and however it may have been acquired, it appears that the doctor's application to study was never remarkable; for all competent judges subsequently agreed in pronouncing him the shallowest of sciolists, so far as knowledge of his profession was concerned.'

Dr Pritchard seems from the first to have been destined for the naval service, in which several of his relatives are said to have held high rank. Two of his uncles are stated to have been admirals, one of his brothers, Francis Bowen Pritchard, was a surgeon in the Navy, and another, Charles Augustus

Pritchard, acted as secretary to the Naval Commander-in-Chief at Plymouth. Pritchard memorialized the authorities of the College of Surgeons to be allowed to offer himself for examination at an earlier period than was at that time permitted; and, his application having been granted, he appeared before the Court of Examiners on 29 May 1846, and, after the usual examination, was admitted a member of the College. He underwent an examination before the Navy Board, was duly gazetted an assistant surgeon in Her Majesty's Navy, and joined H.M.S. *Victory* on 2 November 1846. In this capacity Pritchard made voyages to the Pacific and Northern Oceans and the Mediterranean, during which period he held the following commissions of services: H.M.S. *Collingwood*, 24 December 1846; H.M.S. *Calypso*, 20 March 1848; H.M.S. *Asia*, 13 February 1850; and lastly H.M.S. *Hecate*, 25 September 1850.

It was, it is stated, while serving in the last-mentioned vessel on the home station that Dr Pritchard first met the lady who afterwards became his wife. Miss Mary Jane Taylor was the only daughter of Mr Michael Taylor, a highly respected silk merchant, who resided in Edinburgh. The young lady was at the time staying with her maternal uncle, Dr David Cowan, a retired naval surgeon, who had settled in Portsmouth. During her visit, the *Hecate* came into port, and at a ball which took place shortly afterwards she was introduced to her future husband and destroyer. The young surgeon commenced to pay his addresses, and when he subsequently asked her to become his wife, Miss Taylor accepted him with the full approval of her relatives. The marriage took place in the autumn of 1850, but for some time the young couple were compelled to live much apart. The husband was not possessed of sufficient means to leave the service and provide his wife with a home. He therefore continued to cruise with the *Hecate*, while Mrs Pritchard returned to her father's house in Edinburgh.

Meanwhile his wife's relations were endeavouring to secure for Dr Pritchard some suitable opening on shore as a private practitioner. Such an opportunity was found at Hunmanby in Yorkshire; and in March 1851 he resigned the service and commenced practice in that place, where he and Mrs Pritchard first took up house. Shortly after settling at Hunmanby, Dr Pritchard opened a branch in the neighbouring town of Filey, then a rising watering-place, and was appointed medical officer of the No. 3 district of the Bridlington Union. During his residence there he published various books on subjects connected with the locality, and contributed articles to medical and other journals.

With reference to this period of his career, the following extract from the *Sheffield Telegraph*, published shortly after the trial, is of considerable interest: 'Dr Pritchard, the poisoner, is well known at Hunmanby and Filey, where he practised before his removal to Glasgow. He left those places with a very indifferent reputation. He was fluent, plausible, amorous, politely impudent, and singularly untruthful. One who knew him well at Filey describes him as the "prettiest liar" he ever met with. He pushed his way into publicity as a prominent member of the body of Freemasons, and made that body a means of advertising himself. In the carte-de-visite we have seen of him he is taken in the insignia of the order. His amativeness led him into some amours that did not increase the public confidence in him as a professional man; and his unveracity became so notorious that, in his attempt to deceive others, he succeeded only in deceiving himself. Hunmanby and Filey were much too small for a man of that kind. He was soon found out. His imagination overran the limits of probability, as much as his expenditure overran his means; and, if we are rightly informed, he left Yorkshire in discredit and in debt. It was said of him after he had gone that he spoke the truth only by accident, and seemed to be an improviser of fiction by mental constitution and habit.' Other contemporary local journals comment upon his mendacious character and doubtful reputation during his residence in Yorkshire, which appears to have extended over a period of six years.

In 1857 Dr Pritchard purchased a diploma of Doctor of Medicine *in absentia* from the University of Erlangen. He also became a licentiate of the Society of Apothecaries of London on 1 April 1858. Having sold his practice in Yorkshire, he accepted an offer to act as medical attendant to a gentleman travelling abroad; and in the autumn of 1859 he left England and visited Egypt and the Holy Land, his wife, meanwhile, going back to her parents' house in Edinburgh.

When Dr Pritchard returned from his travels in June 1860, it was decided that he should recommence practice in Glasgow, and he shortly thereafter took up house with his wife and family at No. 11 Berkeley Terrace there. From his appearance among them, his medical brethren in that city seemed to have regarded him with suspicion and dislike. To some of these he brought letters of introduction; but the statements he made as to his previous career and exploits were so manifestly false that they considered him a person unworthy of credit, and one with whom they desired no further acquaintance. Like his most celebrated professional prototype, 'Dr Fell', he appears to have inspired in many of those with whom he came in contact an unaccountable feeling of repulsion, notwithstanding the plausibility of his manners and his indefatigable desire to please. He made several attempts to gain admittance to the Faculty of Physicians and Surgeons, but was unable to find a Fellow to undertake the responsibility of proposing him. In his application for membership of the various medical societies, where the only qualifications requisite were the possession of a diploma and a respectable character, he was equally unsuccessful. He is said to have been grossly ignorant of his profession, while daring and reckless in its practice. Notwithstanding the coldness with which he was treated by his medical confrères, in October 1860 he applied for the then vacant Andersonian Chair of Surgery at the University, alleging in his application that he had had 'many opportunities, in almost every part of the world, of gaining practical experience and promulgating the principles of modern surgery.' In support of his candidature, he submitted numerous testimonials from well-known medical men in England, regarding the genuineness of which there was considerable dubiety. His application was, however, unsuccessful, the appointment being given to Dr Macleod.

Disappointed in obtaining the goodwill and support of his profession, Dr Pritchard now directed his efforts to win a more general popularity. He became a member of the Glasgow Athenaeum, in the affairs of which he apparently took a lively interest, and was subsequently appointed a director of that institution and also an examiner in physiology under the Society of Arts. With a view to attracting public attention, he gave several lectures on various popular subjects, chiefly connected with his travels. A sentence from one of these dealing with his adventures abroad – with him a frequent and favourite theme – has been preserved, and indicates the somewhat startling peculiarities of the lecturer's style: 'I have plucked the eaglets from their eyries in the deserts of Arabia, and hunted the Nubian lion in the prairies of North America.' Another topic upon which he often discoursed was that of the Fiji Islands; but it was unfortunately ascertained – whatever may have been the extent of his knowledge of that interesting group – that the public accounts he gave of them were never twice the same. Dr Pritchard was also wont to boast of an acquaintanceship with Garibaldi, of whom it was his custom to speak with fervent enthusiasm. In proof of his intimacy with that celebrated patriot it is said that, having been absent from Glasgow for some time, he, on his return, exhibited to his friends a handsome walking-stick, bearing the inscription – 'Presented by General Garibaldi to Edward William Pritchard.' One gentleman, however, on being shown this valuable souvenir, at once recognized it as a stick which he had formerly seen in the doctor's possession, but without the interesting inscription. On another occasion Dr Pritchard caused his health to be proposed at a dinner, given in connexion with the Glasgow Athenaeum, as that of 'a distinguished physiologist, and a friend of Garibaldi.' These are typical instances of the doctor's astonishing mendacity, his friendship with the Liberator of Italy being, it is understood, entirely apocryphal.

In furtherance of his scheme, Dr Pritchard at this time became a Freemason, and assiduously cultivated the acquaintance of the local brethren. On 18 March 1861 he was appointed to the Lodge St Mark, of which he was elected Master in the following year; and he was admitted a member of the Glasgow Royal Arch Chapter on 4 December 1861. In the same month he became a Knight Templar in the Glasgow Priory, and also joined the Grand Lodge of the Royal Order at Edinburgh. His fine appearance and insinuating manners are said for a short period to have won him a high place in the estimate of his Masonic brethren; but it was soon discovered that his enthusiasm and zeal proceeded solely from interested motives, and as such were, of course, fundamentally opposed to the principles of Freemasonry.

A singular and suggestive method by which Dr Pritchard is said to have courted that notoriety for which, throughout his whole career, he exhibited an inordinate craving was by having copies of his photograph printed off in large numbers, and supplying these at less than cost price to local stationers for sale. He was also in the habit of distributing copies freely among casual acquaintances; a curious instance of which is recorded in the case of the gentleman with whom he happened to travel to Glasgow on the evening of his arrest and to whom he presented one, which must, in the light of subsequent events, have proved an interesting souvenir.

The following description of the personal appearance and characteristics of Dr Pritchard at this period of his career is taken from a contemporary print: 'As most of our readers are no doubt aware, Pritchard was a tallish, well-built man of a rather striking presence. His features were regular, the forehead being well arched, and the nose aquiline and slightly hooked. The upper part of the head was perfectly bald, but this defect he partially concealed by the careful adjustment of a lock of his light brown hair. One of the most prominent points in his appearance was his beard, which he wore very long, and on the trimming of which he evidently bestowed considerable pains. He dressed neatly, and his manners were characterized by an elaborate, studied politeness – the very perfection, in short, of the *suaviter in modo*.' Personal vanity, and the desire to create a pleasing impression upon those with whom he came in contact appear to have been at all times eminently characteristic of the man; and he seems to have been so far successful as to have acquired a considerable, though not a first-class, practice. It is stated, however, to have been a matter of public knowledge that Dr Pritchard took a profligate advantage of his professional opportunities to make improper attempts upon his lady patients, both married and single; and that one such incident was made the ground of a prosecution, which was only arrested from adverse circumstances overtaking the gentleman whose wife had been grossly insulted.

We now come to the first of those remarkable occurrences which were ultimately to secure for Dr Pritchard the notoriety which, by other means, he strenuously sought. On 6 May 1863 a paragraph appeared in the newspapers setting forth particulars of a mysterious fire which took place the previous day at his house in Berkeley Terrace, whereby a young servant girl in his employment lost her life. It is beyond doubt that, in connexion with his subsequent claim under his fire-insurance policy, Dr Pritchard returned to the Insurance Company, as destroyed, certain articles of jewellery of which no trace could be found among the debris; and that on the company resisting this claim, he ultimately abandoned it, and accepted a small portion of the amount. More uncertainty, however, relates to the part played by him in the tragedy of the girl's death. Dr Pritchard was examined by the authorities in connexion with the affair, and a post-mortem examination of the body took place; and though no further action was taken by them, considerable suspicion appears to have been attached to him at the time, which subsequent events went far to confirm. In commenting on this occurrence after the trial, a contemporary writer observes: 'We may pass over certain coincidences as being merely curious – that, for instance, Dr Pritchard coming to the door (dressed, it is to be presumed, for there is nothing to the contrary in the statement) only after the policeman rang, though he admits having been up a considerable time before that; the absence of Mrs Pritchard and the other maid; the exception on the particular night of his usual act of seeing and questioning the servant as to whether he had been wanted; we say nothing of the difficulty of burning a volume of a book so as to take away all trace of it; and the insurance is too common a thing to deserve much attention. But it requires a large amount of very easy credulity to believe that the girl, under the circumstances stated, would either not have escaped by the door (only a few feet from the bed), or made an attempt in that direction, or at the very worst would not in the lie of the body, and in the contraction or contortion of the muscles, have exhibited some of the ordinary indications of pain. We can easily conceive a case where, by the sudden influx from another quarter of a great body of smoke, a person in a deep sleep may be so suddenly caught by asphyxia as to be choked as she lay, yet even in that case there will always be some contraction or contortion; but in the case we are examining the smoke had its beginning in the room; it was therefore under the law of progress, it was close by the sleeper, and it is scarcely possible to conceive that a young, active woman would not have been quickened by the first touch of asphyxia either to an attempt at escape, or a voluntary or involuntary action of the muscles. Such absolute quiescence as set forth would seem to amount to a physical impossibility. The only presumption which can make the story quadrate with natural laws is that the girl was dead, or under the influence of a soporific, before the fire was kindled. As to the means of the death, or the hand that applied the flame, these must be left to the judgement or imagination of the reader.' Dr Pritchard's record is, however, sufficiently black as it is; and, in the absence of direct proof of his guilt, it would be unjust to credit, or rather debit, him with this additional crime.

Doubtless in consequence of this unpleasant episode, Dr Pritchard removed at Whitsunday 1863 to No. 22 Royal Crescent; and at that term the place rendered vacant by the death of his former housemaid was taken by Mary M'Leod, a girl of fifteen years of age, whose connexion with his establishment was to prove only less fatal than that of her unhappy predecessor. Whatever may have been his relations with the latter, we learn from his own confession that he seduced this girl, during his wife's absence at the coast, in the summer of that year; and the intimacy between them continued, as admitted by Mary M'Leod in her evidence at the trial, until shortly before Mrs Pritchard's death in the spring of 1865.

After remaining for a year at 22 Royal Crescent, Dr Pritchard, at Whitsunday 1864, removed to a house which he had purchased in Clarence Place, then one of the divisions of Sauchiehall Street, where he continued to reside during the events brought out at his trial, and until the time of his arrest. It is interesting to note that this house, situated a few doors west from Mains Street, is within a short distance of Blythswood Square, celebrated as the residence of Madeleine Smith. The agreed-on price was £2000, but £1600 was borrowed on security of the property; and as Mrs Taylor, his mother-in-law, provided a sum of £500 to meet the balance, the doctor acquired his new residence upon easy terms. With reference to the payment of this sum, Mrs Taylor wrote to her daughter Mrs Pritchard: 'I have told him (the law agent) to get the order drawn for the money in two sums, one for four hundred pounds and one for one hundred pounds, so as Edward may hold the hundred in his own hand and pay the other £400 as part of the purchase-money. I have done it in this way so as these lawyers may not get hold of the whole £500, and keep it under some pretence or other. Now, my dear Mary, you must take care that this money is well spent. We have all felt the trouble in getting it; and I have no doubt it would be a source of satisfaction to us all if it is the means of getting Edward forward in life, and much depends on his going on quietly and perseveringly – he is now in a better position, and with his industrious and steady attention to his practice, all will be well. Give him my kind love and earnest wishes for success.' Notwithstanding the fact that his practice appears to have been considerable, he must at this time have been in some financial straits, for Mrs Taylor writes to him: 'Once more let me express the hope that a very short time will relieve you from all this trouble. I will do all I can to push the thing on. My love to Mary and the children. Ever, dear Edward, yours affecty., Jane Taylor.' It further appears from a letter which that lady wrote to her daughter, that the sum she thus advanced was a loan and not a gift, as subsequently stated by Dr Pritchard, for she refers to 'the terms on which I have advanced it, namely, that I am to have a bond over the property, so as to secure the £500 in the event of anything being unfortunate in time coming.' No such security, however, was given at the time; but after Mrs Taylor's death, at the request of her trustees, Dr Pritchard agreed to the loan being so secured for the benefit of Mrs Pritchard and her children.

We also find that from this time onwards Dr Pritchard began to overdraw his bank account, of which he kept two, one with the Clydesdale and the other with the City of Glasgow Bank; and with the view, no doubt, of adding to his resources he, in November of that year, took into residence with him, as pupils and boarders, two medical students named Connell and King.

In the course of the summer of 1864, according to the evidence of Mary M'Leod, Mrs Pritchard had discovered Dr Pritchard kissing her in one of the bedrooms; and in the autumn, as the result of her intimacy with her master, a miscarriage took place, which Dr Pritchard admitted was produced by him. She also stated in her evidence that, on one occasion, he told her that when Mrs Pritchard died, if she died before him and she (M'Leod) was alive, he would marry her.

It was in the month of October 1864 that the condition of Mrs Pritchard's health first attracted the notice of other members of the family. At this time the household consisted of herself; Dr Pritchard; four of their five children; the cook, Catherine Lattimer; and Mary M'Leod, who acted as both nurse and housemaid. The eldest child, a daughter, had been brought up by her grandparents, Mr and Mrs Taylor, and resided with them in Edinburgh. The two medical students, King and Connell, came in the beginning of November. Mrs Pritchard was confined to bed for some time, suffering from sickness and vomiting, which she attributed to a chill; and when somewhat recovered, she went, about 26 November, on a visit to her relatives in Edinburgh. There she remained until

22 December, when she came home to Glasgow for Christmas. During this visit she became much better in health, and continued well until a fortnight after her return, when the distressing symptoms from which she had previously suffered reappeared with greater intensity. The sickness became more persistent, occurring usually after meals – particularly liquid food. From this time onwards she was seldom able to go downstairs to take her meals with the family, and her food was either taken or sent to her room by her husband. During the month of November, Dr Pritchard was proved to have bought tartarized antimony and tincture of aconite, in quantities of one ounce of each; and on 8 December he purchased an ounce of Fleming's Tincture of Aconite, which is six times stronger than the ordinary tincture.

Mrs Pritchard's first serious attack of illness was on 1 February when, in addition to violent sickness, she was seized with cramp, accompanied by severe pain, which left her in a very exhausted state. After this attack, Dr Pritchard wrote to Dr James Moffat Cowan, a retired medical man resident in Edinburgh, and a second cousin of his wife's, requesting him to come through and see her. Dr Cowan accordingly visited Mrs Pritchard on the 7th and stayed all night. He found her better than he had been led to expect, and apparently did not consider her case serious. Dr Pritchard described her illness as arising from irritation of the stomach, and Dr Cowan prescribed a mustard poultice and small quantities of champagne and ice. On the day of Dr Cowan's visit, Dr Pritchard bought his second ounce of tartarized antimony and a further ounce of tincture of aconite. Dr Cowan returned to Edinburgh next day, the 8th; and in the course of that night Mrs Pritchard was again attacked with severe spasms, and at her own request Dr Gairdner was called in. He was puzzled by the case, and was of opinion, from the state of excitement in which he found the patient, that she was intoxicated. To him Dr Pritchard expressed the view that she was suffering from catalepsy, and mentioned that she had been getting stimulants on the advice of Dr Cowan. Dr Gairdner ordered all stimulants to be discontinued, and prescribed a simple dietary and no medicine. He called again next day, found her better, and renewed his advice, but was not asked to repeat his visit. Neither Dr Cowan nor Dr Gairdner observed any symptoms of fever in the case.

Dr Gairdner was, however, very far from satisfied with the treatment which the patient was receiving, and accordingly on the 9th, after his second visit to Mrs Pritchard, he wrote to her brother, Dr Michael Taylor of Penrith, expressing his dissatisfaction and strongly recommending Mrs Pritchard's removal to her brother's house. On Dr Taylor's suggesting that his sister should come to him for a time, Dr Pritchard expressed his perfect willingness that she should do so, but considered that she was not then in a fit state to travel. It need hardly be said that the unfortunate lady was never permitted to visit her brother, which would seriously have interfered with her husband's plans.

On Dr Cowan's return to Edinburgh he saw Mrs Taylor, and recommended her to go to Glasgow to nurse her daughter who, with only two servants in a large household, required, he thought, more attention than she was receiving. Mrs Taylor accordingly proceeded to Glasgow on Friday 10 February, and took up her abode in that fatal house, which she was destined never to leave again alive. The day before she came, her son-in-law bought an ounce of tincture of aconite, his fourth purchase of a similar quantity of that poison within less than three months. Mrs Taylor found her daughter confined to bed and suffering from continued sickness and vomiting; and two or three days after her arrival, Mrs Pritchard had another attack of cramp, though not so severe as on the previous occasion. On Monday the 13th, Mrs Pritchard having expressed a desire for some tapioca, a packet was got from the grocers by her little boy; it was left for a short time upon the hall table; was taken down to the kitchen, either by Mrs Taylor or Mary M'Leod; the cook, Catherine Lattimer, prepared half a breakfast-cupful, and it was then carried upstairs by Mary M'Leod to the dining-room. Whether Mrs Pritchard partook of it or not does not appear; but Mrs Taylor did, and immediately became sick and vomited, remarking, poor lady, with unconscious significance, that she thought she must have got the same complaint as her daughter. It was not proved that Dr Pritchard was in the house when this incident occurred; but in the remainder of the packet of tapioca, which was found in the kitchen press after his apprehension, the presence of antimony was unequivocally detected.

On Thursday 16 February Catherine Lattimer left. She was to have done so on the 2nd, but, owing to Mrs Pritchard's serious illness, she could not leave until another servant was engaged to take her place. She was succeeded as cook by Mary Patterson. She did not, however, leave Glasgow, and was in the habit of calling occasionally to take the children for a walk. Upon the 18th Dr Pritchard purchased another ounce of Fleming's Tincture of Aconite.

Now, Mrs Taylor, though a strong and healthy old lady for her seventy years, had, unfortunately, contracted the habit of taking a preparation of opium, known as Battley's Sedative Solution. She commenced to use this medicine as a remedy for the neuralgic headaches from which she suffered, and the practice had so grown upon her as to enable her to take with impunity considerable quantities of that drug. Shortly after her arrival in Glasgow, she sent the girl M'Leod to have filled for her by the local chemist a bottle which, apparently, she carried about with her for that purpose. On the morning of Friday 24 February Catherine Lattimer called at the house and saw Mrs Taylor, who expressed great anxiety as to her daughter's condition, and said she could not understand her illness. The old lady spent the day in the sickroom – she had been in attendance upon her daughter day and night since she came – and went down to tea with Dr Pritchard and the family in the dining-room at 7 o'clock, after which she wrote some letters in the consulting-room and sent Mary M'Leod out to get sausages for her supper. She then went upstairs to her daughter's bedroom, which she had shared since her arrival – Dr Pritchard occupying the spare bedroom. A few minutes later the bell rang violently, and the servants, on going up, found Mrs Taylor sitting in a chair very ill and trying to be sick. Hot water was brought to effect this, but to no purpose; she quickly became unconscious, and sat with her head hanging down upon her breast. Dr Pritchard was summoned, and, having examined her, he told the boarder Connell to go for Dr Paterson, as Mrs Taylor had been seized with apoplexy and was seriously ill. Accordingly, shortly after 10 o'clock, Dr Paterson appeared in that chamber of death. It was the first time he had been in the house, and the result of his visit, and the course which he saw fit to adopt in regard to it, are among the most remarkable features of this case.

Dr Pritchard met Dr Paterson in the hall, and told him that the old lady, while writing some letters, had fallen from her chair in a fit, and had been carried upstairs to her bedroom. He added that 'she was in the habit of taking a drop' – a deliberate and wicked lie – and said that Mrs Pritchard had been ill for a long time with gastric fever. Dr Paterson then proceeded to the sickroom. Mrs Taylor, who had been lifted on to her daughter's bed, was still alive; but he at once expressed his opinion that she was dying under the influence of some powerful narcotic. He attempted to rouse her, and, a degree of consciousness supervening, Dr Pritchard clapped the poor lady on the shoulder, saying, 'You are getting better, darling', on which Dr Paterson remarked, 'Never in this world.' Dr Pritchard then told him that she was in the habit of taking Battley's Solution, that she had recently purchased a half-pound bottle of that medicine, and that it was highly probable she had taken 'a good swig at it'. Dr Paterson in his evidence gives a striking picture of the occupants of that fatal room. Mrs Taylor was dying, fully dressed, upon her daughter's bed; and, sitting up beyond her, he observed Mrs Pritchard, whom he then saw for the first time, in a state of pitiful agitation and distress; and the conviction forced itself upon his mind that she was under the depressing influence of antimony. He did not speak to her, however, or question her husband as to her condition, but left the house. Shortly before 1 o'clock Dr Paterson was again sent for, but refused to go, as he considered Mrs Taylor's case hopeless.

At 1 o'clock in the morning of Saturday 25 February, a

fortnight after her arrival in Glasgow, Mrs Taylor died. Mary Patterson, with the assistance of Mrs Nabb, a woman who washed for the family, proceeded to dress the body, and in the pocket of the old lady's dress they found her bottle of Battley. While they were thus occupied, Dr Pritchard came into the room and asked for the bottle, which, he said, M'Leod told him had been found. On seeing it he exclaimed, 'Good heavens, has she taken all that since Tuesday!' and cautioned them to say nothing about it, as it might lead to trouble, and it would never do for a man in his position to have it talked about. He then removed the bottle. In it were subsequently detected an appreciable quantity of antimony, and also aconite to the extent, in the opinion of Professor Penny, of about 7 per cent of the entire contents. On the 27th Catherine Lattimer called, and was shocked to hear from Dr Pritchard of Mrs Taylor's sudden death; 'We have a sad house to-day, Catherine,' said the doctor.

On Wednesday 1 March Dr Pritchard met Dr Paterson accidentally in the street and asked him to call and see Mrs Pritchard next day, as he was going to Edinburgh to bury his mother-in-law. Dr Paterson did so; and, from his observation of Mrs Pritchard on that occasion, his previous opinion was confirmed. He made no communication, however, to the unhappy lady as to his belief that her death was being slowly compassed by poison. On the 3rd Mr Michael Taylor, the husband of Mrs Taylor, called on Dr Paterson and said that Dr Pritchard had sent him for the certificate of death. This Dr Paterson declined to give, without stating any reason beyond that to do so would be contrary to professional etiquette. The next day Dr Paterson wrote to the registrar, who had sent him a schedule to fill up, refusing to grant the certificate and characterizing the death of Mrs Taylor as 'sudden, unexpected, and to him mysterious.' The death was accordingly certified by Dr Pritchard himself as follows: Primary cause, paralysis: duration, twelve hours; secondary cause, apoplexy: duration, one hour. No competent medical man would have stated these causes in such an order – apoplexy invariably preceding and producing paralysis. On the 5th Dr Pritchard called on Dr Paterson and said that Mrs Pritchard was greatly benefited by the treatment he had ordered.

From the time of her mother's death, Mrs Pritchard's illness continued its mysterious course. To her dressmaker, Janet Hamilton, who saw her on 8 March, she complained of constant retching, for which she could ascribe no cause; and remarked, poor soul, that it was strange she was always well in Edinburgh and ill at home. To Mrs Nabb she complained of vomiting even in her sleep. Lattimer called and found her very thin and weak, and in great grief at the sudden loss of her mother. During Mrs Taylor's residence in the house she herself attended to her daughter's food, and, shortly after she came, was in the habit of preparing the patient's meals in the bedroom; but since that lady's death Mrs Pritchard's meals were, as formerly, either taken or sent to her by her husband.

It is a curious feature of this extraordinary case that, during the whole course of his wife's illness down to her death on 18 March, Dr Pritchard was in continual correspondence with her brother, Dr Michael Taylor of Penrith, minutely detailing the symptoms of the patient and suggesting modes of treatment. To his father-in-law and daughter in Edinburgh he also wrote with great frequency on the subject of Mrs Pritchard's ill-health, many of his letters, especially those alluding to the death of Mrs Taylor, being couched in language which, in the circumstances, can only be described as of revolting hypocrisy. Writing to his daughter in Edinburgh some time before the death of that lady, Dr Pritchard says – 'Kiss dearest grandma for me – love her and help her all you can, and when the rolling years pass away you will remember my advice and be happier far by doing so than I can positively make you understand now. Pray to our Heavenly Father quietly and alone to spare her to us, to protect you from all harm, and make you a good girl – in due time a Christian woman, and a blessing to us all. Never forget kind friends, those who have an interest in your well-doing.'

On Monday 13 March Dr Pritchard made what proved to be his last purchase of Fleming's Tincture of Aconite; and that evening he sent up a piece of cheese by Mary M'Leod for

Mrs Pritchard's supper. Her mistress asked the girl to taste it, which she did, and at once experienced a burning sensation in her throat, followed by considerable thirst. This cheese was taken down to the pantry; and the next morning the cook, finding it there, ate a small portion, with similar results. She then became violently sick and had to go to bed. On the following night, Wednesday 15 March, Dr Pritchard asked Mary Patterson to make some egg-flip for Mrs Pritchard. While she was beating up an egg in the pantry, he said he would get some sugar for it; and she heard him go into the dining-room, where that was kept, from thence into the consulting-room, and then saw him return and drop two lumps of sugar into the tumbler. When adding hot water in the kitchen, the cook took a spoonful of the mixture, and remarked to Mary M'Leod on its horrible taste. It was then carried by the latter to the sickroom, where Mrs Pritchard drank a glassful and immediately became sick. Meanwhile, the cook experienced the same burning sensations as on the occasion of eating the cheese, suffered intense pain, and vomited frequently during the night.

At midday on Friday 17 March Mrs Pritchard's bell rang violently three times. At the third ring Mary Patterson, the cook, went upstairs to see what was the matter, and why M'Leod, whose business it was to answer the bell, did not do so. Not being sure which bell had rung, she went to the consulting-room, which, though partly open, refused to open further when she tried it. She then began to ascend the stairs, and, on looking back, saw Dr Pritchard at the consulting-room door, who called to her, 'How is Mrs Pritchard now?' and then came upstairs after her, followed by Mary M'Leod. Shortly after this incident Patterson, on returning to the bedroom, saw Dr Pritchard giving his wife something to drink out of a porter glass. At 5 o'clock the same afternoon Mrs Pritchard had a severe attack of cramp, and became lightheaded, speaking of Mrs Taylor as though she were present, and telling the servants not to mind her, but to attend to her mother. At 8 o'clock Dr Paterson was called in, and was greatly struck by the alarming change for the worse in Mrs

Pritchard's appearance since he last saw her on the 2nd. She was at this time quite conscious, and told him she had been vomiting; but Dr Pritchard said she had not, and was only raving. He further stated that she had not slept for four or five days. Dr Paterson wishing to administer a sleeping-draught at once, Dr Pritchard told him that he kept no drugs in the house; Dr Paterson therefore dictated a prescription, which Dr Pritchard wrote out and sent to be made up. Dr Paterson then left; and Dr Pritchard went to bed beside his wife, Mary M'Leod lying on a sofa in the same room. Having been told by him about 1 o'clock in the morning to get a mustard poultice made by Mary Patterson, M'Leod left the room for that purpose; and on the two servants returning with the poultice they found that Mrs Pritchard was dead.

Dr Pritchard insisted that his wife was only in a faint, and wished hot water brought to restore animation, whereupon Patterson observed that hot water was no use for a dead body. He then said, 'Is she dead, Patterson?' and, addressing the corpse, cried out, 'Come back, come back, my dear Mary Jane, don't leave your dear Edward!' He also exclaimed, 'What a brute; what a heathen!' – expressions in which posterity will be disposed to concur – and asked Patterson to get King's rifle and shoot him. He next wrote certain letters and took them to the post, and, on returning, called Patterson up from the kitchen to tell her that his wife had walked up the street with him and had told him to take care of the girls, but had said nothing about the boys; that she kissed him on the cheek and left him. One of these letters, written in reply to a communication which he had that day received from the secretary of the Clydesdale Bank with reference to his account being overdrawn to the extent of £131 12s. 4d., was in the following terms: '131 Sauchiehall Street, Glasgow. Sir – I am fully aware of the overdraft, and nothing short of the heavy affliction I have been visited with since the year commenced – in the loss of my mother, and this day of my wife, after long and severe illness – would have made me break my promise. If you will kindly tell Mr Readman, to whom I am well known, that immediately I can attend to business I will see him on the matter, please ask him if he can wait till after my dear wife's funeral on Thursday. – I am, sir, yours faithfully, Edward W. Pritchard. 18th March, 1865. Alexr. Mathers, Esq.'

On Monday 20 March Dr Pritchard certified the cause of Mrs Pritchard's death as gastric fever, the duration of which he stated to have been two months. Thereafter, he accompanied the body of his wife to Edinburgh, with a view to its interment beside that of her mother in the Grange Cemetery; and for this purpose it was taken to the house of her father, Mr Taylor. There, at Dr Pritchard's request, the coffin was opened in presence of the relatives, and – exhibiting, we are told, 'a great deal of feeling' – the murderer kissed his dead victim on the lips; a scene surely unparalleled in human history. Dr Pritchard then went back to Glasgow, intending to return to Edinburgh for the funeral, which was arranged to take place on the Thursday following. He went, doubtless, well content with the satisfactory issue of his atrocious plot; a few days more and the grave would close over his second victim also, and shroud for ever the evidence of his guilt. But the cup of his iniquities was full; in the very article of success – too late, indeed, to avail his hapless prey – the iron grasp of justice closed upon him; and, as he stepped from the train at Queen Street Station, he was arrested by Superintendent M'Call, on suspicion of having caused the death of his wife.

The authorities had had a busy time that Monday while the bereaved husband was in Edinburgh; an anonymous letter received by the Procurator-Fiscal, which was popularly attributed to Dr Paterson, but which he denied having sent, had set in motion the tardy machinery of the law; and the inquiries which followed resulted in a warrant being obtained for Dr Pritchard's apprehension. At last the light was about to be let in upon the dark secrets of the house in Sauchiehall Street.

One of the first steps now taken by the authorities was, of course, to institute a rigorous search of Dr Pritchard's house, with a view to discover anything which might bear on the circumstances of Mrs Pritchard's death; and various bottles and other articles found in his consulting-room and elsewhere, including the clothes and bed-linen used by Mrs Pritchard during the illness which immediately preceded her death, were taken possession of by the police. A post-mortem examination by Drs Maclagan and Littlejohn of the body of Mrs Pritchard took place on 21 March, with the result that these gentlemen could discover nothing to indicate that the death was due to natural causes; and the following day the prisoner appeared before Sir Archibald Alison, Sheriff of Lanarkshire, and emitted a declaration upon the charge made against him.

The authorities prosecuted their inquiries with dispatch; and, as the result of certain statements made by Mrs Nabb in precognition, disclosing the fact of the illicit intimacy which had subsisted between the prisoner and Mary M'Leod, the latter was apprehended as being concerned in causing the death of her mistress. After a lengthy examination before the Sheriff she was, however, released. An examination of the books of Messrs Murdoch Brothers and of the Glasgow Apothecaries' Company, Sauchiehall Street, at both of which Dr Pritchard had kept accounts, further satisfied the authorities of the propriety of the course they had taken; that examination showing recent purchases by him of tartarized antimony, aconite, and other poisons, in quantities hardly to be explained by the requirements of any ordinary medical practice. The public excitement which ensued upon the prisoner's arrest was intense; and every step of the inquiry that followed was eagerly perused in the local press, which, until the prisoner obtained the services of Messrs Galbraith & Maclay as his agents, daily reported every step taken by the authorities, giving full particulars of the examination of witnesses, and promulgating sensational theories and speculations regarding the case. The prisoner, meanwhile, preserved a calm and unruffled demeanour, and expressed confident hopes that his innocence would shortly be established. The postmortem examination having failed to disclose the cause of death, portions of Mrs Pritchard's body were reserved for chemical analysis; and the remains were interred in the Grange Cemetery on 22 March.

As showing the singular success of the dissimulation so long practised by the prisoner, neither his wife's nor his own relations believed for one moment in his guilt; and many private friends expressed their perfect confidence in his innocence. Public feeling was also in his favour, for up to that time nothing very reliable had been elicited pointing to any motive which might be supposed to have actuated the prisoner in the commission of the crime with which he stood charged; and the belief that the charge might prove to be unfounded was strengthened by the plausibility with which, in his declaration before the Sheriff, he had asserted his entire innocence. The result of the chemical analysis, which reached Glasgow on the 28th, disclosing, as it did, the unmistakable presence of antimony, at once changed the popular feeling; and, as the result of it, the prisoner was now fully committed for trial, and a warrant was issued for the exhumation of Mrs Taylor's body. At first there had not been any suspicion that the death of Mrs Taylor might have been the result of foul play; and had the inquiry into the circumstances attending that of his wife not taken place, there is little doubt, in the case of his mother-in-law's murder, that the perpetrator would have escaped detection.

On 30 March Messrs Galbraith & Maclay undertook the conduct of the defence; and the prisoner having decided to avail himself of the provisions of the Act of 1701, intimation was made, according to the practice then in use, with a view to the prisoner 'running his letters'; the effect of which was to compel the prosecutor to fix a date for his trial within sixty days, and, if an indictment was served within that period, the trial under it would have to be concluded within the forty days immediately following. On the same day Mrs Taylor's body was exhumed, and the result of the post-mortem examination thereon being precisely similar to that of Mrs Pritchard's remains, and equally contradictory of the statement made by the prisoner in regard to the manner of her death, portions of the body were reserved for chemical analysis, upon which the presence of antimony was unequivocally detected. Accordingly, on 21 April the prisoner again appeared before the

Sheriff, and was examined on the further charge of having caused the death of Mrs Taylor. He thereupon emitted a second declaration, and was committed for trial on this additional charge.

The following account of the prisoner's appearance on that occasion is taken from the *Glasgow Herald* of 24 April 1865: 'The prisoner looked somewhat pale, but he still retains the same amount of self-possession that he has exhibited since the night of his apprehension. It may be mentioned that on that occasion, after having been conveyed from the railway station to Mr Superintendent M'Call's apartment, the doctor, previous to retiring to rest, and before the room was vacated by the officers, engaged in prayer. His subsequent behaviour, we have reason to believe, has been one of the calmest possible description. A day or so after his incarceration in the North Prison he seemed to feel a little annoyed that he could not be favoured with a supply of pomatum for the trimming of his beard and hair. The prison regimen has not at all suited his taste.' He appears to have maintained, while in confinement, the plausible and insinuating manners which had hitherto stood him in such good stead, so much so that all who came in contact with him at this time were more or less influenced in his favour, and formed a high opinion of his intelligence. Whether with governors, warders, or police officers, his efforts were bent on producing a favourable impression, with the view of showing the unlikelihood of one so refined and cultivated being guilty of the terrible charges made against him.

On 31 May the indictment was served upon the prisoner, with the following citation: 'Edward William Pritchard, take notice that you will have to compear before the High Court of Justiciary, within the Criminal Court-house of Edinburgh, to answer to the criminal libel against you to which this notice is attached, on the third day of July, one thousand eight hundred and sixty-five, at half-past nine of the clock forenoon.' On 26 June Dr Pritchard was removed from the North Prison, Glasgow, in which he had been confined since his apprehension, and was brought through to Edinburgh by the first train and lodged in the Calton Jail, there to await his trial. The Lord Advocate (Moncreiff), who was to have led for the Crown, was unexpectedly summoned to London upon Parliamentary business on the Saturday before the trial, and the responsibility of conducting the case for the prosecution devolved upon the Solicitor-General (Young). In view of the intense interest and excitement which the case had aroused in the public mind, special regulations in terms similar to those which obtained at the trial of Madeleine Smith, eight years before, were issued, regulating admission to the Court during the proceedings; and on Monday 3 July commenced what was to prove one of the most memorable trials of modern times. The Court was crowded to its utmost capacity when, at 10 o'clock, the prisoner, who was dressed in deep mourning, was placed at the bar and charged with the murder of his wife and mother-in-law, to which in a firm voice he pleaded 'Not Guilty'. His brother, Charles Augustus Pritchard, by permission, occupied a seat beside him in the dock, which he continued to do until the second last day of the trial.

The personal appearance of Dr Pritchard and his demeanour in Court is variously described in the newspapers of the time. One lively reporter writes: 'He is really, as popular rumour has made him out, rather a good-looking fellow than otherwise – with clearly defined features, and a beard to be much admired by the other sex and envied by such portion of our own as may have reason, in this particular of finish to the male countenance, to resent the parsimony of nature; any line of clear, emotional nobility leaving its trace on the physiognomy I confess I failed to catch, but anything surmised of the distinctly sinister in it must, I think, be set down as imported by the eye of prejudice in the observer. He came up frankly; pale and worn from his months of prison, yet cheerful, on the whole, of aspect. He composed himself for the day and looked ever after, so far as I had opportunity to observe him, the most cool and unconcerned person in Court. Unconcerned, with this decorous exception – I observed he almost always wept when, as a fond husband, it was proper that he should be moved – wept, or did something dexterous with his pocket-handkerchief, which might very well pass for weeping.' Another writer observes: 'The prisoner is a tall, stout, well-built man, rather prepossessing, and with sharply defined features. His hair is long and thin, and he is bald nearly to the crown. The large bushy beard which he wears gives to the lower part of his face an appearance of strength that is at variance with the general character of the countenance. The impression conveyed is that of mildness, approaching perhaps to effeminacy. The expression of his face during the day was sad and thoughtful; he seemed cool and collected, and watched the proceedings closely.' The following interesting account is also given: 'His naturally handsome countenance, and a certain plausibility of manner which characterized him, favourably impressed spectators. This was strikingly illustrated by his bearing in Court, particularly in the earlier stages of the trial. None who saw the intelligent, thoughtful, and mild-looking individual seated in the dock on the first morning of the eventful trial could be prepared for anything like the refined and consummate villainy and diabolic cruelty which each day brought to light, until, when the whole murderous plot was laid bare, the assembled auditors saw before them a perfect fiend in human shape. It was only when his unfortunate victim, Mary M'Leod, reluctantly confessed the relations which subsisted between them that the real nature of the man was made known, and that a change might be seen stealing over his features. Before this, the attention which he paid to the evidence was only what might be expected from one interested in the proceedings, but whose fate could in no way be affected by them. With the anxiety which had now evidently taken hold of him, a certain vulpine look might be detected, as he keenly fixed his eyes upon the girl's countenance, when – under the skilful but gentle questioning of the counsel for the Crown, and of the presiding judge – she rent aside the curtain which had hitherto veiled the inner life of that apparently happy home. Throughout the greater part of her protracted examination a change came over the seducer's features. The mild, gentlemanly expression which these had hitherto worn had now in some degree disappeared; and at times one could almost fancy that traces of malignity could be seen, blended with his keen and steady gaze. This was, however, but momentary, as the sinister look speedily gave place to the usual self-complacent, but thoughtful and somewhat benign, expression. Viewed in the light of the evidence, his demeanour throughout was studied, and designed to deceive the spectators. The only piece of real humanity which peeped out during the five days of the trial was when two of his children, the one a girl of fourteen and the other a boy of eleven, were placed in the box by his counsel to speak to the kindly feelings which subsisted between him and his wife and mother-in-law. Even his hardened nature was overcome, and what had all the appearance of genuine tears trickled down his cheek. This was the one vulnerable spot in the villain's breast, and the scene altogether was such as none who witnessed it will soon forget.'

The case for the prosecution, splendidly handled by the Solicitor-General, was built up with such skill and closeness as to leave practically no loophole for doubt. Not a superfluous witness was examined, and hardly a superfluous question put to any of those in the box. The evidence adduced for the Crown incontestably established that the deaths of both ladies were due to poison. In the case of Mrs Pritchard, it was proved beyond dispute that she died of chronic antimonial poisoning – her body being impregnated with that drug; although the evidence in Mrs Taylor's case, if quite as complete, was not so cumulative and irresistible. The case being one of circumstantial evidence only, no direct act of administration could be proved against the prisoner; but it was amply demonstrated that he alone had the means, opportunity, and skill requisite for carrying through the double crime; and his gratuitous falsehoods regarding the illness and deaths of his victims, both to the registrar and others at the time, and afterwards in his declaration, disposed of the question of his guilt.

The only unsatisfactory link in the strong chain forged by the prosecution was their inability to suggest a motive sufficient to account for the murder of both wife and mother-in-law. The financial motive alleged – a life-rent interest, to the extent of two-thirds, in a sum of £2500 – was manifestly inadequate; and that the prisoner desired to be rid of his wife, so as to marry the servant girl whom he had long before seduced, was equally inconclusive. Mrs Taylor was probably swept from his path because her presence interfered with his elaborate scheme for the destruction of her daughter; although her discovery of the intimacy with M'Leod, as stated in his confession, may have been an additional factor. It is also possible that Mrs Taylor's suspicions may have been aroused as to the cause of her daughter's mysterious illness, for it is to be remembered that, soon after her arrival, she herself prepared in the sickroom the food which the invalid required and shared her daughter's bedroom, to the exclusion of the prisoner. If she indeed hinted at these suspicions to her son-in-law, her fate was sealed. The real motive which actuated Dr Pritchard in taking his wife's life has never been discovered.

The defence, unable to put a single medical man in the box to controvert the testimony of the Crown doctors, had to rely mainly on the antecedent improbability of such a murder being committed by a man of the prisoner's position and education upon relatives with whom he lived on the most affectionate terms, coupled with the failure of the prosecution to suggest a convincing motive. It was a significant fact that the prisoner's counsel called no witnesses to character. The line adopted by Mr Rutherfurd Clark in endeavouring to fix the guilt of the murders upon the girl M'Leod was, in some quarters, adversely commented upon at the time; but, as the Solicitor-General had impressed upon the jury that the perpetrator must have been either the prisoner or Mary M'Leod, he would seem to have been justified in his line of argument. In dealing with the case of Mrs Taylor a strong effort was made – in view of the difference of opinion expressed by the medical witnesses for the prosecution as to the precise nature of the poison which caused her death – to suggest that she might have died from an overdose of her own medicine; but the distinction was too naïve for the jury, satisfied as they were of the fact that antimony and aconite had been introduced into it by hands other than her own. The appearance of the prisoner's unfortunate children in the box, instead of helping the case for the defence, must, one thinks, have removed from the minds of the jury any remnant of pity for their wretched father.

Three diaries kept by Dr Pritchard were produced in Court, but were only referred to by the prosecution for the purpose of fixing certain dates. Some of the entries in these had obviously been made by the prisoner with the view of their being used as evidence in his favour in the event of any inquiry; but so grossly hypocritical were their terms that they were not even alluded to by his own counsel.

The most remarkable feature of the trial was unquestionably the statements made in evidence by Dr Paterson; which earned the severe strictures of the counsel for the prisoner in his address, and the grave censure of the Lord Justice-Clerk in his charge to the jury. To these were added the almost unanimous condemnation of the attitude which he had seen fit to adopt and defend in relation to the case of Mrs Pritchard by the newspaper press of the United Kingdom, in the columns of which, for some time after the trial, appeared numerous letters animadverting upon his conduct. The doctor did not remain silent under this shower of adverse criticism, but prepared and sent to the newspapers an elaborate *apologia*. That Dr Paterson's singular sense of what was due to professional etiquette did not, however, prevent him stating the facts fully when in the witness-box was fortunate for the ends of justice.

The evidence for the prosecution occupied the first three days of the trial; by midday on the fourth the evidence for the defence was completed, the remainder of the sitting being taken up with the addresses of counsel; and on the fifth (and last) day of the trial the Lord Justice-Clerk delivered his charge to the jury. On the conclusion of the lordship's masterly review of the evidence, at a quarter past 1 o'clock, the jury retired to consider their verdict; and after the absence of an hour (during which the prisoner was removed to the cells below the Court-room) they returned to Court, their foreman, Mr George Sim, announcing the following as their verdict: 'The jury unanimously find the prisoner guilty of both charges as libelled.'

On the declaration of the verdict the prisoner clasped his hands together, but exhibited little outward emotion. A few moments later, however, he became faint, and leaned for support upon the shoulder of the policeman sitting at his right; but on being given a glass of water he appeared to revive. During an interval of twenty minutes occupied by the recording of the verdict and sentence, the prisoner made a strong effort to bear up, and maintained his composure in a remarkable degree. These formalities completed, the Lord Justice-Clerk addressed to the unhappy man a few earnest and solemn words, exhorting him to repentance of his crime, the prisoner meanwhile standing up and bowing at intervals as if in assent. His lordship then, assuming the black cap, pronounced sentence of death in the impressive Scots form; and the prisoner, having again bowed to the bench and also to the jury, was conducted down the stair leading from the dock, which he descended with as much composure as he had exhibited on being brought up to hear the verdict.

The following account is given by an eye-witness of the effect upon the prisoner of the able and eloquent addresses of the opposing counsel: 'Somewhat curious it was, during the speeches of the Solicitor-General assailing him and of Mr Clark in his defence, to watch the deportment of the prisoner. Mr Young's address he followed with the closest attention. No emotion was exhibited, save that now and then, when something damaging was stated, one could see a quiver about the lips and a droop and sinking of the pained eyelids. When Mr Clark, on the other hand, in his defence, proceeded to enlarge to the jury on the impossibility of such a monster in human shape, and sketched in strong rhetoric his supposed conduct to the wife of his bosom, his whole face broke, as it were, and after a spasmodic effort at suppression, he wept.' The effect produced on the prisoner by the Lord Justice-Clerk's charge to the jury is not recorded, but it must soon have been apparent to him that it finally disposed of any chance of his acquittal. It was in the highest degree careful, complete, and exhaustive, abounding in subtle insight into special points of the case untouched by those who had previously dealt with it, and was in every respect worthy of so great a judge.

At half-past 3 the prisoner was brought upstairs from the cells to the prison van, which was drawn up at the witnesses' entrance to the Court. A large crowd had gathered in the High Street, excited by the chance of getting a glimpse of him; and, notwithstanding the efforts of a strong cordon of police to keep the Parliament Square clear, considerable numbers got into the piazza. As he issued from the door of the Court-house the prisoner took off his hat and bowed to the assemblage. He walked to the prison van with a steady step, and was then driven to the Calton Jail, the van being followed by a large crowd all the way to the prison. Next morning he was removed to Glasgow by the 10 o'clock train, from which he was taken at Cowlairs, to avoid the crowd awaiting his arrival at Queen Street. From thence he was driven to Glasgow without attracting observation, and placed in the North Prison, the scene of his former confinement.

Very different now was the convict's demeanour from what it had been when he left for Edinburgh. Then he was cheerful and confident, never expressing himself as other than certain of regaining freedom after his trial, when he intended to leave Scotland and reside abroad. Indeed, when his agent, while on the way to Edinburgh, showed some anxiety as to the result of the trial, the prisoner said, 'Keep up your heart: we will return to Glasgow together.' He took with him to Edinburgh a photograph of a family group, including himself, his wife, their children, and his mother-in-law, which he frequently exhibited to the warders and others, taking pleasure, we are told, in pointing out the various members of the family by name. Now his over-confidence gave way to a prostration of mind and body; and he continued during the whole of the next day lying in a sort of stupor, without speaking to those around him. On Monday the 10th, having somewhat recovered, he was visited by his brother, sister, and eldest daughter; and also received the ministrations of the Rev. R. S. Oldham, incumbent of St Mary's Episcopal Church, Renfield Street, of which he formerly had been a member. To this gentleman he made the first of his confessions.

From this time the convict is said to have become more composed, and to have occupied himself with reading the Bible and other works of a religious character. He was frequently visited by the Rev. Dr Norman Macleod of the Barony Parish Church, the Rev. Dr Millar of Free St Matthew's, and the Rev. J. Watson Reid, and was by these gentlemen induced, on 19th July, to make a further and more full confession of his guilt. It will be observed that this document, which includes an exhaustive list of those to whom he professed his indebtedness for kindness or services rendered to him since his apprehension, contains no reference to the counsel who appeared for him at his trial. He is said to have stipulated, however, that this confession should not be given to the world until after his execution — a request in which we can still trace his old ambition to gain, so far as possible, the favourable opinion of his fellows. A further example of this may be found in the fact that it was not until making his third confession that he could bring himself to acknowledge the murder of Mrs Taylor, which hitherto he had strenuously denied.

In Dr Pritchard's case it is to be noted that, unlike more fortunate criminals, no attempt whatever was made on his behalf with a view to obtaining commutation of the capital sentence. The doctor's day for winning the popular vote was long since over, and public sympathy was reserved for the unfortunate family whom his evil deeds had plunged in grief and shame. It is stated that, as the fatal day approached, the convict intimated his intention of making a speech from the scaffold, a proceeding which would have been eminently characteristic of his former love of notoriety; but, yielding to the representations of the reverend gentlemen who were attending him, he agreed not to address the public.

On Monday the 27th Dr Pritchard was removed from the

North Prison, Duke Street, to the South Prison, in front of which, upon Glasgow Green, the execution was to take place the following day. There the convict was frequently visited by the Revs. Mr Oldham and Mr Reid, as also by the Rev. Mr Doran, the chaplain of the jail. His time is said to have been chiefly occupied in reading the Bible and writing various letters. One of these, addressed to his brother-in-law, Dr Michael Taylor, was in the following terms:

27th July, 1865.

Farewell, brother, I die in twenty hours from this. Romans viii. 34 to 39 verses.

Mary Jane, Darling Mother, and you, I will meet, as you said the last time you spoke to me, 'in happier circumstances.' Bless you and yours, prays the dying penitent,

EDWARD WILLIAM PRITCHARD.

During the last hours that he spent on earth, the convict maintained an even placidity of demeanour, spoke confidently of his assurance of being saved from perdition, and avowed his readiness to die the death he had deserved.

Meanwhile, the arrangements for the execution were in progress; and Calcraft, the public executioner, arrived in Glasgow to superintend the erection of the scaffold, which the workmen commenced to put up at 2 o'clock on the morning of Friday 28 July, upon which day the unhappy prisoner was to suffer the last penalty of the law. Considerable interest attaches to the execution of Dr Pritchard, as being the last public execution which took place in Glasgow, if not in Scotland. It is a singular reflection that, less than a century ago, such a shocking and degrading spectacle could have been publicly enacted in a civilized country in presence, it is said, of 100,000 onlookers without one dissentient voice being raised in protest against it.

By permission of the magistrates and prison authorities, Mr Alexander Stewart, of the Edinburgh Phrenological Museum, was permitted to take a cast of the convict's head immediately after his execution. The body was thereafter interred in the graveyard of the prison, where, scratched upon a stone, the letter 'P' alone distinguishes it from those of other malefactors who have met a similar doom, and await, in that resting-place, their summons to the Great Assize.

Thus perished ignominiously upon a public scaffold, by the hands of the common hangman, one whom many in that vast assemblage must long have known only as the urbane and courteous gentleman, the genial lecturer, the kindly physician, and the amiable and pious philanthropist. The strange thing is that a life largely spent in endeavouring to earn, however undeservedly, the approbation of others should end thus, amid the execration or indifference of thousands of his fellow-citizens; and that the name of Dr Pritchard should for all time be associated with a deliberate cruelty and dissimulation unequalled even in the dark pages of the history of crime.

The single redeeming feature presented by a character, in other respects, of unexampled villainy is the convict's affection for his children, which, among so much else that was false and mendacious, appears to have been perfectly sincere. The fondness subsisting between him and his eldest daughter, who visited him frequently in prison till shortly before his last day, was specially strong; and it is touching to read of the poor child writing a letter to one of the officials, begging him to be kind to her 'dear papa'. With this exception, however, no criminal career of which we have any record exhibits a more shocking combination of wickedness, hypocrisy, and blasphemy than that of the man who, leaving the deathbed of his murdered wife, methodically entered in his diary a prayer to the Holy Trinity to welcome her whom his foul hand had, but a moment before, relentlessly done to death.

Robert Wood

· 1907 ·

BY

BASIL HOGARTH

I

I т has been said many times that the Camden Town Murder is the classic British crime of this century; and certainly a strong case for its pre-eminence over most other murders might easily be made out. The trial of Robert Wood at the Central Criminal Court, Old Bailey, in December 1907, for the alleged murder of a street prostitute, Emily Dimmock, in Camden Town is unique in many respects. To the layman interested in the psychological aspects of murder, the case must prove of abounding interest; while, to the purely legal mind, it furnishes a remarkable precedent of the first instance in which an accused murderer, availing himself of the facilities to give evidence on his own behalf bestowed by the Criminal Evidence Act of 1898, successfully maintained his plea of not guilty. Public opinion on the case – sane public opinion – was thus ably posited by a contemporary leader writer in the *Daily Chronicle*: 'To the moralist and to every serious-minded citizen who considers the state of society, how terrible are the sidelights which the case throws on life in London! Of "scandals in high life" we always hear much, and the publicity which they inevitably attract is perhaps out of proportion to their proper dimensions. Here in this case we have the limelight thrown upon scandals in low life, and it is a saddening and sickening spectacle that is revealed. How awful is the life-picture of the murdered woman – "the lowest of the low", as they called her, passing at the end of the week as the wife of one man and for the rest of it consorting promiscuously, as the evidence showed; leading what is called a "gay life", and ending it with her throat cut by some stray companion. We need not follow up the theme into the other by-ways of human folly, vice, depravity, and squalor which the evidence opened up to the public gaze. Englishmen are proud of their civilizing mission among the "inferior races" in the "dark" countries of the world. We are not among those who would ridicule or discourage such work. But is there not some civilizing to be done nearer home? There are savages, as we call them, who would be ashamed to live the life that is led sometimes in Camden Town, and Camden Town is but the particular locality upon which this case has chanced to throw the flashlight revealing the seamy side of low life in London.'

Camden Town is not beautiful. It possesses, in fact, a strong resemblance to a place once described by Arnold Bennett as 'A dingy and sordid neighbourhood where existence was a dangerous and difficult adventure in almost frantic quest for food and drink and shelter, where the familiar and beloved landmarks were public-houses, and where the immense majority of the population read nothing but sporting prognostications and results and, on Sunday mornings, accounts of bloody crimes and juicy sexual irregularities. A hell of noise and dust and dirt, with the County of London tramcars, and motor lorries, and heavy, horse-drawn vans sweeping north and south in a vast clangour of iron thudding and grating on iron and granite beneath the bedroom windows of a defenceless populace.'

There is a street in Camden Town called St Paul's Road which, somehow, has become disentangled from the noisier streets in the neighbourhood. Traffic has almost ceased to circulate here, and in its shabby-genteel privacy it is like a forgotten garment, left faded and worn. At about a quarter past 11 on the morning of 12 September 1907 a rather elderly lady might have been seen knocking at the door of No. 29 in this street. Her name was Mrs Shaw, and she had travelled from Northampton by an early train to pay a visit to her son 'Bert', who had but recently married. She was admitted to the house by the landlady, Mrs Stocks – as yet the young couple could not afford a house of their own – who told her that, despite the lateness of the hour, her son's wife was still in bed. About a quarter of an hour later her son himself put in an appearance. He was a well-set-up young man, employed as a dining-car cook on one of the restaurant cars of the Midland Railway. It was his custom to return home each morning with the train leaving Sheffield at 7.20 a.m. bound for St Pancras, and he used to arrive at St Paul's Road between 11.30 a.m. and noon.

After greeting his mother and the landlady, Shaw went from the kitchen into his own apartments to rouse his wife. He knocked at the door, but received no response. When he tried to open the door, he found that it was locked. This unusual circumstance aroused his suspicions. Returning to the kitchen, he received a duplicate key from the landlady, who followed him through. In the parlour they saw around them evidence of a rapid search through the drawers, which had apparently all been hurriedly ransacked, as their contents were strewn about the floor in confusion. Folding doors led to the bedroom; in the lock of the door there was usually a key; but that too was missing this morning, and frantic knocking failed to elicit a response. Now thoroughly alarmed, the young man smashed in the wooden panels of the bedroom door. He stepped into the room and saw that the bedclothes were huddled together in a heap: on the floor a pool of blood had trickled down towards the skirting boards. Rushing to the bed, Shaw tore aside the sheets and discovered the dead body of his 'wife', completely nude, lying face downwards. A gaping wound had been inflicted in the throat, the fatal thrust having almost dismembered head from trunk. The bed was soaked with blood.

Although the venetian blinds were drawn, a few shutters had been half-opened, and through this aperture filtered a gleam of sunshine. This shaft of light was directed on to a sewing-machine on the top of which lay a postcard album, partly open, with some of its contents scattered on the floor. The presence of that postcard album in the bedroom, with some of the postcards torn out, puzzled Shaw, for it had always been kept on a small table in the front room, a treasure prized by the dead woman. He made a quick search through the bedroom and the parlour and found that a number of things had disappeared. So far as he could then remember, he found that a gold watch, a silver cigarette-case with his initials stamped on it, a silver 'curb' chain with a small glass charm, and a purse were among the things unaccounted for. Later he found that a wedding ring and keeper belonging to the murdered woman were missing also; yet on the top of the chest of drawers there were two gold rings. There was a washstand in the bedroom containing a jug of water and a basin, and on the back of a chair facing it there was cast a damp flannel petticoat which bore traces of blood. On the wooden rack of the washstand a white towel was folded, clean and dry. The remains of a meal, probably supper, stood on the table in the parlour. Four empty stout bottles, two plates, two knives, and two forks, and a few used dishes suggested a visitor at supper.

A murder is an unpleasant event to discover at any time. But it was especially distressing for young Shaw at this time. Perhaps it would not have been quite so awkward if his mother had not chosen to visit him that very morning; perhaps it would not have been so difficult if it had happened in his own house. As it was, he knew that there would have to be a lot of irksome explanations. What called for discreet explanation was the fact, as yet unknown to his mother and the landlady, that he was not really married in the legal sense. The girl who passed as his wife was in fact one he had picked up from the streets. Her name was Phyllis Dimmock and her past history, he knew, would not bear too close an inspection.

Shaw had known Phyllis for two years before she came to live with him. She was a street prostitute. When they arranged to live together, it was on the understanding that Phyllis, whose real name was the less euphonious Emily Elizabeth Dimmock, would abandon her calling and settle down to a liaison with him. They had lived together for nine months, and, so far as he knew, the arrangement had worked admirably. But Shaw, whose work took him away each night, did not know that Phyllis had never to any considerable extent altered her mode of living. Doubtless, from her point of view, the arrangement seemed perfect, because it combined the security of marriage with the varying rewards of freelance easy virtue. What could be more simple, during the absence of Shaw each night, than to slip out of their apartments and resume her profitable calling? There is no doubt that Shaw was genuinely surprised when he learned later from the police investigations the nature and extent of the woman's duplicity.

Thus the true story of his association with Dimmock must now come to light. It was hardly a pleasant prospect for him; but he called a doctor and the police.

Dr John Thompson, the divisional surgeon of police, arrived at the house a little after 1 in the afternoon. The first thing that attracted his attention was the quantity of blood that had flowed from the wound. The bedclothes were saturated and a stream of blood had infiltrated the mattress, finding an outlet on to the floor, where hours of slow dripping had caused a large pool to settle in the direction of the fireplace. The reclining position of the body on the bed showed no evidence of a struggle. In fact, except in one remarkable particular, it was the position of one who had died painlessly in sleep. The one unusual feature was that the left arm was folded underneath the back, a position in which normal, comfortable sleep would have been impossible. He came to the conclusion that for some reason, never satisfactorily established afterwards, the arm must have been forced back into that unnatural position by the murderer. The nature of the wound, and the absence of a weapon, discounted any suggestion of suicide. The wound itself was very deep, an incised cut extending from beneath the lobe of the left ear to the lobe of the right. The carotid artery, the windpipe, and the jugular vein, as well as the pharynx down to the spine, had all been severed cleanly down to the dorsal vertebrae; the head was only held on to the trunk by a few muscles that had escaped the knife. Taking all these things into consideration, the surgeon advanced the opinion that the weapon employed must have been extremely sharp, powerful, and used with tremendous force and deliberation.

The body was cold and rigid, rigor mortis having set in. It is always a matter of difficulty to ascertain with precision, from the appearance of death-stiffening alone, the length of time which has intervened since death, and, as near as possible, Dr Thompson could only fix the time of death as having occurred between seven or eight, but not more than nine, hours previously. This would put the murder as having occurred some time between 4 and 6 o'clock in the morning. He carefully examined the room for other blood stains, and found two spots of congealed blood on the wash-hand stand and another spot on a jug. In the basin there were water and blood, and on the petticoat thrown over the chair back he also detected the presence of blood. A towel folded on the handrail of the wash-hand stand appeared to be free from blood stains, and later analysis in the laboratory confirmed this fact. Although the murderer must have utilized the jug of water, as the blood stains eloquently testified, there was not a trace of blood on the handle.

The police were extremely alert in their inquiries. Before nightfall they had acquired a stock of useful information concerning the movements of the murdered woman on the day before her death. She had passed the greater part of that day, which was a Wednesday, in washing and ironing linen. A little while after 4 o'clock in the afternoon Shaw went out to catch his train to Sheffield, as was his regular habit. After he had gone Phyllis was seen in the yard at the back of the house taking down the clothes from the wash-line. Later in the evening, about half-past 7, Phyllis came through into the kitchen and was seen to be wearing a light-brown skirt. She had curling pins in her hair. She returned to her own rooms, after a few minutes' casual conversation with the landlady, and half an hour later the latter and her husband heard the slam of the front door, indicating that Phyllis had gone out for the evening. As near as they could fix the time, she must have left the house at a quarter past 8.

In the same house there also lived a widow named Alice Lancaster, a clerkess. She could not say anything about the movements of the deceased woman on the Wednesday, but she was able to tell the police that on the same morning, shortly before 8 o'clock, she had taken two letters from the postman, addressed to 'Mrs B. Shaw, 29 St Paul's Road, Camden Town', and had slipped them under the door of Shaw's apartments.

No one had heard anything unusual or suspicious during the night. Mr Stocks had an alarm clock in his bedroom which was set to go off at twenty minutes to 5, but he did not rise until forty minutes later. If there had been any strange sounds, then he would assuredly have heard them. Mrs Stocks knocked at Dimmock's door about 9 o'clock that morning. Receiving no response, she concluded that her boarder was having a 'lie-in', and thought no more of the matter until the arrival of Shaw and the episode of the missing keys. There were a number of keys in the possession of the dead girl: a key for the front door, which she always kept in her purse, one for the parlour, which was usually kept on the inside of the door, and one for the bedroom door, also kept in the lock, and the keys of the folding door. All these keys, except one that was later discovered, were missing.

At first the police were inclined to regard Shaw with suspicion. But he was able to account for every detail of his movements from the moment he left the house on the Wednesday afternoon at 4 o'clock until the time of his return at 11.30 the following morning. He had a complete alibi, corroborated by his employers. Whoever had committed the crime, it was established beyond a shadow of doubt that Shaw had had nothing to do with it.

In spite of the lack of material which the police had at their disposal, they were yet in possession of the main facts of the dead woman's history by the following day. They obtained in a few hours knowledge which she had successfully hidden from Shaw during the period of her cohabitation with him. And they found one man who furnished a valuable clue.

The history of Emily Elizabeth Dimmock provides another unfortunate instance of the familiar spectacle of real life plagiarizing fiction. George Moore, in his most imaginative mood, never penned a page of *Esther Waters* that was more vivid than the life story of this butterfly of the streets. She was twenty-three years old when she died, having been born at Walworth, the youngest in the family of fifteen. Later the family removed to Wellingborough, where, at an early age, the girl commenced work in a straw-hat factory. Soon she left this for domestic service, entering the house of a family in East Finchley as a general servant. She appears to have been a rather fascinating girl, and no doubt she felt the long hours of domestic service chafing and irksome. At any rate, she quickly slipped into an easier way of earning money, in which the glamour of paint and powder played a part. Tall and slim, always attractively dressed, with pleasant ingratiating manners, she was a favourite among her associates, and before long she had consorted promiscuously with many men recruited from different classes. Phyllis played the piano – rather well, if the testimony of her various landladies, 'protectors', and stray associates is to be believed. She was fond of collecting postcards, which she preserved in an album, and her large collection, including as it did hundreds of postcards posted in remote corners of the globe, indicated the extent and variety of her paramours, many of whom were military and naval men stationed in dismal barracks and obscure foreign ports. She lived at many addresses in her short career, and at one time had been the inmate of a brothel kept by a person named Crabtree, in Bidborough Street. Other addresses at which she resided for brief periods included Euston Road, Manchester Street, Gower Street, Harrison Street, and Gray's Inn Road. All of which suggests that her clientele was assembled in the main from the submerged depths of London 'night life'.

When Shaw first suggested that she might come and stay under his protection, he was fully aware of her previous history; but, as has been mentioned, it was an implicit understanding between them that, in return for his gift of board and shelter, she was to abandon her former mode of livelihood. She kept up a pretence of faithfulness to Shaw, but it was really her custom, after he had gone to work each night, to slink to her old haunts in Euston Road and pick up such stray

admirers as were not averse to paying for a night's adventure.
If she found someone satisfactory, she would return to the
apartments in St. Paul's Road late in the night, after the landlady was safely in bed, and surreptitiously introduce her
visitor, who would retreat from the house in the early hours
of the morning. Her favourite rendezvous was the 'Rising
Sun', a public-house in Camden Town, where, with friends
and associates, it was her wont to beguile the hours of waiting
for men of leisure and ready money. It was in this 'Rising
Sun' tavern that the police first got into touch with a man
named Robert Percival Roberts, who was later to become a
figure of considerable importance in the case. Roberts was a
ship's cook who had been paid off in the previous month. On
the Sunday before the crime he had met Phyllis in the bar of
the 'Rising Sun'. He was clearly a desirable companion for
her, for he was then in the midst of the pleasant process of
liquidating a sum of £38, his savings from a recent voyage.
Roberts went with Dimmock to her apartments and stayed
the night there. He left at half-past 7 on the Monday morning.
The hospitality apparently delighted him so much that he
spent the following two nights, Monday and Tuesday, in the
same fashion, parting company with a couple of sovereigns
and the price of a bottle of whisky for this pleasant lodging.
He did not spend the Wednesday night with her as it happened that she had arranged to accommodate another guest
that night. To the police this seemed a rather strange story,
and doubtless would not have been believed but for the fact
that Roberts, like Shaw, was able to produce a cast-iron alibi,
proving conclusively that on the Wednesday evening he had
slept at a temperance hotel. The proprietress of the hotel and
a fellow-boarder corroborated this, and he was automatically
eliminated in the search for the murderer.

Roberts was able, however, to give the police a valuable
clue that proved the real starting-point in their investigations.
On the Wednesday morning, just after he rose, he heard a
knock at the door. Two letters were then pushed under and,
picking them up, he handed them to Phyllis. One was from a
lady's tailor, a circular advertisement; the other was a private

letter. After reading it, she passed it over to Roberts, who read part of it. He was able to recall the contents. The tenor of the message was: 'Dear Phyllis, – Will you meet me at the "Eagle", Camden Town, 8.30 to-night, Wednesday? – Bert.' There was also a postscript to the letter, but he was not permitted to read this. When Roberts had finished reading, the woman rose, went to a chest of drawers, and took from out of one of the drawers a postcard which she handed to him. It was a picture postcard bearing on one side the portrait of a woman embracing an infant. The reverse side contained both the address and a message which read: 'Phillis [sic] darling, – If it pleases you, meet me, 8.15 p.m. at the [here there was a sketch showing a rising sun]. – Yours to a cinder, Alice.'

Roberts noticed that the letter and the postcard were both written in indelible lead, and from a comparison decided that the handwriting was the same in both. The girl then took the letter and the tailor's circular, put them together in an envelope, and set fire to them with a match, throwing them into the empty fire-grate. She put the postcard back into the drawer. The reason for burning the one and keeping the other is obvious – the letter signed in a man's name would undoubtedly have aroused Shaw's suspicions had he come across it; the postcard, signed 'Alice', was innocuous – and, moreover, she was in the habit of collecting postcards.

In the fire-grate of the bedroom a detective had already found the charred remains of a letter, and although most of it had been destroyed, there still remained occasional letters and words which could be deciphered, corroborating Roberts's story in material respects. The postcard album and the hasty search were now explained. The murderer had evidently been seeking the postcard. The police searched thoroughly for it, but in spite of their efforts nothing came to light. They interviewed hundreds of persons who had known the dead woman, and followed up innumerable clues that petered out; and for a while it looked as if the investigation would end in stalemate. Then it chanced that Shaw made an important discovery. In packing his things away, before leaving his rooms, he had to empty the chest of drawers. Each drawer had a lining covering the bottom improvised out of a folded sheet of newspaper. As he was removing one of these linings he came upon the missing postcard for which the police had searched so long in vain, and immediately communicated his discovery to them. The postcard was then exhibited to Roberts, who recognized it as the one that Dimmock had shown to him on the Wednesday morning.

With this tangible clue in the hands of Scotland Yard, the hunt was up, and efforts were redoubled to secure an arrest. As none of the intimate acquaintances of the dead woman could shed any light on the handwriting, the police had to fall back on other means of establishing the identity of the writer. There were three other postcards in the album the handwriting on which bore a marked resemblance to that on the 'Rising Sun' postcard, and so the Commissioner of Police ordered facsimiles of these four postcards to be sent to various prominent newspapers in the hope that their reproduction in the press would lead to the identification of the writing. Along with these facsimiles, the Commissioner sent a letter in which he remarked: 'The attached postcards are believed to have direct bearing on the case of Emily Dimmock who was found murdered at 29 St Paul's Road, Camden Town, on the night of 11th instant. Any person recognizing the handwriting should at once communicate with New Scotland Yard or any Metropolitan police station.'

Among the newspapers to which Scotland Yard supplied facsimiles of the 'Rising Sun' postcard was the *News of the World*. In the *News of the World* there appeared two facsimile reproductions of the 'Rising Sun' postcard, over which was the challenging caption 'Can You Recognize This Writing?' As a stimulus to detection the proprietors offered a reward of £100 to the person or persons who could give such information as would lead to the identification of the handwriting in the facsimile.

Thus it happened that on the morning of Sunday 29 September 1907 several million people from Land's End to John o' Groats saw the reproduction of the 'Rising Sun' postcard. Among these millions there was a young lady named Ruby

Young who lived at Earl's Court and euphemistically designated herself an 'artist's model'. When she saw the facsimile she cut it from the paper and put the cutting into an envelope. She also wrote a letter, to which she attached the clipping, and laid the letter on a table with the intention of posting it later in the day. But the letter was never posted, for that same evening, between 8 and 9 o'clock, a young man called on her and saved her the trouble. The young man was an artist-engraver, and his name was Robert William Thomas George Cavers Wood. He had scarcely set foot inside her room when he burst out: 'Ruby, I'm in trouble.' Taking the envelope from the table, the girl opened it, drew the enclosed clipping out, and handed it to her visitor with the remark: 'That is your handwriting.' He did not deny this, but offered to explain.

The gist of this narrative was that one Friday evening in September, while in Camden Town, he was walking up Euston Road with a friend of his, and they called at a public-house known as the 'Rising Sun'. While he was in the bar, a girl came up to him and asked for a penny to insert in a mechanical organ. He gave her a coin, and later she asked for a drink in a friendly way. Meanwhile his friend went away, and the girl was left alone in the bar with him. While they were drinking an urchin came into the bar, offering picture postcards for sale. The girl, who called herself 'Phyllis', wanted to purchase a postcard from the boy, but the young artist stopped her, saying that they were common and that he had some which he had brought from Bruges. He showed her a selection. She chose one bearing a reprint of a picture in which a woman was fondling a child in her arms. She asked him to send it to her after he had written 'something nice' on it. He could not think of anything on the spur of the moment, but he recalled that he had arranged an appointment with his friend who had just left, so he wrote down a few words in the style of an appointment. He was about to sign it in his own name when she stopped him with a gesture of confusion, telling him to subscribe it 'Alice'. He promised to post it, but as he had no stamp at that moment he put it in his coat pocket. They had another drink, and then he left the 'Rising Sun'.

The matter, according to the young man's explanation, would have ended there had it not been for a strange coincidence. The next day he happened to be walking along Great College Street in Camden Town on his way to the office of the Gas Light and Coke Company when he came upon the girl who had been in the bar the night before. She was disappointed that he had not sent the card, and he again promised to do so. They walked a little way along the street and then parted. He posted the card on Sunday night and thought no more about the matter. Then he called at the 'Rising Sun' on the Monday night, and who should be there again but his acquaintance 'Phyllis', who came from the other side of the bar and greeted him. She left him, saying that she would come back shortly. As he had nothing better to do he hung about the bar, and waited some time. Eventually, as she did not reappear, he went outside and was about to go home, crossing the street for that purpose, when he saw her talking to a lame man. As soon as she caught sight of him she turned to her companion and said: 'I'll see you later when the "pub" closes.' She then came over to him and they went back to the bar and had a few drinks. He then left the bar. 'That,' said Wood, 'was the last time I ever saw the girl.' It was a plausible story, speciously told, and for the moment Ruby Young was satisfied. She did not therefore apply for the £100 reward, and she promised not to identify the handwriting.

There was another who recognized the elegant penmanship on the postcard; a foreman, called Tinkham, in the employment of a glass-works in Gray's Inn Road. When Mr Tinkham saw a placard exhibiting a large-size reproduction of the script, he immediately recognized it as that of an artist who worked for the same firm. The artist was, of course, Robert Wood, who had been employed for fourteen years along with Tinkham as a pattern designer. The foreman approached Wood and, when challenged, Wood admitted writing the postcard. He then gave an explanation that was in all material respects the same as that previously tendered to Ruby Young. Wood also added that his old father was in a poor way of health, and should it come to his knowledge that his son had been at all mixed up in such an unpleasant business there might well be disastrous results. He asked the foreman, as a personal favour, to keep the matter quiet. The latter, who had a great liking for the young man whose courteous manners and kind disposition had made him a general favourite in the works, promised to do so.

Thus the power of the press was defeated, and Fleet Street failed to recruit from its army of amateur detectives two persons who alone could shed light on the authorship of the 'Rising Sun' postcard.

The 'Rising Sun' after the murder became the rendezvous of morbid sightseers, as well as a place of increased interest to its old habitués, among whom were many ladies who had been friendly with Phyllis Dimmock. The police pursued their inquiries and elicited some interesting facts concerning the male friends of Phyllis Dimmock. The wife of a printer, a Mrs Emily Lawrence, whose friendship with Phyllis was so intimate as to extend as far back as 1899, described a young man whom she had often seen with Dimmock. She had occasionally seen them together in the 'Pindar of Wakefield', a public-house in Gray's Inn Road, and, a few nights before the murder, she had seen them together in the bar of the 'Rising Sun'. On Monday night 9 September Mrs Lawrence called at the 'Rising Sun' along with a friend, Mrs Smith. This young man was in the bar, and after he had inquired of them if they had seen Phyllis, he invited the two ladies to have a drink. Mrs Smith said to him, jocularly, 'Don't tell Phyllis we have had a drink with you or she will be jealous.' In a little while Phyllis came in, and the young man sat down with her. Eventually they left together, and the girl announced that they were going to the Holborn Empire. But Phyllis looked very nervous and confided to Mrs Lawrence that she did not like him at all. Later in the course of the evening the four met again in the bar, slightly before midnight. The girl said that they had not been to the variety show at all, but had spent the night in another public-house, the 'Adam and Eve'.

This information was very significant, for the police had been interviewing persons who had seen this strange young man in Phyllis Dimmock's company on the three nights immediately preceding the murder. Many witnesses came forward and, as in each case their accounts tallied, the authorities were able to circulate the following description of the mysterious companion: 'About 30 years of age. 5 feet 8 inches in height. Has a long thin blotchy face and sunken eyes. He was wearing a blue serge suit, a bowler hat with a somewhat high crown, a double collar, and a dark tie. He is a man of good education and of shabby-genteel appearance.'

They were also able to incorporate an important mark of identification into that description, for a carman named Mac-Cowan came forward with a most remarkable story which, if true, would inevitably lead to an arrest. MacCowan, who lived in Chalk Farm, was out of work early in September, and he was in the habit of setting out early in the morning in search of employment. He used to wait for a friend of his, a man named Coleman, who was also out of work, and together they would set out on their quest. On the morning of the murder, at about twenty minutes to 5, he left his house in Hawley Street and walked in the direction of Brewery Road. To get there he had to pass through St Paul's Road, and he arrived there about twelve minutes to 5. As he was passing down the road he heard footsteps behind him. Turning round, he saw a man leaving the gate of No. 29. He watched the man go down the road in the opposite direction from Brewery Road. Although MacCowan did not actually see the man's face, he noticed that he wore a dark overcoat, with the collar turned up, and a hard bowler hat. What particularly attracted his attention, however, was a peculiarity in the man's walk. There was a pronounced jerk of his shoulders as he moved. He carried his left hand in his pocket, and he was a stiff-built man of 5 feet 7 inches or 8 inches.

Of course, the police had kept in sight the fact that a prostitute's calling brings her into the company of many strange men, but what impressed them in the conduct of their investigations was that, although many of her male friends had been interviewed and had succeeded in proving to the police that they were not concerned in the murder, a number of persons, most of them habitués of the 'Rising Sun' inn, came forward and supplied a description of this man with the sunken eyes and the shabby-genteel appearance. The press day by day continued to supply the public with titbits about the Camden Town Murder; but, in spite of the optimistic assurances of several daily papers that an arrest was imminent, there was no concealing the fact that Scotland Yard were marking time. They possessed the description of their man, sufficiently circumstantial and precise in detail, but, among the thousands of people in London who were daily meeting with the suspect, there was no one so far who could supply information as to his whereabouts. And they could do little but continue to ask for the writer of the 'Rising Sun' postcard.

We must not, however, lose sight of Ruby Young, the artist's model, who plays an important rôle in this drama of Camden Town. For almost three years she had been on intimate terms with her artist friend Robert Wood, there being something in the nature of an irregular union between them.

Robert Wood was an artistic designer, who had risen from a very subordinate position in his firm to a responsible post. He was able to augment his salary with freelance cartoon drawing for the press, and seems to have had plenty of money. His father was an elderly Scot who had been a compositor for twenty-five years on the staff of the Edinburgh *Scotsman*. Shortly after the birth of their son Robert his wife died, and Wood went to London, where, with his large family of twenty, he settled in the St Pancras district. The father's employment in London with Messrs Eyre & Spottiswoode was excellent and secure, so he married again.

Robert was thus brought up in London. He went to the Thanet Church School, St. Pancras, where he proved a clever and sociable boy, winning a number of school prizes. He attracted the favourable notice of a Dr Kent Hughes, then a house surgeon at St Bartholomew's Hospital and a friend of Wood's schoolmaster. When the boy was old enough to leave school, the physician secured a situation for him as an assistant steward at the Australian Medical Students' Club in Chancery Lane. Here the youngster showed considerable aptitude in sketching and reproducing illustrations from medical and surgical textbooks. In fact, so great was his skill, that he was frequently called upon by the students and medicos who frequented the club to draw diagrams and illustrations for them. Ultimately the club was disbanded owing to serious bank failures in Australia caused by improvident financial speculations. The number of Colonial students coming to London was suddenly restricted almost to *nil*, and among those who were in this country, many were compelled to return to Australia owing to serious losses.

In consequence Robert Wood was dismissed from his post at the club, and, in response to an advertisement, applied for a vacancy in the sand-glass works of Messrs J. R. Carson, a fairly large firm employing a hundred men, whose premises were then at 58A Gray's Inn Road, London. His work here consisted of designing figures and decorative patterns suitable for fancy glassware. In fourteen years he had risen from a humble position to that of one of the leading employees in the firm. He was of an exceptionally amiable disposition, kind and courteous to all who worked with him, and he won for himself a place in the affections of all, both his employers and his fellow-workmen having the highest regard for him. There was no doubt about his cleverness in drawing. Some two years before William Morris died, he had chanced to come across some of the young man's designs, and had been greatly impressed by their originality and the strong promise for the future of which they gave indication. Morris was introduced to Wood, and encouraged him to continue his creative work, giving him certain technical advice on decorative matters.

It may have been that he had too much money to spend, or that his tastes ran in a peculiar direction, but his relations with Ruby Young were of a very questionable nature. They had been for two years extremely intimate, and improper relations had habitually occurred between them. And although Wood was aware that his sweetheart was sometimes following the calling of a prostitute in the West End of

London, he did not apparently consider this fact of sufficient importance to warrant a break in their relations. They did eventually separate, but for a reason unconnected with Ruby Young's profession.

Ruby Young lived with her mother, and when the latter removed from Liverpool Street, near King's Cross, to Earl's Court, it can only be supposed that Robert Wood found the distance from St Pancras rather trying. Hitherto, one of the most charming aspects of his relations with Ruby Young had been that she lived so near to his home – only a stone's throw away. At any rate, as months went by, Robert Wood's ardour began noticeably to cool. Where formerly he had met her at least twice during the week, and had spent the greater part of the week-end with her, he now found it difficult to meet her even once in a fortnight.

At the end of July 1907 there was a definite rupture, the cause being jealousy. For some time Ruby had caught stray wisps of gossip indicating that her young man's attentions were not wholly confined to herself, and one day she chanced to meet him with a female companion. There was, of course, a quarrel, and the two did not see each other again until August, when they met by chance in the street. Wood had been holidaying in Belgium – it was his custom to take his vacation abroad – and he had much to tell her. They talked for half an hour or so. What precisely happened at that meeting we do not know. But certainly no arrangements were made to renew their former relations. Apparently they were now little more than casual acquaintances, meeting only when chance should happen to bring about the encounter, and confining their conversation to superficial small talk.

Ruby Young did not see Wood again that month. But on Friday 20 September, a week after the discovery of the murder in Camden Town, she received a telegram from him in these words: 'Meet me at Phit-Eesi's to-night 6.30. – Bob.' Phit-Eesi's was a bootshop in Southampton Row, and in the old days of their intimacy they had frequently met there. Expectant and rather intrigued by the unexpected summons,

Ruby Young went to their old meeting-place at the appointed hour. When she arrived at Phit-Eesi's, Wood was waiting. He had scarcely exchanged the usual polite greetings when he burst out, 'Ruby, I want you to help me. If any questions are ever asked you by any one, will you say that you always saw me on *Monday* and *Wednesday* nights?'

This was a strange request to make of a discarded sweetheart, and Wood's obvious anxiety aroused her curiosity. She asked for a reason, but he evaded the question. Ultimately, after a fruitless effort to try and extract the reason for this unusual request, and following upon much coaxing and persuasion, the girl agreed to his suggestion. They went to a teashop and had a little refreshment, during which the artist urged on Ruby the absolute necessity of saying, if ever she should be approached by anyone, that he always spent Monday and Wednesday nights in her company. When she had finally consented and her curiosity was to some extent assuaged, they left the restaurant. Wood explained that he had to see a Mr Lambert, a friend of his employed as an assistant in a bookseller's shop close by, and they parted at the Underground Station in Leicester Square.

If Ruby Young had possessed the novelist's omniscience and could have played the part of an eavesdropper, her curiosity would have been provoked even more than it was. For when Wood left her he immediately went back to No. 106 Charing Cross Road, where he saw his friend, Mr Lambert, a bookseller's assistant. Wood's first remark was: 'I have seen Mr Moss, the head man at the works, and he has been talking about the Camden Town murder. If Mr Moss says anything to you, will you tell him that we met and had a drink, but leave the girl out?' Lambert's mind carried him back to the night of 11 September, which was the Wednesday immediately preceding the murder of Phyllis Dimmock. On that night, shortly after 9, Lambert had been in the bar of the 'Eagle', a tavern situated opposite the Camden Town Station. He was rather surprised to see there his friend Robert Wood, alone with a young lady, whose rather untidy appearance impinged itself on his memory. He noticed that she was still wearing Hinde curling-pins in her hair, and the girl, in some confusion, seeing that Lambert had observed her head-gear, proffered an apology, saying, 'Hope you will excuse my dress as I have just run out.' When Lambert asked Wood what brought him there, the latter's non-committal reply was that he had business to attend to. The bookseller remembered that when he left the bar of the 'Eagle' that same night, the girl and Wood, whose business, whatever it was, did not seem to be of a pressing nature, remained behind. He had not noticed the features particularly, and although some sort of formal introduction passed between them he had not regis-tered a mental note of her name at the time. But he realized now that this must have been the girl who was murdered. No wonder the young artist, whose family was so strait-laced in many respects, wished to avoid all connexion with the case. 'I tell you', Wood insisted, 'that I can clear myself, only I don't want it to come to my father's ears. He is an old man and in poor health.' Lambert agreed to keep silent, and there-upon dismissed the matter from his mind.

As Ruby Young did not overhear the dialogue between Wood and Lambert, she also gave the matter no further con-sideration. The week-end passed with nothing particular to distinguish it. While no further developments were recorded in the press, rumours were circulating freely, and were ac-corded the fullest publicity. An old man who had committed suicide in the Tottenham Marshes was said to have been a bearded individual whose frequent visits to Dimmock had aroused the suspicions of one of her many landladies. This gentleman, who was passed off as 'Uncle', had a generous habit of leaving the girl a sovereign after each visit. This was the man, it was conjectured, who had murdered Emily Dim-mock, and who had then taken his own life in a fit of remorse. There was no more truth in this catchpenny solution of the mystery than in any of the other 'alleged confessions' and 'hourly arrests' so assiduously discovered by the battalions of diligent reporters and special investigators who swarmed round Camden Town and New Scotland Yard.

On Monday morning Ruby Young received a postcard

from Wood, which contained the following message: 'Sweetheart, – If it is convenient for you, will you meet me as before at Phit-Eesi's, 6.30, and we will have tea together and then go to the theatre, which I hope will be a little ray of sunshine in your life – Good-bye.' They went to the Prince of Wales Theatre. When they came out, and were separating to catch their respective homeward vehicles, Wood suddenly said to her: 'Don't forget now. Mondays and Wednesdays.' She did not see him again until he called at her house on the following Sunday, which was 29 September, the day on which the Sunday newspapers were flooding the country with the facsimile reproductions of the 'Rising Sun' postcard. It was to be seen on every hoarding and each newsboy carried enlarged copies of the card.

We have already seen how Ruby Young first came to know that Wood had previously become entangled in the Camden Town affair. When she heard the story of Wood's encounter in the 'Rising Sun', she divined the reason for his telegram and his strange requests; she realized then that she was being asked to assist in concocting a false alibi. There was something about this which rather stuck in Ruby Young's throat. She suggested to Wood that he ought to go to the police, but he said: 'I cannot prove where I was on the Wednesday night, that's why I can't go to them. On the Tuesday night I was with my brother Charles the whole of the evening, but on the Wednesday I was out alone, walking, and no one was with me who could speak for me.' There was considerable discussion between them, and once again Wood asked the girl to stick to the story about Monday and Wednesday nights. After a while, not without misgivings, she gave way to his pleading. They put their heads together and formed their plan of campaign. The girl said: 'The best thing for me to do is to say that I met you at 6.30 at Phit-Eesi's, and we had tea at Lyons' Café, and then after tea we went down Kingsway to the Strand and straight on to Hyde Park Corner. Then we'd better say we walked along the park straight out to Brompton Oratory, and got there at half-past 10. We will say that we parted there: you went back by tube to King's Cross and got back home just before midnight.' Wood thought this story was excellent. When he left that night, she travelled with him in the tube as far as Piccadilly Circus. In the train she confided to him that she was again feeling nervous about the story she was to tell, because it had now occurred to her that others might have seen her elsewhere on the Wednesday night. 'If my name gets into the newspapers,' she said finally, 'it will hurt my mother.' Wood assured her and once more she was mollified.

On the Tuesday following, at lunch-time, as she was passing through Museum Street, where Wood's elder brother Charles lived, she met Robert. He reminded her of her promise. The next day she saw him again, and once more he referred her to the arrangement. His insistence was now beginning to annoy her, and she replied tartly, 'Yes, I'll be true! Don't bother me! It's getting on my nerves.'

So Ruby Young was a woman entrusted with a secret; and, although she did not contemplate for a moment betraying Wood's trust, most of the pleasure in a secret for her, like many other women, was the illicit pleasure to be derived from its partial exposure to a confidential friend – not to be repeated, of course. That was exactly what Ruby Young did. Some days later she breathed a word of Wood's dilemma to a friend. That friend mentioned it, in confidence, to a journalist on the staff of the *Weekly Dispatch*. It was manna from heaven to him, and he immediately got into touch with Ruby Young. No doubt the pressman besprinkled his conversation with vague references to accessories after the act, and principals in the second degree, for, on 4 October, Inspector Neil, who was in charge of the inquiries into the case, received a message by telephone. The upshot of this was that he went to the Piccadilly Tube Station and saw outside the artist's model, Ruby Young. What she told him supplied the missing link in the police chain.

At 6.30 on the evening of 4 October, as Wood was leaving the premises of the London Sand Blast Glass Works in Gray's Inn Road, he was met by Ruby Young, who shook hands with him. As she did so, Inspector Neil approached them, made himself known to Wood, and asked him to step into a waiting cab. Before they drove off Wood said to Young: 'I have to go with this gentleman. If England wants me, she must have me. Don't cry, but be true!'

The destination of the cab was the police station at Highgate, and on the way Wood stated very emphatically that he had not made any secret about the postcard with the sketch of the rising sun. He said, after being cautioned: 'My young brother, or my stepbrother, called my attention to the handwriting of the postcard when it came out in the Sunday paper. I told them it was *like* my handwriting, but I knew at the same time that I wrote the card, and the same night I had a chat with my brother Charles, a conscientious sort of chap who lives at Museum Street, and his wife, Bessie. I was advised to go to Scotland Yard. But about that time I was very busy at the office with the work of the chief, who was away on holiday at the time. My brother then said that the next best thing to do was to write a letter, addressed to one of us, care of the poste restante at the G.P.O. We sent the letter, addressed to Charles, and it stated that I acknowledged writing the postcard, and giving my reasons for not coming forward. Now I want you to get that letter, inspector, because it shows that I did not conceal the matter.' Neil took a note of the address. It was: 'Charles Carlyle Wood, Poste Restante, St. Martin's le Grand.' Wood then went on to give an account of his relations with the dead woman, and this account was precisely the same story that he had already told Ruby Young. But he made one vital mistake. Not knowing that Ruby Young had been questioned, he thus explained his movements on the night of Wednesday 11 September: 'On Wednesday I left work about 6.20, and went straight home, and afterwards walked up to Holborn with my sweetheart, Ruby Young, who had called for me. We had tea in Lyons, remaining there until about 8 or 8.30 p.m. After strolling about the West End I bade her good-night at Brompton Oratory and returned by tube to Holborn. I then walked home from there, and arrived, as near as I can say, about midnight.'

Wood was detained at the police station, and on 5 October

he was put up for an identification parade and identified by a number of persons, whose statements contradicted in several material essentials the statement made by Wood to Inspector Neil. He was identified as having been in the 'Eagle' tavern on the Wednesday night, and several women said that they knew Wood to have been acquainted with Dimmock for fifteen months before September 1907. Ruby Young also told the police about Wood's anxiety over the Mondays and Wednesdays matter; and they also became aware that he had attempted to close the mouths of Lambert and the works foreman. As a result, on 6 October he was formally charged with the murder.

From the police point of view the identification parade on 7 October clinched the matter. They had in attendance MacCowan – he who had told them about seeing a man leaving a house in St Paul's Road shortly before 5 o'clock on the morning of the tragedy. A number of men were assembled. MacCowan could not identify any one of them. Then a police official gave the order 'March', and MacCowan immediately noticed that one of the men in the parade had the same peculiar twitching of his shoulders as the man he saw emerging from the gateway. He identified Wood by his walk, without hesitation.

The inquest had commenced on 30 September before Dr Danford Thomas, the coroner for Central London, at St Pancras Coroner's Court. On 7 October Wood was brought before the magistrate at Clerkenwell Police Court, and charged with the murder. An application for bail at £2000, put forward by his solicitor, Mr Arthur Newton, was objected to by the police, and refused by the magistrate. The verdict of the coroner's jury on 28 October was circumspect in wording. It was: 'We find that the deceased Emily Elizabeth Dimmock met her death by wilful murder, and that the evidence we have received is sufficient to commit the accused for trial.' Meanwhile, at the Police Court, the magisterial proceedings had been going on. The police knew that a conviction was going to be difficult to secure and, accordingly, after the first formal charge and evidence of arrest, the proceedings were directed by the Senior Counsel of the Treasury, Sir Charles Mathews. In spite of the clever defence of the accused's astute solicitor, and the indication of an alibi, Wood was sent forward for trial.

The accused's employers immediately put a sum of £1000 at the disposal of the defending solicitor in order to brief counsel. Thus he was in a position to secure such leaders as he chose without regard to expense. The trial ought to have come before the November Sessions, but, as the Police Court proceedings had not then terminated, an application to postpone the trial was made on 20 November by Mr Huntly Jenkins before Mr Justice Ridley, who granted the extension of time craved for, and the trial was accordingly fixed for the December assize.

2

On December 1907 the Grand Jury, charged by Sir Forrest Fulton, K.C., had before them the depositions in the case of *Rex* v. *Wood*, and having considered them they returned a true bill against the prisoner. The trial commenced on 12 December at the Old Bailey, in the new building, which had been opened by King Edward in the preceding January.

The proceedings aroused unprecedented interest. The long delay before any arrest had been made, the 'gay' life of the murdered woman, the mystery surrounding the case, as well as the romantic interests involved and the apparent betrayal of a lover by his mistress – all these features combined to render the trial of overpowering interest for many people. On the opening day the Court-room was thronged. All the available space was occupied. Many famous novelists, dramatists, and society leaders were present. Prominent in the gangways reserved for distinguished visitors were such celebrities as G. R. Sims, H. B. Irving, A. E. W. Mason, Bart Kennedy, Sir George Alexander, Sir A. W. Pinero, Oscar Asche, Seymour Hicks, Mr Willard, and G. B. Huntley. At the solicitors' table, along with Mr Arthur Newton and the prisoner's elder brother, Charles, sat Sir Hall Caine, then fresh from his triumphs in the theatre. The trial opened before Mr Justice

Grantham, and it was a common sight during the conduct of the proceedings to see judges like Sir Albert Bosanquet and Judge Rentoul sitting on the Bench with the presiding judge. Counsel for the Crown were Sir Charles W. Mathews, Senior Counsel to the Treasury, Mr (later Sir) A. H. Bodkin, and Mr I. A. Symmons; for the defence, Mr (later Sir) Edward Marshall Hall, K.C., led Mr Herman Cohen, Mr Huntly E. Jenkins, and Mr J. R. Lort-Williams.

An unusual incident occurred at the opening of the trial, Sir Edward Marshall Hall challenging two jurors, named Arnold and Reid. Both were compelled to leave the box, and as the challenges were peremptory, the leader for the defence was not bound to explain his objection to the gentlemen whom he challenged. (It is to be hoped that Sir Edward was not merely following the time-honoured principle of the Irish barrister who explained to a delighted judge that he challenged any juryman who looked at all intelligent!)

The opening speech for the Crown was temperate, yet very closely reasoned. Sir Charles, in a voice that has been described as exceedingly grating and unpleasant to listen to for a number of hours consecutively, outlined the case against the accused; he stressed the fact that Wood had attempted to suborn a number of possible witnesses, and in many ways had tried to tamper with potential evidence, and stop evidence reaching the police through normal channels. Sir Charles put the character of the accused very fairly before the jury. He told them that Wood undoubtedly possessed a most excellent character and that he had served one firm, the London Sand Blast and Glass Company, for an uninterrupted period of fourteen years, during which time there had never been the slightest complaint made against him, either in his capacity as workman or in any moral way. But he submitted that, although he was to his fellow-workmen, as well as to his family at Frederick Street, a model worker of an affectionate disposition, he was really living a double life and his spare time was spent in a very different fashion. Sir Charles also pointed out that it was an essential part of the structure of the Crown case that Wood had known Dimmock long before the day mentioned by him in his statement to Inspector Neil. He then elaborated the account already given of the request made by Wood to Ruby Young asking her to swear that on the nights of Monday and Wednesday he was always in her company. The Crown relied on this attempt to suborn witnesses and concoct a false alibi as a clear indication of guilt on Wood's part. Vital importance was attached to the similarity of handwriting between the decipherable remains of the charred fragments and the 'Rising Sun' postcard, which was admittedly in the handwriting of the accused. Clearly, if the jury were satisfied that the handwriting of the charred fragments was the identical handwriting of the postcard, then the letter received by Dimmock, and read by the ship's cook, Roberts, who had stayed there for two consecutive nights before the murder, must be in the handwriting of the accused. If so, it showed that he had made an appointment with her to meet him at the 'Eagle' tavern on the night of the murder.

The Crown attached great weight to the fact that Dimmock was not dressed on the Wednesday night as she would have been, smartly and attractively, if she had been going out to pick up a man from the streets that evening. She had her curling-pins in her hair. They were found still in her hair when the alarm was raised next morning, and were observed by three independent witnesses: (1) By the landlady, Mrs Stocks, who saw Dimmock with her hair in curling-pins at 7 o'clock on the Wednesday evening just before she heard the front door slam; (2) by a barmaid in the 'Eagle', who recognized Dimmock as being in the bar on the Wednesday night, and overheard her say to one of her male companions, 'Excuse me for being so untidy'; and (3) by the bookseller, Lambert, who had seen Dimmock and Wood together in the 'Eagle', and who remembered that the girl made an apology for her apparent untidiness, saying something about having come out in a hurry. The inference to be drawn from these facts, according to the Crown, was that Wood, intending to murder Dimmock either late on Wednesday night or early on Thursday morning, sent her a letter making an appointment for a public-house where he thought he would not be known. As it chanced, however, he was observed. The hair-curlers pointed to the fact that the girl, having fixed an appointment for that night, did not trouble to dress up as she would have done had she been going out to attract a casual man.

The other important evidence in the Crown case was that of MacCowan, whose evidence and identification, if accepted, showed that Wood was in the neighbourhood of St Paul's Road at a time when, according to medical evidence, the murder had just been committed. Sir Charles Mathews strongly impressed upon the jury that the identification was excellent because it was a peculiarity of walk that had been described to the police long before any of the descriptions appeared in the newspapers, and because the witness unhesitatingly picked Wood out from a number of men merely by his walk and without reference to any facial characteristics. Moreover, his reference to the peculiarity in the accused's walk was corroborated by Ruby Young, who said that there was undoubtedly a peculiar feature in his walk, and agreed with MacCowan's description of it as a 'jerking or nervous twitching of the shoulder forward when walking.'

The state of the apartment on the morning when the discovery was made, in the belief of the Crown, pointed to certain obvious inferences which pressed onerously against the accused. The half-opened shutters of the venetian blind had been opened by the murderer in order to obtain a light sufficiently strong to enable him to search through the postcard album. What would there be in a postcard album that made it necessary to make so thorough a search at a time when every additional minute that the murderer stayed in the house was drawing nearer to the hour of possible detection? Clearly there was in that album something which, if left behind, was a valuable clue to the identity of the murderer. Wood had admittedly written a postcard, and the subterfuges he had subsequently resorted to in order to avoid his being known as the writer of it proved conclusively, in their opinion, that he realized what a dangerous clue it was. With regard to the missing articles, they had obviously been taken in order to simulate the appearance of a robbery and start the police on a false track. But robbery as a plausible motive could be discounted at the outset, for otherwise why should a thief leave behind him what were probably the most valuable of all Dimmock's possessions – the gold rings? In addition, the futile efforts made by the accused to suborn Ruby Young, the bookseller, Lambert, and others showed that he had something to conceal. The presumption raised by this conduct was that Wood was guilty of the crime of murder.

Any suspicion that might seem to fall on either Shaw or Roberts could be dispelled, as both men could prove beyond dispute where they were at the time of the murder. A suggestion had been made at the Police Court by Mr Arthur Newton, the solicitor for the defence, that the man responsible for the murder might be an associate of Dimmock known as 'Scotch Bob', who had been known to utter threats against the murdered woman. Sir Charles Mathews had caused exhaustive inquiries to be made, and, if required, he was prepared to put into the box this man, 'Scotch Bob', who could prove that at the time of the murder he was employed in a hotel in Scotland. There was a further point stressed by Sir Charles before he concluded his speech. Wood had always maintained the attitude that he knew nothing whatever about the crime; but a warder who had charge of him while in prison heard him say, after one of the identification parades, 'If it comes to a crisis, I shall have to open out.'

The plans prepared and produced by Sergeant Grosse were called in question by Marshall Hall, in cross-examination, his point being that the power of the lights that shone in the vicinity of 29 St Paul's Road had been tampered with to such an extent as to suggest that it was a brilliantly lit locality, when in fact it was very badly lighted. The whole of his cross-examination of this witness was directed towards laying a foundation for his subsequent cross-examination of Mac-Cowan, who was the most damaging of all the Crown witnesses. Marshall Hall wished to show that, apart from the lights supplied by the local electricity company, there was no available light power in the neighbourhood; and that, as the street lights had been turned off at a time before MacCowan left the house, and as according to the evidence of MacCowan himself it was a morning of drizzling rain, it necessarily followed that the opportunities for intelligent and reliable identification were so small as to be practically negligible. It was Marshall Hall's determined and consistent attitude all through the trial that the case for the Crown was manufactured and bolstered up by rotten evidence, a glaring example, in his opinion, of what happens when 'vaulting ambition o'erleaps itself'.

His success with the first official police representative was a splendid augury. The officer was compelled to admit that the plan which was prepared by him gave the impression that St Paul's Road was in the full glare of a powerful row of lights coming from a railway siding, when in fact there was a fairly continuous row of houses in between. This row of houses was not shown clearly on the map. Thus anyone who looked at it would conclude, in the absence of any explanation to the contrary, that the side of St Paul's Road on which No. 29 was situated was lit up by a brilliant ray of light. Again, at the railway bridge, from which the light was said to come, a wall at least 9 feet high, which would prevent much light from escaping, was not marked on the plan. Marshall Hall did not hesitate to press the point home:

'Q. You know it was a dark, muggy morning. If the electric standards were extinguished at that time (4.37), they would be useless for the purpose of light at five to five? – A. Yes. Q. Is it not the case that, this being so, you have been specially asked to prepare a map that would show, as your evidence suggests, a sufficiency of light coming from the railway forty feet below the road?' It is not surprising that no immediate answer was returned to that question.

It is of interest to notice that, although Marshall Hall often cross-examined Crown witnesses like Shaw and Roberts on their moral credit, with disastrous effect, the leading counsel for the defence did not try to bring home the guilt of the crime to any one. He was too shrewd an advocate to prejudice his client's case in that bungling fashion. If an accused sets up a defence that he is not guilty, but that either X, Y, or Z could be, he puts himself in a very perilous position, for, if he fails to prove the guilt of X, Y, or Z, the jury are apt to conclude that this very failure by itself is a proof of the accused's own guilt. Apart from the extreme technical difficulty involved when a defending counsel has to defend his own client with one hand and, with the other, prosecute some other individual (without the resources of the Crown), there can be no doubt that such a dual defence, if it fails, rebounds on the head of its author. An interesting example of the converse process occurred at the Old Bailey trial of 'Scotty' Mason, who was convicted in May 1923 of the murder of Jacob Dickey, a taxi-driver. In that case the Crown counsel, Sir Richard Muir, had to sustain the dual rôle of prosecuting the accused and defending his chief witness, Vivian, whom the defence accused of actually committing the murder. Although Sir Richard was successful in his onerous task, and the accused was convicted, the element of doubt that entered into the case resulted in the reprieve of Mason. Marshall Hall did not attempt to postulate: 'Wood cannot be guilty, because X or Y or Z is the guilty party, as I will now proceed to demonstrate to you.' He merely said: 'The facts which the Crown have brought forward are insufficient to enable you to condemn any one.'

Marshall Hall's questions often appeared on the surface to suggest that X or Y might have committed the crime. In reality, they were directed not to that end, but merely to show that things looked so black against X or Y that either, as a precautionary measure of self-protection, might well be prepared to take the opportunity of casting suspicion on someone else. Taken in this light, the cross-examination of the ship's cook, Roberts, was an inspired masterpiece of subtle forensic legerdemain. The damning feature of this witness's evidence was patently his identification of the handwriting on the charred fragments. According to Roberts, these charred fragments were the ashen remains of a letter which was received by Dimmock, who exhibited it to him, and which contained a specific assignation to meet the writer within the 'Eagle' bar, opposite Camden Town Station, on the Wednesday evening. This was very inculpatory evidence if once accepted by the jury. The cross-examination, therefore, was at first directed towards ascertaining Roberts's whereabouts on the night of the crime. Roberts was forced to admit that things looked very black against him – so black, in fact, that he would inferentially clutch any straw that would help him out of his danger. The rest was deceptively easy: a suggestion was put to Roberts that his identification of Wood had been obtained from a description supplied to him by a witness in the case, and was not a spontaneous identification, followed up by a suggestion that there had never been a letter of assignation at all but that it was a figment of his imagination invented in order to plant a false clue. Two curious facts came out in cross-examination: (1) The letter was signed 'Bert', and the accused always signed letters 'Bob'; (2) the letter, according to Roberts, contained a message that was so brief that it would easily go on one page. Yet the charred remains prove conclusively that, whatever they were originally, there was writing on the four sides of the two leaves. Moreover, the writer was so cramped for space that he had to crush some of the words upside down into one of the corners.

It would be difficult to find a better illustration of a dangerous witness being disarmed by an adroit cross-examiner; it was a splendid example of the most polished technique of skilful cross-examination. This cross-examination was obviously piercing the armour of the Crown, for on the second day two witnesses were introduced to speak to Roberts's movements on the night of the murder. Strategically, this was an error, for in his closing speech Marshall Hall neatly turned the tables on this testimony by stigmatizing the Crown case as proving X to be guilty simply on the inference that A, B, C, and D had alibis that were satisfactory to the police, whereas X's alibi was not!

MacCowan's evidence had already been severely shaken at the magisterial proceedings by Mr Newton. At the Old Bailey, Marshall Hall drew out the following vitally significant points: (1) That the street lights were turned off at 4.37

and that as MacCowan did not, on his own admission, leave his house that morning until 4.40, the lights could not have been on. Therefore the opportunities for observation must have been very few, especially as, according to the witness, it was a thick, drizzly morning; (2) the witness spoke of the morning as drizzly, but the weather records showed that the week of 7 September was the hottest of that year, and that no rain fell on either the day preceding the murder or on the day of the murder itself. Therefore, the witness's powers of recollection were demonstrably at fault; (3) the witness admitted that he had not seen the man with the peculiar walk coming down the steps of the house in St. Paul's Road. He had seen him on the road. Therefore it did not of a certainty follow that the person he saw had in fact emerged from No. 29. He might have been a casual passer-by.

The testimony of Inspector Neil was not much shaken, but, on the other hand, it was of an administrative nature and added little to the quota of substantial evidence at the disposal of the Crown.

Ruby Young's evidence was mainly connected with the attempts of Wood to concoct the false alibi. The manner in which Marshall Hall elegantly disposed of this point is instructive: 'With regard to that arrangement, have you ever thought that, having regard to the evidence of Dr Thompson, who places the time of the murder at 3 or 4 in the morning, the alibi Wood arranged with you from 6.30 to 10.30 on the evening previous to the murder, would be a useless alibi for the murder, but a perfect one for the meeting of the girl?' The witness confessed that, although it did not strike her in that light at the time, she saw the possibility of such an explanation when it was put to her.

A group of witnesses, including Mrs Lawrence, Mrs Smith, Gladys Warren, and a man named Crabtree, were called with the object of showing that Dimmock and Wood were intimate for months before the night of 6 September, which Wood adhered to as the date of his first meeting with Dimmock. It was on the evidence of these witnesses that the case against Wood really revolved, and as their testimony requires particular study, it will be better to deal separately with it later.

Towards the end of the fourth day the case for the prosecution was closed by the calling of their last witness, the mysterious 'Scotch Bob', who proved his alibi beyond dispute. After a fruitless appeal by Marshall Hall to the judge to decide that there was no case to go to the jury, the leading counsel for the defence outlined his reply and indicated the nature of his defence. The mainstay of that defence was an alibi spoken to by the accused, and corroborated by a number of other witnesses, whose testimony was, in counsel's submission, not only credible, but incontrovertible. He hinted that the murder could only be the work of a maniac, a sadist such as used to prowl in the night haunts of Whitechapel a few years before. He relied on the excellent character borne by the accused to rebut the suggestion of any sexual mania.

There was no credible motive for Wood having committed the crime. None of the missing articles had ever been traced to him, and there was no sign of a weapon in his home at Frederick Street. The only factors that could possibly implicate Wood as a possible criminal were: (1) The charred remains alleged by the Crown to be a letter of assignation; (2) the identification of Wood by MacCowan as the man he had seen in St Paul's Road on the morning of the murder; (3) the attempts to suborn Lambert and Tinkham, the foreman at the glass-works; (4) the untruthful statement made to the police; and (5) the concocted alibi. Factors (3), (4), and (5) all bore a single construction susceptible of an innocent explanation. They were attempts made to conceal the fact of the accused's low relations with depraved persons. Being a young man, held in high esteem, he had in a sense been occasionally indulging in a double life. To his fellow-workmen and his family he appeared an upright and honourable young man leading a model life; the other side of the picture was that he had had intimate relations with Ruby Young and had met one or two undesirable women whom he would have been ashamed to acknowledge knowing to his father and colleagues. All that the so-called subornation of Lambert amounted to was a request to 'leave the girl out of it'. The alibi with Ruby Young was clearly useless if it was intended as an alibi to cover the time of the commission of the murder: it was only an alibi to get him out of a meeting on the Wednesday night with Dimmock. With regard to the false statement to the police, when he made that statement, he thought that it would clear him of the low association. Undoubtedly it was deception; but it was not the cunning deception of a callous, maniacal murderer. Marshall Hall maintained that it was the transparent duplicity of a young man of overweening vanity who was truly ashamed of his lapse from the virtuous path, and wished to conceal his association with an unfortunate of Dimmock's class.

The charred fragments were undoubtedly in Wood's handwriting. They were not, however, parts of a letter of assignation, but merely sketches and little notes drawn on scrap paper for his own amusement, which Dimmock by some means had secured. The letter relied on by the Crown was invented by Roberts to divert suspicion from himself – perhaps on to young Shaw. The signature 'Bert' was significant; if Wood had written the letter he would have signed 'Bob'. Factor (1) could be disposed of in this fashion.

The identification by MacCowan, factor (2), was in Marshall Hall's view 'the flimsiest and most unsatisfactory evidence of identity ever put before a jury in any Court of justice in the world.' If it were true, it turned solely on a peculiarity of walk described in circumstantial detail. Counsel was prepared to call sixty-five fellow-employees of Wood who would deny that there was the slightest peculiarity in Wood's walk. He did not suggest that MacCowan was lying. On the contrary, he agreed that MacCowan had seen a man, but that man was not even remotely connected with the murder. He was a railwayman, named Westcott, going to work. Westcott would be called, and the jury would see for themselves that he was a broad-shouldered young athlete, an amateur boxer, who walked with a noticeable swing.

Admittedly Wood had been on terms of intimate relationship with Ruby Young. He swore that he had not been immoral with Dimmock; but even the most casual association with a prostitute like Dimmock was disgusting in the eyes of good-living people like his father and brothers. So he had lied, more for their sake than for his own. He had been immoral and he had told a few lies, yet that was a long way from proving that he was necessarily a murderer on that account. The most that the lies could suggest was vague suspicion – and the jury were not entitled to convict on suspicion.

It was a splendid defence, the production of a marvellous forensic technique, and in architectonic structure Marshall Hall himself never improved on it. There was not a question that had not its appropriate answer, not a doubt but had its resolution on a perfect cadence.

When, towards the end of Mr Justice Grantham's summing-up, the learned judge gave his own view of the case for the prosecution: 'In my judgement, strong as the suspicion in this case undoubtedly is, I do not think that the prosecution has brought the case home near enough to the accused,' his charge was interrupted for several minutes by a storm of applause which burst forth from spectators in the Court, in spite of the stentorian rebukes of uniformed ushers. This was, of course, repeated when the jury brought in their not guilty verdict, and after the trial, when Robert Wood left the dock, there occurred such a 'scene' as has rarely, if ever, been paralleled in the records of our assizes. The Court sat until late in the evening of the final day and the verdict of the jury was not announced until close on 8 o'clock. Crowds thronged Newgate Street, and the streets in the vicinity of the Court were impassable: traffic was brought to a standstill. All London was waiting for the verdict, in the mean streets of Camden Town and in the palatial residences of Mayfair. Millions were engulfed in a colossal wave of mass hysteria. Theatrical performances were interrupted to announce the verdict when at last it was flashed through the telephone wires. At a West End theatre Mrs Beerbohm Tree (as she then was) rushed breathless on to the stage. 'I have just arrived from the Court,' she gasped, 'the Court where young Robert Wood stood in peril of his life. I am glad to be able to tell you that the jury found him not guilty.' When the cheers died away, she continued: 'I am pleased to hear the reception of the tidings I have brought. While the jury were out, we seemed to hold our breath, and we hoped, but we feared perhaps the jury would after all ... I was one of those who burst into tears, others burst into cheers which were taken up, echoed and re-echoed by thousands on the streets ...'

In its cheap sentiment and crude melodrama this farrago of maudlin emotions would be difficult to equal. It reads for all the world like one of the more boisterous pages of Sinclair Lewis or Upton Sinclair pouring astringent satire on some criminal process of Gopher Prairie or Zenith City. After the trial a vast cordon of policemen escorted Wood and his relatives to a near-by restaurant. From the balcony of the teashop the appearance of the bearded figure of Wood's father was the signal for a furore of cheering. At length, amidst the applause the old man was heard to announce: 'I thank the public for their enthusiastic reception of me, and for the kindness which they have shown to me and my family in this very trying case. ...'

After the successful defence Marshall Hall was inundated with showers of letters and telegrams congratulating him on his splendid fight. He himself remarked afterwards: 'It has been a most extraordinary case. I have always been convinced of the innocence of Wood. He is certainly a remarkable young man, and his coolness and courage throughout have been beyond anything I have ever seen. He was actually engaged in sketching the judge during the absence of the jury. His ability, by the way, is wonderful. There was an unfortunate difference of opinion on the last day about the calling of witnesses Sharples and Harvey. Sir Charles Mathews did offer to call although I was not aware of it. I appreciate greatly the courtesy I received from Sir Charles; and the first to congratulate me were Mr Williamson of the Treasury, and Mr Bodkin. The conclusion of the case produced a very remarkable scene. I tried to get to the dock to congratulate Wood, but was unable to reach him on account of the crowd. I heard him several times attempting to thank me, and I received the profound thanks of his father and elder brother.

Every one shook hands all round when the verdict was given. The scene, especially the cheering outside, was more like an election than the end of a criminal trial. I must express my thanks to my juniors and to my solicitor for their great assistance in what has certainly been one of the most remarkable cases in modern times.'

In startling contrast was the attitude of the mob towards Ruby Young, who was generally regarded in the light of their popular hero's temptress. It was well known that, had that infuriated mob outside the Court laid hands on her, they would have killed her without compunction. The authorities managed, however, to get her out of the Court unnoticed. On the suggestion of Sir Herbert Austin she changed into the clothes of a charwoman, and, with two detective sergeants at her side, she escaped to Ludgate Hill, unrecognized by the prowling hordes of hooligans who were lying in wait for her. The majority of ill-informed people seemed to labour under an impression, perfectly erroneous, that Ruby Young had betrayed Wood for the sake of the £100 from the *News of the World*. Ruby Young said afterwards: 'It has come to my ears that I am supposed to have received £100 from the *News of the World* for information concerning the 'Rising Sun' postcard issued on 29 September. I wish to contradict this statement as I have never received a penny from any one. It is against my nature to accept such a kind of reward. Perhaps the rumour arises in this way. My attention was first called to the facsimile of Robert Wood's handwriting in the postcard reproduced in the *News of the World*. On the Sunday it was published I received my copy in the ordinary way, being a regular reader. I was at once struck with the identical handwriting of my boy friend. I also noticed at that time that a reward of £100 was offered. I never thought for the moment of betraying Robert Wood for the sake of that money. On the same day he called on me and, as I have already stated at the trial and before the coroner, at the very time he called, my letter to him enclosing a cutting from the paper was on the table. I drew his attention to the matter. Later on I confided my secret to a friend and became the unhappy witness of his arrest. The stories about my accepting the reward – blood money as it is commonly called – have been most distressing to me.'

What happened to Ruby Young afterwards history does not record. She soon disappeared from the public eye. As for Robert Wood, he remained a nine days' wonder, and then his celebrity dwindled. He found it convenient to change his name, and in the passing of years he was forgotten, the mention of Camden Town, of Emily Dimmock, of Ruby Young awakening no responsive echo in the public ears. The man who had been for a brief moment a public idol soon was nothing more than a vague recollection, arousing only casual and indifferent comment.

Such is the ephemeral fame of a popular hero!

3

Many years have passed, and it is now possible to approach this case with a sense of that dispassionate objectivity which was so noticeably absent at the actual trial. One of the gravest objections that can be urged against the British system of trial by jury is the fact that it is impossible to disentangle from the circumstances of the case the surrounding elements of prejudice which the atmosphere and temper of the epoch necessarily breed. Nothing is more detrimental to the solution of a difficult judicial problem – especially where the solution of that problem depends on the correct statement of isolated facts from which inferences are derived, often trivial and meaningless in themselves, but convincing in cumulation – than the infusion of psychological elements which tend to banish impartiality.

There can be no doubt that at the trial of Robert Wood in 1907 there was a distinct leaning towards the accused; and the friendly attitude of the public eye at large was inevitably communicated to the members of the jury. Thus, in reconsidering this remarkable case after this lapse of time, we are in a position undeniably superior to that of the jury who sat in the Central Criminal Court in 1907. Admittedly we do not have the various witnesses before us to help us to decide the measure of credibility to be attached to their stories; but the lack of oral testimony will be more than compensated for by the avoidance of that unscientific party spirit and rancour which was in such obvious evidence at the trial.

The case for the Crown was purely circumstantial; its web of circumstance was spun with gossamer lightness, so fine as to be almost too weak to bear the structure of a prosecution. The argument was tenuous, it involved a reciprocal process of eliminating several potential murderers by exclusion and exhaustion, and it connected the prisoner with the crime by certain elements – scraps of evidence which, to yield a positive result, demanded the closest correlation. The case against Wood depended on the intersection of the following strands of evidence: (1) That a letter was written by him to Dimmock making an assignation for the Wednesday night at the 'Eagle' public-house; (2) that the charred remains found in the fire-grate at 29 St Paul's Road were fragments of that letter; (3) that Wood was seen by MacCowan emerging from the house after the murder had been committed.

It was desirable also to prove that Wood already knew and was intimate with Dimmock. While it was not imperative to know this – the murderer need not necessarily have known the woman at all – if it could be shown that Wood knew Dimmock before 6 September (the date at which he fixed the beginning of their acquaintance), the effect would be to strengthen the indictment in two vitally important respects. In the first place, it would establish a nexus between Dimmock and Wood, from which a glimmer of motive, whether jealousy or otherwise, might be invoked; and, secondly, it would follow that the accused in his statement to the police was deliberately lying on a material particular. This statement, containing vital untruths, might then be represented as a tissue of calculated lies; and the interpretation would be that the murderer was attempting to cover his traces.

For this purpose the Crown called an elaborate cycle of witnesses, whose testimony was intended to show that Dimmock and the accused were intimate over a period of some eighteen months before the woman died: (1) Gladys Warren is called to prove that she knew of their acquaintance, and she cites specific occasions when she saw the pair together; (2) Crabtree, the keeper of a disorderly house, is called to prove that Wood was a constant visitor of Dimmock when she was an inmate of his brothel; (3) Lindham is called to speak to occasions on which he saw Dimmock and Wood together in the 'Rising Sun' public-house; (4) Mrs Lawrence is called to prove that she had seen them together in the 'Pindar of Wakefield' public-house. This quartette has seen evidence of intimacy between the artist and the dead woman on at least eight different occasions ranging over a period of eighteen months before the murder. The four witnesses are not known to one another. They have each individually identified Wood. If their testimony is to be rejected, these four witnesses, all strangers to one another, must be lying or mistaken. Reason revolts at either explanation. The law of parsimony in logic forbids us to invoke a remote solution when an obvious one is close at hand. True, the witnesses are all of a poor, and perhaps a depraved, class; but it has yet to be shown that truth, like love, flies out of the window when poverty comes in at the door.

Crabtree was admittedly a brothel-keeper and a convicted horse thief, but is his testimony automatically vitiated by that fact? In his eloquent speech to the jury, Marshall Hall argued that the appearance of such a disgusting specimen of humanity for the Crown was a tacit admission of the weakness of their case. The answer to that is painfully obvious. If Wood's associates were brothel-keepers and gin-sodden sluts, what could the Crown do but call them? The Crown were not, after all, responsible for Wood's friendships. Is there to be a yardstick of morality by which Crown witnesses alone are to be measured and rejected if they do not conform to a reasonable standard of purity? Even, however, if the evidence of Crabtree be discredited, there still remains that of the other three, whose standards of moral rectitude were not on a lower plane than that of the accused himself.

The 'Rising Sun' postcard, we have seen, played an important part in the early days of the mystery; but its function in the Crown case at the Old Bailey trial is not extremely important, except in this one particular: whoever committed the murder searched through the album in vain for a postcard. The inference is that he regarded the postcard at the time as a dangerous piece of evidence which he could not afford to leave behind. As we know, he did not find the card. The remarkable fact is that Wood later confessed to having sent a postcard, although his first steps were to conceal from the police all information that might lead to his being identified as the writer of it.

The charred letter is important, not so much because it proves a meeting at the 'Eagle' (for this could be, and was in fact, proved *aliunde* at the trial), but because it affords proof of a definite appointment made by letter. Wood's own explanation of this letter is worse than unconvincing; it is incredible. He admits that it is in his handwriting, but cannot explain its purport except as 'sketches and funny sayings'. He is quite certain that it is *not* a letter, but is unable to give any explanation *why* he is sure it is not a letter. On the charred fragments there is not the slightest indication of a sketch and there seems to be nothing in the nature of a funny saying. On the contrary, the fragments contain these syllables: 'ill ... you ... ar ... of ... the ... e ... Town ... Wednes ... if ... rest ... ... excuse ... good ... fond ... Mon ... from ... the.' We have the evidence of Roberts, the ship's cook, who swore that he saw portions of a letter sent to Dimmock, on the Wednesday morning. The text, so far as he read it, was: 'Dear Phyllis, – Will you meet me at the bar of the *Eagle* at Camden Town 8.30 to-night, Wednesday. – Bert.' This certainly fits in with the decipherable words on the fragments.

The suggestion of Marshall Hall that Roberts was inventing this letter is untenable. The fact that two letters did arrive on the morning before the murder is corroborated by Mrs Lancaster, a lodger in the house at St Paul's Road, who slipped them under the bedroom door. There were charred fragments in the grate which contain words that will bear the construction of an assignation. These fragments are admittedly in the handwriting of the accused. Yet he can only suggest that they are sketches, which obviously they are not. So here Wood would appear to be concealing the truth. If Roberts had been lying, how could he have invented words almost identical to those which appeared on the charred fragments? Roberts supplied the police, be it remembered, with the text of this letter long before the charred fragments had been in fact deciphered. Roberts was not in the confidence of the police and could not have been aware that they had even discovered any fragments at all. It is unthinkable that he had invented such a letter and that the charred fragments discovered later contained words which by a mere coincidence, were similar to those invented by Roberts. Most investigators will therefore feel compelled to admit the truth of the first and second premises of the case for the Crown.

The third premise is MacCowan's identification of Wood, and here the patterned sequence of incriminating circumstances becomes involved. MacCowan's description of the peculiarity in the walk of the accused is corroborated by both Inspector Neil and Ruby Young. Moreover, MacCowan certainly identified Wood at the parade on 7 October on this mannerism of gait. Identification is, however, one of the *quaestiones vexatae* of criminal jurisprudence. In all cases involving personal identification there is invariably abundant material present for founding cross-examination of the type so much to the forefront during the Wood trial. It depends on variable, inconstant factors, such as eyesight, climatic conditions, visibility and illumination, facial or bodily peculiarities, the possibility of a duplication of those peculiarities in other persons, ability of the identifier to describe accurately the mannerisms by which he is able to distinguish the particular person from others of similar build, the ability of that person to retain a clear mental vision of the person he has seen, the length of time between the identifier seeing the suspect and the identification parade, the possibility of external influences (photographs, newspaper descriptions, conversations with other witnesses, etc.), as well as the actual conditions under which the identification parade is conducted.

In the present case, not only were the witnesses divided as

to whether or not Wood possessed a peculiarity of walk such as would impinge itself on MacCowan's memory, but a young man named Westcott was provided by the defence, who alleged that he was the man whom MacCowan actually saw. There are, however, grave objections against Westcott's testimony: (1) As Westcott could not identify MacCowan, there is no substantial, convincing proof that he saw MacCowan – he may have seen someone else, possibly the murderer; (2) Westcott's evidence was not forthcoming spontaneously, whereas MacCowan's was: (3) MacCowan, in his very first statement to the police, said that the man whom he saw in St Paul's Road was wearing a hard bowler hat. Westcott usually wore a cap. Therefore the man whom MacCowan saw was not Westcott, unless MacCowan was mistaken in his reference to the bowler hat. In a dispute as to the relative merits of the powers of observation of these two witnesses the honours must be awarded to MacCowan, who not only supplied a description of the man he saw but later picked him out at an identification parade; whereas Westcott, when asked to identify the man he had seen, failed.

It would seem, therefore, that we are on fairly safe ground in ignoring Westcott's contribution to the case. That favourite epithet of the defence – 'Lying or mistaken' – might be applied as well to Westcott as to any other witness of the trial.

It is not proposed to discuss at length the alibi put forward by Wood. From a legal point of view, the dictum of a famous Irish judge on the alibi question might be quoted: 'An alibi, if it be true, is the best defence that can be put forward. But, on the contrary, if it turns out to be untrue, it amounts to a conviction';[1] and this from a later case: 'But from the facility with which it may be fabricated it is commonly regarded with suspicion and sometimes unjustly so.'[2] It is essential to fix the time within precise limits. In an interesting case tried in Scotland and reported by Alison, the jury were directed to disregard an alibi because it appeared that all it proved was that the accused went to bed at a certain hour and was found

[1] Per Baron Daly in *Rex* v. *Killen*, 28 State Trials, 995, at p. 1040.
[2] *Rex* v. *Robinson*, [1924] Old Bailey Session Papers 423.

there the next morning. As the distance from the scene of the crime was only two miles, the alibi did not preclude the possibility of the accused having arisen in the night, returning to bed after he had dispatched his victim.[1] The possibility that the same thing happened in this case cannot be ruled out and must be taken into consideration in investigating Wood's alibi.

It will be noticed that the defence brought out the gentle disposition of the accused, stressing his refinement and good character. Still, the exemplary character of the accused, even if it be established, does not carry us one step further. A host of examples of murderers who led model private lives could be furnished. Evidence of good character in a capital charge counts for nothing. In any event, as Mr Justice Grantham pointed out, it was useless to put forward any claims to superlative character on Wood's behalf.

The last question is: How far can Wood's lies and efforts to conceal material evidence be reconciled with his attitude of innocence? The attempted suppression of evidence is properly regarded as a gravely prejudicial circumstance. Following the leading legal authorities on this point, 'it is to be interpreted as a consciousness of guilt and a desire to evade justice.'[2] The fact that an accused tells lies to the police is not, of course, proof that he is guilty. Much depends on the enormity of the lies, and the question arises: Did the accused realize at the time of his lying that his position was really serious? Many people will tell a lie when they consider the occasion unimportant. There seems to have been a tendency, of recent years, to minimize the adverse effect of such lies on the principle *nemo adversarium armare tenet*. In the famous 'Green Bicycle' case (*Rex* v. *Ronald Light*, Leicester Assizes, 1920) the accused gave lying accounts to the police on several occasions. At the trial he admitted the falsehoods, but said

---

[1] *His Majesty's Advocate* v. *Frazer*, 2 Alison, 'Principles of the Criminal Law of Scotland', at p. 625.

[2] *Rex* v. *Crossfield*, 26 State Trials, at p. 217; *Rex* v. *Donellan*, (1781), dictum of Puller, J.; *Regina* v. *Palmer*, 1856 Session Papers, Central Criminal Court.

that, not wishing to be implicated, and anxious to avoid causing his mother any worry, he simply told the lies in order to get out of the business. Light was acquitted. On the other hand, in the amazing Sacco-Vanzetti trial in America, the falsehoods told by both accused as to their whereabouts on the night of the crime for which they were indicted were founded on by the Commonwealth of Massachusetts as incriminating proof of their guilty minds, in spite of the fact that the accused, as illiterate aliens, might well have underestimated the seriousness of lying to the police.[1] The question to be decided is whether deliberate lies told to the authorities are evidence of a deep-rooted 'consciousness of guilt', or merely indicative of a mind that takes to lying as the line of least resistance. Wood's explanation, that his false alibi with Ruby Young was merely to conceal his association with an immoral person like Dimmock, and so avoid social ostracism, seems quite plausible until we remember the character of Ruby Young, who was in fact known to the police. It then becomes the proverbial route from the frying-pan into the fire.

Here, then, is an intricate problem calculated to provide mental gymnastics for every armchair detective. Who killed Emily Dimmock? The reader must evolve his own solution of this mystery of Camden Town since Time, despite the popular assurance to the contrary, cannot now be relied upon to tell.

[1] *Commonwealth* v. *Sacco & Vanzetti*, 1921, before Thayer, Ju.

READ MORE IN PENGUIN

In every corner of the world, on every subject under the sun, Penguin represents quality and variety – the very best in publishing today.

For complete information about books available from Penguin – including Puffins, Penguin Classics and Arkana – and how to order them, write to us at the appropriate address below. Please note that for copyright reasons the selection of books varies from country to country.

In the United Kingdom: Please write to *Dept. JC, Penguin Books Ltd, FREEPOST, West Drayton, Middlesex UB7 OBR*

If you have any difficulty in obtaining a title, please send your order with the correct money, plus ten per cent for postage and packaging, to *PO Box No. 11, West Drayton, Middlesex UB7 OBR*

In the United States: Please write to *Penguin USA Inc., 375 Hudson Street, New York, NY 10014*

In Canada: Please write to *Penguin Books Canada Ltd, 10 Alcorn Avenue, Suite 300, Toronto, Ontario M4V 3B2*

In Australia: Please write to *Penguin Books Australia Ltd, 487 Maroondah Highway, Ringwood, Victoria 3134*

In New Zealand: Please write to *Penguin Books (NZ) Ltd,182–190 Wairau Road, Private Bag, Takapuna, Auckland 9*

In India: Please write to *Penguin Books India Pvt Ltd, 706 Eros Apartments, 56 Nehru Place, New Delhi 110 019*

In the Netherlands: Please write to *Penguin Books Netherlands B.V., Keizersgracht 231 NL–1016 DV Amsterdam*

In Germany: Please write to *Penguin Books Deutschland GmbH, Friedrichstrasse 10–12, W–6000 Frankfurt/Main 1*

In Spain: Please write to *Penguin Books S. A., C. San Bernardo 117–6° E–28015 Madrid*

In Italy: Please write to *Penguin Italia s.r.l., Via Felice Casati 20, 1–20124 Milano*

In France: Please write to *Penguin France S. A., 17 rue Lejeune, F–31000 Toulouse*

In Japan: Please write to *Penguin Books Japan, Ishikiribashi Building, 2–5–4, Suido, Bunkyo-ku, Tokyo 112*

In Greece: Please write to *Penguin Hellas Ltd, Dimocritou 3, GR–106 71 Athens*

In South Africa: Please write to *Longman Penguin Southern Africa (Pty) Ltd, Private Bag X08, Bertsham 2013*

READ MORE IN PENGUIN

There are nine volumes in the classic Famous Trials *series, now re-issued in Penguin.*

Famous Trials Volume 1   Edited by Harry Hodge

The four murder trials in this volume, each a *cause célèbre* in its day, continue to fascinate and intrigue us decades later.

Here are four vastly different characters, led to the dock by very different circumstances. Madeleine Smith, a spirited young woman, was accused of administering arsenic to her lover. Oscar Slater was sentenced to death for the alleged murder of a woman whose very name he may never have heard, yet he outlived the judge who presided. Mild Dr Crippen dismembered his wife's body and buried the remains; his capture was due to the tenacity of a police detective. And Dr William Palmer, a cruel and brutal man, was the first person to be brought to trial for strychnia poisoning.

These remarkable, factual accounts not only enlighten us as to the workings of the legal systems of the day, but also illuminate the darker side of the human mind.